Current Issues in Clinical Psychology

Volume 1

Current Issues in Clinical Psychology

Volume 1

Edited by
ERIC KARAS

Alder Hey Hospital
Liverpool, England

Plenum Press • New York and London

ISBN 0-306-41362-0

Based on lectures presented at the Annual Merseyside Course in Clinical Psychology, held September 25–27, 1981, in Merseyside, United Kingdom

PREFACE

In January 1980 a 'Refresher Course in Clinical Psychology' was held in Liverpool. The aim of the course was to apply a contemporary perspective to issues of significance and interest to clinical psychologists in Britain, and more specifically to afford the opportunity for past graduates in clinical psychology from Liverpool University to meet together to share their working experiences.

Following the success of this event it was decided by the Mersey Regional Group of Clinical Psychologists to embark upon a long term project; The Annual Merseyside Course in Clinical Psychology, as a means to provide a post-qualification training forum for practitioners of clinical psychology and related professions. In the tradition of the refresher course, it was designed to impart to its delegates and to readers of this book, the most recent ideas in a variety of fields of enquiry within clinical practice and theory.

The growing emphasis on post-qualification training from within the clinical psychology profession marks an important milestone in its development and the inception of this course reflects this growth by fulfilling its further purpose of providing a regular platform from which national and international innovations and developments can be presented and discussed.

The proceedings of the inaugural Annual Merseyside Course in Clinical Psychology is the first volume in a series addressed to issues specifically selected for their current significance to the development of clinical psychology. The book is intended to stand in its own right and the series will develop into a composite text with the quality of being regularly updated.

This volume covers five areas and all the papers have been invited from leading clinicians and researchers in their respective fields. The papers have been presented here in the order in which they were delivered to the conference delegates and are imparted in the original styles of their individual authors. Each section

v

has an introductory paper and it is to these that I shall leave the description and setting of the sections.

Some additions and changes to the original conference format have been made for publication. The first is the inclusion of the chapter by Barrie Jones who is Regional Tutor to clinical psychologists in the Mersey Region. His paper on post-qualification training was especially invited as a fitting beginning for Volume I of the series. In addition two of the introductory chapters namely those by Bill Barnes and Dorothy Fielding and by Glyn Owens have been written by Merseyside psychologists with a special interest and expertise in the area under discussion. The other introductory chapters have been written by the chairpersons of the respective symposia. Finally, although he was not a speaker at the conference, Mike Dewey was invited to prepare a written paper on computer applications. As Lecturer in Psychological Statistics at the University of Liverpool, he is a valuable resource for psychologists on Merseyside on the subject of computing.

The conference was attended by close to two hundred people and apart from clinical psychologists it drew members of a variety of related professions. I believe that the conference was enjoyed by those who attended and hope that this record will prove both stimulating and useful to clinical psychologists and others, no matter what their level of experience or where they practise.

ACKNOWLEDGMENTS

I first wish to thank my colleagues, the organising committee of the first Annual Merseyside Course in Clinical Psychology for the industry and dedication that made the event a success. They are, Bill Barnes, Alick Bush, Dorothy Fielding, Barrie Jones, Miles Mandelson, Ray Miller, Glyn Owens, Lyn O'Sullivan, Steve Parry, Dave Pilgrim, Peter Pratt and Peter Slade. Particularly, I wish to mention the guiding spirit of Ray Miller who kept us all under control and functioning as a team.

I also thank the contributors both to the conference and to this publication for taking part and for responding to my anxieties about deadlines.

I appreciate the support of those organisations who gave financial encouragement to the event, enabling us to pass on to the conference delegates the advantage of reasonable fees.

My gratitude goes to Ann and Miles Mandelson, Ann for typing the camera-ready copy and Miles for acting as a safety net for my many proof reading and editing omissions.

Finally, I thank Dr. Robert Andrews and Ms. Madeleine Carter of Plenum Publishing Corporation for their patience and tolerant advice.

CONTENTS

POST-QUALIFICATION TRAINING

Further Training for Clinical Psychologists 3
   R.B. Jones

LEGAL AND FORENSIC ISSUES IN PSYCHOLOGY

Legal and Forensic Issues in Psychology -
    An Introduction 17
   R.G. Owens

Sexual Crime: Trivial? Serious? Treatable? 23
   D.J. West

Sexually Explicit Materials and Their Therapeutic Use 29
   M. Yaffe

Forensic Psychology and the Clinician 41
   L.R.C. Haward

Current Theories of Crime 53
   H.J. Eysenck

ANOREXIA NERVOSA: COUNSELLING AND SELF-HELP GROUPS

Anorexia Nervosa: Counselling and Self-Help Groups -
    An Introduction 67
   E. Bromley

The Role of Counselling and Self-Help Groups in the
    Management of Anorexia Nervosa 73
   P. Slade

Counselling for Clients with Anorexia Nervosa 83
   G. Edwards

The Value of Self-Help Groups in Anorexia Nervosa 95
   P.M. Hartley

COMPUTER APPLICATIONS AND BIOFEEDBACK IN CLINICAL PSYCHOLOGY

Computer Applications and Biofeedback in Clinical Psychology -
   An Introduction 107
   J.B. Ashcroft and R.G. Owens

The Microprocessor in Clinical Psychology: Technical and
   Ethical Aspects 111
   S. Lovie

Psychological Testing: The Way Ahead 121
   A. Elithorn

Computers: Decision-Making: Clinical Psychology 135
   M. Dewey

A Computer Controlled Biofeedback System: Effects of
   Inversion of the Feedback Signal on Heart Rate 147
   H. McAllister

INTERNAL EVENTS AND PROCESSES WITH PARTICULAR REFERENCE
TO DEPRESSION

Internal Events and Processes with Particular Reference to
   Depression - An Introduction 161
   B. Barnes and D. Fielding

Resistance to Change 171
   D. Rowe

Depression Caused by Arrested Intellectual Development 179
   N. Symington

Pattern of Change in Mood and Cognition with Cognitive
   Therapy and Pharmacotherapy 185
   I.M. Blackburn and S. Bishop

Is All Behaviour Modification 'Cognitive'? 207
   C.F. Lowe and P.J. Higson

LONG TERM CARE

Long-Term Care - An Introduction 231
    F.M. McPherson

Initiatives in Long-Term Residential Care 241
    J. Hall

From Token Economy to Social Information System: The
        Emergence of Critical Variables 253
    D. Fraser

Why Don't Clinical Psychologists Working with the
        Mentally Handicapped do Psychology? 263
    C. Cullen, P.A. Woods and L. Tennant

Voices from the Institution 281
    D. Brandon

Index 295

POST-QUALIFICATION TRAINING IN CLINICAL PSYCHOLOGY

FURTHER TRAINING FOR CLINICAL PSYCHOLOGISTS

R.B. Jones

Fazakerley Hospital
Liverpool

Since its inception in the 1940's clinical psychology in the United Kingdom has undergone a series of changes (Hetherington, 1981). If anything the rate of change and development has been accelerating, the publication of the Trethowan Report (DHSS, 1977) being particularly important in providing further impetus to the diversification in the practice of the profession. In addition to their traditional service role in psychiatry and mental handicap, clinical psychologists now provide input to a variety of medical specialties, from paediatrics to geriatrics and cosmetic surgery to orthopaedics. Practitioners now respond to a range of health needs at a community level and come into contact with a wide variety of clients and many other disciplines.

Further changes in response to needs will undoubtedly take place in the future. Indeed the value of our relatively recent move into primary care and the way we are presently operating is already being questioned (McPherson, 1981). The increasing recognition that there is unlikely to be an expansion in numbers of clinical psychologists in the UK to match the demand for services is leading to new ideas about how the service should be delivered (Hawks, 1981).

Developments in knowledge and skills are also taking place. The integration of cognitive processes and behaviour change methods (e.g. Beck, 1970) for example, has led to a concentration of effort in applying this to clinical populations (e.g. Blackburn and Bishop, 1981; Woodward and Jones, 1981). A close relationship between research and clinical practice has traditionally been regarded as a cornerstone of clinical psychology; it is imperative therefore, that practitioners keep abreast of new ideas and applications.

3

The emphasis in clinical psychology must be on the likelihood of, and propensity for change. One means of ensuring that practitioners keep in touch with developments is through further training. That the importance of further training is recognised is demonstrated by agreement in the profession on the desirability of training after qualification (British Psychological Society, 1977). Post-qualification training is clearly a matter of vital importance, yet only limited progress has been made so far in the UK in providing such training in any structured and coherent way. Some attempts have been made to identify more precisely what the needs are, and this must be the first step.

Needs

Training schemes leading to the initial qualification in clinical psychology can only hope to provide a broad coverage of the theoretical and practical content of clinical psychology. There is a clear need for formal training, by suitable courses, to be continued at the immediate post-qualification level and, in view of the ever changing nature of the profession emphasised above, to be available for practitioners at all stages of their careers.

Post-qualification training must also be concerned with the provision of varied experience in the field. This leads to questions concerning specialisation. What degree of specialisation is desirable, and at what stage in an individual's career specialisation should take place are questions that have been considered at some length by Hall (1980). He concluded that "any emergent consensus on the extent, location, standardisation and breadth of post-qualification training needs to be paralleled by a similar consensus on post-qualification specialisation".

For recently qualified practitioners the most appropriate means of marrying the two aspects of post-qualification training - training by formal courses and the provision of varied clinical experience - is to have their posts recognised as training posts. Unfortunately there are practical difficulties in this. These have been detailed by Kat (1981) and include the change in employment regulations that would be necessary, the cost implications and the restriction in growth that would be imposed by less psychologists being able to take up independent posts.

For the immediate future, therefore, the onus will have to remain on each clinical psychology department to ensure that their recently qualified staff receive a range of experience in the field. However, if agreement could be reached on what is regarded as an appropriate range of experience, this would be of value. Three general aims of the Basic Grade period, which seem eminently sensible, have been suggested by Hall (1980). They are: i) to

provide one major clinical commitment to ensure involvement beyond
that experienced during training, ii) to provide clinical experience
with trial periods in different fields to which the individual might
wish to move and, iii) to allow for the development of other clinical, research and administrative responsibilities. It is worth
noting that periodic trial periods in other fields would be useful
for all grades of staff, heads of department included.

In addition to the provision of further practical experience, a
planned organisation of training courses for practitioners is
urgently needed. It is in the development of these courses that we
can usefully apply ourselves at the present time for both our
immediate and future benefit. An important initial concern is to
determine the appropriate content of post-qualification courses.

Content

Four areas on which post-qualification training might focus
have been suggested by Watts (1980). These are: training for work
with specialised populations, for example in child health or neuro-
psychology; training in specialised clinical techniques such as
psychotherapy; training in clinical research in which the pursuance
of clinically relevant Ph.Ds was emphasised; and preparation for the
responsibilities of senior grades.

The emphasis appears to be on training for newly qualified
psychologists. It is tempting to believe that once a certain level
of seniority has been reached, the need for training ends. However,
this does not recognise the necessity of keeping abreast of the
sort of rapid changes taking place in the profession. It is important, therefore, to have a broader perspective and consider post-
qualification training for practitioners of all levels of experience.

A recent publication on training policy (British Psychological
Society, 1982) embraces the view of training as a continuous thread
running through each individual's career. It identifies two kinds
of post-qualification training that should be regarded as obligatory.
The first concerns refresher courses aimed at keeping all members
of the profession in touch with developments, not only in their
own specialised fields but in all aspects of clinical psychology.
I would envisage these being courses of between two days and one
week in length.

The second involves training in skills necessary for senior
posts. Fairly short courses and workshops - perhaps no longer than
one day - would be needed to provide training in skills such as
those required in administration and management, supervision,
liaison, and service and manpower planning. This reflects one of
the areas previously identified by Watts (1980) and is clearly

aimed at recently qualified psychologists. Experienced practitioners would also benefit, although their participation is likely to be mainly as teachers.

Also identified is a further kind of post-qualification training, not regarded as obligatory but related to the needs of the individual. This subsumes two of the categories put forward by Watts - training for work with specialised populations and training in specialised clinical techniques - and could usefully be called training in specialised skills and knowledge. A diversity of training vehicles is needed to satisfy the varying needs of practitioners at different stages in their careers, from short intensive courses to formal part-time training over a period of years.

Unlike Watts (1980) the BPS publication (1982) does not single out research as a subject for post-qualification training even though, with the exception of some psychologists who have carried out full-time research, by the end of pre-qualification most clinical psychologists still have relatively limited research experience and perhaps not a full grasp of research methodology. It is true that expertise in research is developed by active participation and that many practitioners become involved in collaborative and individual research. Nevertheless, courses in the methodology of clinical research would be of great value for qualified clinical psychologists. Such courses need not be regarded as a special category of post-qualification training but could also be subsumed under the heading of training in specialised skills and knowledge.

In summary, the content of post-qualification training falls into three major areas: refresher courses for all practitioners, training in preparation for senior posts and training in specialised skill and knowledge. This latter area can be further subdivided into training for work with specialised populations, training in specialised clinical techniques and training in the methodology of clinical research.

It can be seen that while the emphasis is on continued training for recently qualified clinical psychologists, post-qualification training is appropriate at all stages of experience. The relevance of training in the identified, major areas for practitioners of different levels of experience can be summarised as follows:

Area of training	Relevance
1 Training in preparation for senior posts.	For recently qualified clinical psychologists only.

Area of training	Relevance
2 Provision of varied clinical experience.	Mainly for new practitioners, but experienced practitioners would also benefit from occasional periods in other fields.
3 Training in specialised skills and knowledge.	For all practitioners, but especially applicable to those at recently qualified end of spectrum of experience.
4 Refresher courses.	For practitioners of all levels of experience.

Present Opportunities

Some idea of the opportunities for further training that are currently available can be obtained by consulting the Diary Notes published monthly in the Bulletin of the British Psychological Society detailing forthcoming events of a scientific, professional and educational nature. No more than a brief glance is needed to reveal that such events are not only available, but, indeed, plentiful. The Diary Notes for the first six months of 1981 carried announcements for 34 conferences, 18 scientific meetings, 16 work- shops, 9 seminars, 7 courses, 7 lectures, 6 symposia, 1 congress, 1 consultation, 1 convention, 1 day event and 1 educational prog- ramme.

Given the apparent abundance of meetings, conferences etc. that may have potential for providing post-qualification training, how does the practitioner, who is likely to have limited funding and study leave available, decide which are likely to be most beneficial? This may not be too difficult for experienced practitioners who can base their choices on previous experience and information gleaned from others. However, newly qualified clinical psychologists may have considerably more problems, and a series of bad choices early on may significantly blunt their enthusiasm.

One tactic might be to select by looking at their titles a number of events that look promising as post-qualification training vehicles and then contact the organisers for further details before deciding which to attend. Yet the survery of Diary Notes shows that there is an array of different titles which makes the initial dec- ision of "promising" far from straightforward. For example, should one plump for something labelled a symposium, or is a conference more likely to extend one's knowledge and expertise? What is meant by a consultation or a one day event? Would attendance at a series

of short events - lectures, seminars, scientific meetings - be more
beneficial than attending a conference lasting several days?

The other factor influencing choice is, of course, the requirement of the individual; some will be looking for a general course
and others for something more specific. Even where this property
is concerned the labels give little in the way of firm guidance.
For example a conference might be expected to cover a greater range
of subjects than a symposium, but this is not invariably the case.

An alternative tactic might be to abandon the Bulletin's Diary
Notes altogether in favour of the Division of Clinical Psychology's
tri-monthly Newsletter. Unfortunately this is even less helpful.
Instead of confusion being created by the welter of notices, there
is a paucity of announcements. The two Newsletters published during
the first six months of 1981 each carried a single announcement for
the same educational event.

Practitioners, therefore, must use the Bulletin's Diary Notes
and news announcements together with notices that arrive, apparently
at random in the post. A useful guide might be to single out those
events that are labelled courses or workshops. These labels at least
make the training intention clear. Furthermore, of the 16 workshops
and 7 courses announced in the Diary Notes in the first half of
1981, almost all covered topics of relevance to clinical psychologists.

It must be concluded that a number of suitable post-
qualification training events are available nationally in the UK,
but that they are certainly not organised or advertised in any
coherent way. In addition no guidelines are available to help
practitioners in selecting courses and workshops that most closely
meet identified training needs.

At a local level post-qualification training is also being
carried out. However, there would appear to be considerable variation in the adequacy of what is provided in different parts of the
country. This makes it difficult to draw any general conclusions.
It might be helpful, therefore, to look at post-qualification
training in my own Region - the Mersey Region - and to consider
this as one model of what can be organised locally.

We have two major courses. One is the Annual Merseyside Course
in Clinical Psychology, a refresher course held over three days and
advertised nationally. The other is a two year part-time University
based course leading to a Diploma in Psychotherapy. These are
supplemented by occasional one day and half-day courses. Topics
for these are put forward by the clinical psychologists in the
Region, which ensures that local needs and interests are covered.
Every one to two years a Regional supervision workshop is held

which reflects the involvement of all departments in the supervision of probationers on the Liverpool University based clinical psychology training course.

Special provision is made for Basic Grade psychologists with a series of meetings and seminars covering their own particular needs. We have noticed that a brief experience of working full time in the Health Service is sufficient to make Basic Grades acutely aware of the needs to augment their knowledge of the structure and management of the NHS and to develop further their skills in management and formal communication.

These small scale local events have the advantage of requiring very little financial input. Local expertise can be drawn upon. When an outside speaker is required the Regional Education and Training Department provides financial support. Their endorsement of our post-qualification training programme has proved particularly helpful in encouraging individual practitioners' employers to grant study leave and travelling expenses.

A further, not inconsiderable beneficial spin-off from these local training events is that it enables us to invite other disciplines to participate and attend, so fostering inter-professional relationships and co-operation.

Future Developments

Undoubtedly the most pressing requirement is for structure and coherence for post-qualification training. Only through this will it become possible to identify areas of need that are not being covered by nationally available courses. The establishment of the Practitioner Training Sub-Committee in 1980 by the Clinical Division of the BPS was a firm step in the right direction. The Committee provides a forum in which ideas on training can be developed; its main aims can be seen as the identification of training needs and the fostering of activities to meet these needs. It is still early days for this Committee, but it has produced some useful information from which conclusions can be drawn about the organisation of further training. Cullen (1981) reported the results of a survey carried out under the auspices of the Committee into supervision workshops. Two of the major findings were of general importance for training.

It was found that the majority of supervision workshops were one-off, rather than regular events or part of a planned series. If post-qualification courses are to be successful they will need to be organised regularly by the same body of people. In this way the organisers can profit from their own experience with the aim of improving the courses they offer. New formats can be tried; those that do not work well can be discarded and successful ones further improved. For example we are experimenting on the Annual Merseyside Course with a session in which several different theoretical view-points are presented on the one issue. Regular courses may also allow themes to be developed from year to year.

The other finding concerned the absence of attempts to evaluate the success of supervision workshops. This is pertinent to all post-qualification courses and workshops. The delineation of aims by the organisers is essential both broadly, in terms of the identified major areas of post-qualification training, and in more detail. This will then allow evaluation to be carried out, again by the organisers but also by a national body, using agreed criteria. The Professional Affairs Board of the BPS has produced criteria for the assessment of post-qualification courses in psychological therapy (British Psychological Society, 1981). It should not be difficult to determine guidelines and assessment criteria for other types of courses, such as refresher courses, that are intended to meet the main areas of training need. Perhaps there is a role for the Clinical Division's Practitioner Training Sub-Committee in developing these guidelines and criteria and in monitoring courses and workshops in the same way that pre-qualification courses are systematically assessed. It should, however, be possible to adopt a similar and briefer assessment procedure.

If a number of courses are to be organised regularly or as a series and to be monitored, there is a strong argument that they should be based on major centres. These major centres need not be permanently determined, but might change periodically. Edinburgh, Liverpool and Exeter might each put on annual refresher courses for five years, with co-ordination of content between centres and from year to year; three other centres might then take over for the next five years and so on.

Finance for training will continue to be an issue. In the longer term if post-qualification training for clinical psychologists becomes accepted as mandatory, study leave and expenses will then be available for individuals as of right. For the foreseeable future, however, it will remain with heads of departments to negotiate financial support for the further training of their staff. Much further training will continue to take place at a local level, but individuals will require financial support to attend major national training events.

These major courses and workshops will have to be self-financing from the fees they charge. It is important that they flourish. Therefore, as well as meeting the academic and professional requirements of post-qualification training, they will need to be popular amongst practitioners. Organisers will have to pay due attention not only to academic content, but to the presentations of the individual contributors. It is all too easy for speakers to fall into obvious traps such as presenting a paper in the format of a journal article (Edwards, 1982). The importance of other factors, such as providing opportunities to socialise, establish contacts and informally interchange ideas and information should also not be underestimated.

The use of the words "course" and "workshop" which clearly imply training, might help persuade employers to give financial support to individuals. If a system of monitoring major courses by a committee of the Division of Clinical Psychology can be instituted, finance to attend those courses endorsed should be easier to acquire. Such endorsement would also be important in pointing practitioners towards those events that will provide the best in post-qualification training.

The publication of proceedings of refresher courses is valuable. Not all practitioners can attend a major refresher course each year, but nevertheless more could benefit if published proceedings were available.

For the future we might also consider the introduction of a further training qualification. Feldman (1976) suggests a qualification comparable to the American ABEPP (Associate of the Board of Examiners in Professional Psychology), perhaps for intending principal level psychologists. Exchange clinical placements between Districts, Regions or even countries might also facilitate development in the profession, and the idea of lengthy study leave or a sabbatical year would no doubt be greeted with enthusiasm by practitioners.

Conclusions

Post-qualification training is most readily seen as applicable to newly qualified clinical psychologists, but it has been argued that it is just as important for practitioners of all levels of experience. Three broad areas of training can be identified: general refresher courses, training in preparation for senior posts and training in specialised skills and knowledge.

Some training at both local and national level is currently available. Local training should continue to be geared to meet local needs; the organisation of post-qualification training in the Mersey Region is put forward as one possible model. There is an urgent need for a coherent structure of post-qualification training at a national level with courses covering the three broad areas being provided at major centres. It is suggested that these nationally available courses be assessed in the same way as pre-qualification courses, but using an abbreviated assessment procedure.

Courses that meet agreed criteria would be endorsed, which would be advantageous in directing to them practitioners in search of post-qualification training. Unless post-qualification training becomes mandatory, financial support for individuals will remain discretionary. In the present situation, endorsement of courses as approved training vehicles may also assist practitioners in securing financial support to attend from their employers.

Recently qualified practitioners should continue to be given a range of clinical experience to extend that obtained during pre-qualification training. Guidelines for this range of experience are needed.

With the professional role and activities of clinical psychologists constantly changing and developing, there will also be a continual need to reappraise post-qualification training. Other possibilities for the future might include a post-training qualification for entry to senior posts and long term study leave comparable to that granted to academic staff.

REFERENCES

Beck, A.T., 1970. Cognitive Therapy: Nature and relation to behaviour therapy. Behaviour Therapy, 1: 184-200.
Blackburn, I.M. and Bishop, S., 1981. Is there an alternative to drugs in the treatment of depressed ambulatory patients? Behav. Psychother., 9: 96-104.
British Psychological Society, 1977. Postgraduate training in clinical psychology: Optimal length and format of training. Bull. Br. Psychol. Soc., 30: 284-285.
British Psychological Society: Professional Affairs Board, 1981. Criteria for assessment of post-qualification courses for applied psychologists in psychological therapy. Bull. Br. Psychol. Soc., 34: 130
British Psychological Society, 1982. Training in Clinical Psychology: A Statement of Policy. Bull. Br. Psychol. Soc., 35: 153-155.
Cullen, C., 1981. Supervisors' workshops: Report of a survey conducted by the Standing Committee on Practitioner Training. Div. Clin. Psychol. Newsletter, 33: 21-22.
DHSS, 1977. "The Role of Psychologists in the Health Service. The Report of the Sub-Committee". HMSO, London.
Edwards, J.R., 1982. The psychology of the conference. Bull. Br. Psychol. Soc., 35: 89-91.
Feldman, P., 1976. Clinical training. Div. Clin. Psychol. Newsletter, 18: 20-23.
Hall, J., 1980. And post-qualification specialisation. Div. Clin. Psychol. Newsletter, 27: 13-16.

Hawks, D., 1981. The Dilemma of Clinical Practice: Surviving as a Clinical Psychologist. In McPherson, I. and Sutton, A., 1981. "Reconstructing Psychological Practice". Croom Helm, London.

Hetherington, R., 1981. The changing role of the clinical psychologist. Bull. Br. Psychol. Soc., 34: 12-14.

Kat, B., 1981. Training Policy. Div. Br. Psychol. Newsletter, 32: 32-35.

McPherson, I., 1981. Clinical Psychology in Primary Health Care: Development or Diversion. In McPherson, I. and Sutton, A., 1981. "Reconstructing Psychological Practice". Croom Helm. London.

Watts, F. 1980. Post-qualification training. Div. Clin. Psychol. Newsletter, 27: 10-12.

Woodward, R. and Jones, R.B., 1981. Cognitive restructuring: A controlled trial with anxious patients. Behav. Res. & Ther., 18: 401-407.

LEGAL AND FORENSIC ISSUES IN PSYCHOLOGY

LEGAL AND FORENSIC ISSUES IN PSYCHOLOGY - AN INTRODUCTION

R. Glynn Owens

Sub-Department of Clinical Psychology
University of Liverpool

The involvement of clinical psychologists in forensic issues
is not new, as indeed is unsurprising given the reliance of the law
upon psychological concepts (e.g. "intent"). In recent years,
however, there has been an increasing scope for the psychologist
concerned with the workings of the law. Such an increase has, in
the United Kingdom, been reflected in such things as the establishment by the British Psychological Society of a Division specifically
concerned with such issues, the Division of Criminological and Legal
Psychology, established in 1977.

Today psychologists, including clinical psychologists, can be
found in a wide range of legal settings. Academic psychologists
contribute to the teaching of courses on criminology. Clinicians
can be found working in each of England's four Special Hospitals,
established for the treatment under conditions of security of
offenders deemed to be mentally abnormal and detained under one or
other sections of the 1959 Mental Health Act. Psychologists also
work with the Home Office, in such institutions as prisons, borstals,
detention centres etc. Such psychologists come from a variety of
backgrounds including research, clinical and occupational psychology.
Finally it should be noted that psychologists are to be found involved
in the work of research units specifically concerned with forensic
issues, including the Home Office Research Unit and the Special
Hospitals Research Unit.

This wide range of forensic applications is well reflected in
the contributions to the present symposium. Much of the concern of
psychologists in the criminological field has been with various
aspects of sexual behaviour. Both Professor West and Mr. Yaffe
address themselves to this topic, albeit from somewhat different

perspectives. Professor West points to the wide variation between
cultures in what should be regarded as sexual offences, and by
implication the extent to which these change with changes in societal
mores. Such changes are still to be seen; at the time Professor
West was writing his paper for example, homosexual behaviour was an
offence in Northern Ireland and had only recently ceased to be one
in Scotland. By the time of publication Northern Ireland had
followed the rest of the United Kingdom in permitting such behaviour
under limited circumstances. Yet much variation remains even between
neighbouring countries; in the United Kingdom, for example, the age
of consent for homosexual activities is 21, yet in France it is 16
(the corresponding ages of consent for heterosexual intercourse are
16 and 15).

Perhaps the most striking point at which psychology and the law
meet is that of the notion of consent. Consent as commonly defined
is involved, as Professor West indicates, in a substantial proportion
of those offences classed as sexual offences. The law, however,
specifies circumstances under which such consent cannot legally be
given, the most obvious of these being where consent is given under
duress or by someone legally considered to be too young to give
such consent.

At least some psychologists, however, have gone further than
this in proposing a wholly determinist view of human behaviour.
Skinner (1971), for example, has equated 'freedom of choice' with
control by schedules of positive reinforcement, and quotes the
example of the United States' Agricultural Adjustment Act. Here
the US Government in the 1930's, in an effort to reduce agricultural
output, offered payment to farmers for what constituted, in effect,
an agreement not to produce food. An initial ruling of the Supreme
Court recognised that the irresistibility of positive inducements
was equivalent to an unconstitutional coercion on the part of the
government. This ruling, however, was later reversed on the grounds
that "to hold that motive or temptation is equivalent to coercion
is to plunge the law into endless difficulties". In respect of
such things as consent to sexual behaviour, such a perspective
implies at the very least that the notion of consent be treated
with caution and evaluated not only in the light of whether threats,
but also irresistible inducements are involved. Such a perspective
is reflected in Professor West's reference to paedophiles' use of
sweets and the like as bribes to children. As yet it is far from
clear how the legal system might be expected to cope with such
conceptual problems - the "endless difficulties" of the Supreme
Court ruling.

Related to the general problem of consent is the notion that
the law will often prohibit behaviour seen as harmful to the individual even when that individual wishes to indulge in such behaviour.
Such things as the control of drug abuse fall obviously into this

category, but with sexual behaviour, too, parallels may be found. In particular the prohibition of sexual activity with children is seen as necessary for their protection even when they do not themselves perceive such a need. (Notably children may not be the only ones; many researchers, too, have been surprised by the failure of childhood sexual activity with adults to produce lasting effects. Methodological difficulties abound, of course, but the research is nevertheless instructive, with even early research finding few harmful effects under certain circumstances e.g. Bender and Blau, 1937.)

For the time being, then, the notion of consent, whilst difficult, seems not to admit of any simple solution. Questions of who may consent, and under what circumstances, seem likely to remain with us for some time. In the meantime, the observation that so many "crimes" are perpetrated upon willing victims suggests that legal, commonsense and psychological notions are still far from agreement.

A similar conflict is apparent when considering Professor West's comments on rape. The observation that serious physical injury is relatively infrequent in rape victims appears paradoxical in the light of the generally accepted notion that rape constitutes an extremely serious offence. One possible resolution of this paradox involves the consideration of the psychological effects of rape, often considered to be more extreme and permanent than most physical effects. In addition to this feminists have pointed out that the "victims" of rape extend beyond those individuals on whom the attack is actually perpetrated to the vast majority of the female population, who may quite realistically feel like prisoners, unable to go out without an escort. Such writers tend to have little sympathy with the "victim blaming" approach discussed by Professor West in the context of the attacker who revolts against sexuality following seduction or attempted seduction.

Professor West's final points concerning the difficulties both of clinical and research work in this area underline a concern of many forensic workers. Much early work on treatment was difficult or even impossible to evaluate because of the pressures placed on offenders to show that they had been 'cured'. Such factors have probably contributed greatly to the failure of many therapies to live up to early promise (e.g. aversion therapy). Such difficulties are compounded by the ethical problems involved in therapy and research, when the notion of consent, already seen to have many complex aspects, is further complicated by the pressures operating upon offenders. Such issues call for caution in the conduct and evaluation of both therapy and research.

Ethical problems of course have been raised whenever sexual behaviour or material is under consideration. Mr. Yaffe, in his

paper, points to the fact that such issues, in addition to legal
issues, arise even when such materials as films and photographs are
used for clearly therapeutic purposes. Nevertheless it has been
possible to use such materials to help several groups of clients
with their sexual difficulties, and the clinician will find much in
Mr. Yaffe's paper of interest and relevance. Of course, the therapeutic use of sexually explicit materials also raises questions
regarding possible harmful effects of exposure to such stimuli.
Warnings of the potential dangers of such material have often been
made by moralists concerned with sexual behaviour, but as Mr. Yaffe
points out in his paper, such warnings do not find reliable support
in the research literature. At present, therefore, such material
seems likely to prove of considerable value to the clinician, Mr.
Yaffe's paper indicating a range of likely applications.

It would of course be a mistake to assume that forensic psychologists' only interest was in sexual behaviour. The day-to-day
role of the forensic psychologist involves a number of different
activities, and Professor Haward, in his paper, describes how such
a role applies to the activities of the civil and criminal courts.
The four categories of activity he describes will be familiar to
many forensic psychologists. Some may wish to add to these an
additional category, concerned with the acceptability of forms of
evidence presented to the court. Thus the present author has on
occasion been called upon to present a basis on which statements
made by defendants may later be called into question by a defence
counsel unhappy with the content of such statements. Some of these
will correspond to the categories described by Professor Haward;
for example a recent case involved a defendant who was said to have
read a statement written for him by a police officer. The testimony
of the present author that the defendant's specific reading disability would preclude the reading of such a statement was accepted
by the prosecution as a basis for "lightening the file", i.e.
removing the defendant's statement from the prosecution case. Such
an example corresponds in part to Professor Haward's "clinical
role". In a rather different example the present author was able
to argue that the circumstances under which a statement had been
taken were such as to call into question its veridicality, and as
a result the statement was again omitted from the prosecution's
case. The relationship of such a role to those described by
Professor Haward is perhaps less clear. That the involvement of
psychologists in court procedures does not always have a happy
ending, incidentally, is highlighted by a recent case, interestingly
involving the symposium's remaining speaker (Tunstall et al., 1982).
Here the evidence of psychologists in court was not only subject
to dispute by other psychologists, but various professional issues
e.g. the confidentiality of test materials came to be seen of
importance, an issue considered in some detail by Professor Haward.
In such circumstances it is clear that the psychologist may often
despair of the legal system, reacting with frustration and possibly

antagonism. Under such circumstances it becomes important to remember that the psychologist with something worthwhile to contribute to a case may still feel obliged to make such a contribution despite the risk of such contribution being disregarded. On this basis it is perhaps unsurprising to see Professor Haward concluding that court work may be "challenging, frustrating, salutory, time-wasting and sometimes addictive ...but ... never dull".

Considering, however, what may be considered the opposite extreme to the day-to-day activities of the courts, Professor Eysenck provides an overview of the ways in which psychology may be seen to contribute to the wider area of criminological theory. Professor Eysenck has come to be known as a champion of the role of genetic and biological factors in human behaviour, and his theory of criminal behaviour, first presented in detail almost twenty years ago, (Eysenck, 1964) remains one of the few attempts to produce a comprehensive psychological theory of criminal behaviour. Of course attempts have also been made to produce theories based upon non-psychological bases, and some of these are considered briefly by Professor Eysenck. The role of relative poverty, for example, is called into question with figures reflecting changes in the distribution of wealth in the United Kingdom failing to parallel a claimed change in the incidence of criminal behaviour. It remains to be seen whether, given the methodological difficulties of comparing crime rates over such a long period of time, such an argument will prove convinving, although those interested in such issues may wish to make more detailed studies themselves. Professor Eysenck's sources on national wealth distribution are not specified in his paper, but those concerned with such issue may wish to note that a regular breakdown of the distribution of national wealth is published by no less a source than the Inland Revenue in their annual statistics. Over recent years these have failed to show any substantial change in the national distribution of wealth, an observation which may be of value in considering the merits of theories relating such data to criminal behaviour.

Professor Eysenck's basic theory, that criminal behaviour can arguably be seen to have both genetic and environmental components is unlikely to be disputed by most workers familiar with the field, even if exception is taken to the processes he postulates by which such factors may operate. At the very simplest level, few people would reject the notion that genetics operate as a factor affecting such things as physical ability, strength, etc.; to the extent that such factors are involved in criminal behaviour at least a minimal genetic contribution must be accepted. Perhaps the question of most interest is not the extent to which environmental and genetic factors currently operate, but rather the extent to which each of these factors may currently set limits on the achievements possible within society. With our present state of knowledge the prospect of a Utopian crime-free society must sadly still seem remote.

Perhaps one of the most striking features of the present symposium, then, is the extent to which in the short space of four presentations such a wide range of psychological activities in forensic matters may be illustrated. It is as yet too soon to say whether forensic psychology has exhausted its possible roles, but it is nevertheless clear that the psychologist is rapidly becoming an integral part of the legal system. The four papers of the present symposium form a useful overview of some aspects of psychology's legal role.

REFERENCES

Bender, L. and Blau, A., 1937. The reaction of children to sexual
     relations with adults. Amer. J. Orthopsychiat., 7: 500-518.
Eysenck, H.J., 1964. "Crime and Personality". Routledge and Kegan
     Paul, London.
Skinner, B.F., 1971. "Beyond Freedom and Dignity". Knopf, New York.
Tunstall, O., Gudjonsson, G., Eysenck, H.J., and Haward, L., 1982.
     Professional issues arising from psychological evidence
     presented in court. Bull. Brit. Psychol. Soc., 35: 329-331.

SEXUAL CRIME: TRIVIAL?   SERIOUS?   TREATABLE?

D.J. West

Standards of sexual conduct are highly culture-bound.   In parts
of the United States, solitary masturbation was, until recently, a
crime.   In countries governed by Mohammedan laws adultery is still
a serious crime.   Consensual homosexual behaviour between adult
males is still a crime in most legislation within the United States,
as it was until earlier this year in Scotland and still is in
Northern Ireland and the Irish Republic.   The age at which a female
becomes a legitimate target for sexual intercourse varies remarkably
from one European country to another.   In our own relatively recent
history the age was twelve, now it is sixteen.

The belief that our own criminal law is used solely, or even
mainly, to protect citizens from forcible sexual molestation is far
from reality.   Recent Home Office research (Walmsley and White,
1979) has established that a very substantial proportion (some 43
per cent) of all convictions for serious sexual crime concern
incidents in which the participants are fully consenting.   The
reason is that the law is widely used as an instrument for the
enforcement of moral standards, in particular to prevent youngsters
becoming participants in sexual activity, and to prevent homosexual
behaviour in places open to the public.   The vast majority of so-
called victims of sexual crime are consenting girls and boys or
adult males making homosexual contact in public conveniences.   Even
excluding the common offences of street soliciting by female prostitutes or 'indecent exposure' by males (neither of which count as
'serious' offences in the Home Office classification) it is only a
minority of prosecutions for sexual crime that concern forcible
assaults.

According to the Criminal Statistics for England and Wales,

23

serious sexual crimes known to the police have actually decreased
over the past decade, although almost every other crime has become
more frequent and crimes of violence against the person have more
than doubled. Among offences classified as both serious and sexual
the crime of rape, although it has increased significantly in recent
years, remains at less than 6 per cent of the annual total (1,225
out of 21,107 in year 1980). This represents an incidence per head
of population less than a thirtieth of that recorded in the FBI
Uniform Crime Reports for the whole of the United States.

The much commoner crimes of indecent assault upon a female, or
unlawful sexual intercourse, are usually non-violent and often consensual activities. The police exercise considerable discretion in
instituting prosecutions when the age difference between the participants is not large, but even so many of the male offenders are
teenage youths having contacts with girls of fourteen to sixteen.
When younger female children fall victim to a prosecuted sex offence
it is usually with an adult in her entourage, such as a parent,
relative, family friend or lodger. Although violent or even
homicidal sexual attacks upon children are not unknown, and hit the
headlines whenever they occur, the vast majority of paedophylic
behaviour is in the nature of minor indecencies, sometimes procured
by bribing the young girl with sweets or other small gifts. Actual
sexual penetration is unlikely to occur, except sometimes within the
safe confines of the nuclear family; but then, if detected, it may
be prosecuted as incest, which is considered particularly grave.

Boys who become involved with adult males more often do so
outside the home, either with strangers encountered in cinemas,
parks, amusement arcades or other public places, or with adults with
whom they have some organisational contact, such as teachers, youth
leaders, and staff of residential institutions. Since the legal age
of consent to homosexuality is twenty-one, sexual contacts with
adolescent boys are probably more likely, when detected, to lead to
prosecution than are contacts with girls of similar age. The
adolescent participants in sexual offences, both male and female,
are not infrequently runaways from home who are either looking for
a bed or hoping to maintain themselves by prostitution.

The courts tend to deal with sex offenders quite severely.
They are more likely than most other types of offenders to be
imprisoned and to receive long sentences. Although, among males,
convictions for indictable sex offences represent less than 2 per
cent of all convictions for indictable offences, sex offenders
comprise about 5 per cent of the population of sentenced male
prisoners. Sex offences involving young boys or girls attract
heavy sentences, perhaps because of the widespread idea that premature sexual contacts makes for sexual maladjustment. Anxiety
about boys being seduced into permanent homosexuality is especially
acute. Such limited factual evidence as is available suggests that

such risks are greatly exaggerated. Retrospective questioning of groups of normal young persons of both sexes reveals that a substantial minority have had early sexual experiences with older persons without this having appeared to have had any influence upon their development. Naturally, the courts tend to see the worst cases, namely those in which the child has felt intimidated and has laid a complaint, or those in which the child has formed an intense, lasting but inappropriate emotional friendship which has drawn the disapproving attention of parents. It is the preferential selection of the latter type of situation for prosecution which may give an exaggerated impression of the prevalence of children eager to have sexual contact with an adult.

Even rape, the sexual crime considered most serious, does not usually have quite the horrific connotations commonly attributed to it, as a recent survey based upon details culled from police files from six English counties over a five year period clearly demonstrated (Wright and West, 1981). Although some degree of force or threats were usually employed, physical injury requiring medical treatment occurred to less than 6 per cent of the victims. About half the offenders were acquaintances or friends of the victim, and the unwanted sex act, which often took place in the home of the victim or offender, was usually preceded by some kind of social interaction.

Having emphasised the banality of much that passes for serious sex crime, it needs explaining with equal vigour that a small minority of sex offenders are potentially very dangerous, especially if frustrated in their approaches or threatened with denunciation to the police. Some are compulsively repetitive in seeking out victims and some find sadistic enjoyment in causing their victims as much pain or humiliation as possible. A number of very violent attacks that occur in the context of a sexual encounter are actually expressions of revulsion against sexuality, as in murders of prostitutes or homosexuals by men who have allowed themselves to be tempted into acts they consider sinful and in conflict with their self-image.

Treatment on medico-psychological lines would be inappropriate for many sex offenders. It seems sometimes that the law is in greater need of adjustment than the offender. For instance, on occasion the police decide to prosecute consensual sexual behaviour between two youngsters of approximately similar age. In such cases, not even the wishes of irate parents can properly justify invoking the criminal law, with all that may involve by way of stress and stigma, for the control of behaviour widely regarded as natural and age-appropriate. It is also arguable whether the employment of police officers to challenge women on the streets, or to spy upon men's conveniences, are profitable exercises, or whether it might not be more economical to deal with these problems as they arise, that is when a member of the public is affronted and complains.

The great majority of individuals prosecuted for a sex offence for the first time never appear before the courts again for another sex offence. From the standpoint of public policy in the allocation of scarce resources, it would seem extravagant, where the initial offence is of a rather trivial kind, such as an act of indecent exposure, for the courts to call for clinical investigations on individuals unlikely to be reconvicted. On the other hand, once a sex offender has been reconvicted, even for a trivial sex offence, the likelihood that he will go on being reconvicted for similar offences becomes quite high, and inquiries as to the need for specialist treatment are certainly justified.

Offenders can be roughly divided between those whose primary interest is in consensual relations with mature persons of the opposite sex, and those with inclinations considered deviant, such as paedophyles, exhibitionists, incestuous fathers, lovers of adolescent youths and sadistic men who obtain maximum satisfaction when their sexual partner is forced against her will or made to suffer. Crimes of a sexually deviant nature are not uncommonly committed by individuals who are not sexually deviant in this sense, but who are frustrated in their attempts to secure an appropriate partner. Socially alienated, inadequate, or excessively inhibited persons, or sufferers from mental or physical handicaps, or ageing men who have lost their partners and are too old to find another, are all to some extent vulnerable. They may turn to children, not because that is their true preference, but because such contacts seem easier and, in the short term, less threatening.

Sexual assaults or rapes of mature females are sometimes committed by similar types of individual, as a result of difficulties experienced in obtaining access to a consenting partner. More often, however, the offenders in these cases are merely young, impulsive, predatory and poorly socialised. Working class males with a history of convictions for non-sexual offences predominate. Their problems, if any, lie in their inability or unwillingness to abide by the social rules governing either courtship or property, rather than in any disturbance in the sexual sphere.

Clearly, these different types of problem demand radically different treatment approaches. In some cases, judicious non-intervention may be much the best policy, or else simple reassurance that an isolated instance of inappropriate sexual behaviour that happens to have come to public notice does not mean a lifetime of sexual maladjustment. In many more cases, social skills training, basic sex education, role playing of courtship routines, or even practice with volunteer surrogates, may be sufficient to overcome the frustrations that have led to the disapproved behaviour. When the root problem is a true fixation upon some deviant form of sexual

expression, a reorientation of sexual preferences may be the
appropriate therapeutic goal. Psychologists have developed a range
of techniques for orgasmic reconditioning. It would not be practicable to review all these methods here, suffice to mention that they
include electrical aversion therapy, shame therapy, covert sensitisation and masturbatory conditioning. In recent years psychologists
have placed less emphasis on the negative aspects of change, that is
the suppression of unwanted desires by aversive routines, than on the
positive encouragement of appropriate responses. Unless the patient
can learn to enjoy some acceptable form of sexual expression, the
suppression of a deviant habit is unlikely to be either satisfying or
permanent. Manipulation of orgasmic responses is most likely to
prove successful with patients who already have some acceptable
sexual interests or experiences to build upon. For example,
exhibitionists who are married and capable of heterosexual intercourse, but who tend to resort to their deviant routine when
something goes wrong in their marital relationships, are relatively
easy to treat by means of aversive methods, because they do have a
realistic alternative. Much more difficult to convert are men with
an exclusively homosexual orientation who have never had any
experience of or sexual interest in the opposite sex. Age preferences are somewhat easier to change, so that men fixated on boys are
sometimes more readily guided towards older males than towards
females.

The therapist needs to be eclectic. For example, a behaviour
therapy routine without simultaneous counselling for a co-existing
marital problem would be relatively unprofitable. Psychotherapy
and behaviour therapy are not mutually exclusive in practice,
however much their theoretical models may conflict. Indeed, even
to understand the nature of the problem, and the complex fantasies
that underpin deviant behaviour, a very trusting and intimate
relationship with the patient is a necessary prerequisite. In some
cases, particularly those in which the relationships with the
opposite sex are fraught with emotional and personality conflicts
rather than sexual inhibitions, psychotherapeutic delving may be
absolutely essential. Some compulsively aggressive sex offenders
are not sadistic sexual deviants who must produce pain to achieve
orgasm, but rather mysogynists with an insecure masculine self-image.
They feel put down and humiliated by women and have a great urge to
dominate their victims in acts of revenge.

Treatments of all kinds are best applied in circumstances of
complete freedom, with the patient cooperating voluntarily without
external pressures, and with the possibility of putting into practice
in real life the new attitudes or interests developed during therapy.
Unfortunately, in penal settings that ideal is often unattainable.
Prospective clients may be detained for long periods in sex-
segregated institutions where the inmate subculture is highly

antagonistic to sexual deviants and towards any man who confides in the authorities. Treatment under such circumstances can be virtually impossible. Even when conditions within an institution are relatively favourable, uncertainty about release dates and difficulty in arranging continued attention after release can mitigate against successful treatment.

Sex suppressant chemotherapy with female hormones or anti-androgens are necessary for the control of very serious offenders who are otherwise uncontrollable and whose prospects of release into the community would be much less without this measure. Even so, such an approach is a confession of failure, an amputation rather than a restoration of function. Moreover the unwanted side-effects of oestrogens, and even of high maintainance doses of cyproterone acetate, are very considerable, and the efficacy of the drugs for the control of all forms of sexual behaviour is open to question.

The results of treatments for sex offenders are peculiarly difficult to evaluate by means of the only criterion of interest to the public, that is a reduction in recidivism. The basic recidivism rate for sex offenders is so much lower than that of the generality of non-sex offenders that large samples are necessary to produce a statistically significant effect. Moreover, since the tendency to recidivism among sex offenders, though small, is very lasting, a long period of follow-up is necessary. Yet another complication is that sex offences, being highly covert activities, may continue for a long time before detection. It is essential, in order to make a valid comparison, that treated and control groups should be under the same degree of surveillance, which is difficult to arrange if one group is under after-care supervision and the other is not. Finally, in this context, as in all issues of treatment in criminology, random allocation of cases between treatment groups and control groups is extraordinarily difficult to achieve. Notwithstanding all these difficulties, the validation of short-term effects, such as a changed pattern of sexual response registered by the penile plethysmograph, or the relief of social anxiety or partial impotence, justifies a degree of optimism about the possibility of long-term benefit. Unfortunately, until specialist treatment units are available within the penal system capable of undertaking bold and consistent therapeutic experimentation and evaluation, we shall never know the answer.

REFERENCES

Walmsley, R. and White, K., 1979. "Sexual Offences, Consent and Sentencing". Home Office Research Study, 54. HMSO, London.
Wright, R. and West, D.J., 1981. Rape - A comparison of group offences and lone offences. Medicine, Science and the Law, 21: 25-30.

SEXUALLY EXPLICIT MATERIALS AND THEIR THERAPEUTIC USE

M. Yaffe

Guy's Hospital
London

INTRODUCTION

Why should this subject be included in a forensic symposium?
Essentially because it impinges upon legal standards, in addition
to both moral and behavioural, and like soccer and politics drives
most people to extremes of opinion. It is particularly interesting
that sexually explicit material is considered to violate the legal
code for it deals with the representation of sexual activity rather
than the behaviour itself, or at least the consequences of viewing
material (Miller, 1982), an area that has received much publicity
and scrutiny over the past decade.

This paper will cover several related issues: a description
of the types of material used clinically, how they are used, and in
what situations, and the ethical implications of their therapeutic
use. As the reader will appreciate, the adjunct use of sexual
material over the past ten or so years represents just one of the
major developments and advances in sex therapy since Masters and
Johnson (1970) first published details of the techniques they had
developed for the treatment of sexual dysfunction. Others include
the treatment of clients without partners either singly or in groups,
and using vibrators to increase sexual arousal and arousability
(Yaffe, 1980).

Sexually explicit materials comprise depictions or representa-
tions of sexual objects and situations - rather than the objects and
situations themselves - and can be classified into erotic art, sex
education material or pornography, i.e. material expressly designed
to produce sexual excitement and often without aesthetic content;
each of these kinds of materials can relate to either heterosexual

29

or non-heterosexual arousal. In the therapeutic context, materials employed, usually film, photograph or videotape, have been specifically prepared for purposes of sex education or therapy (e.g. National Sex Forum Films of San Francisco), compared with commercially available pornography.

Over the past few years three major reviews of the therapeutic applications of sexually explicit material have been published (Bjorksten, 1976; Gillan, 1978; and Yaffe, 1982) and all report its positive contribution when used with particular populations in specified ways as a complement to other procedures. But what differentiates sexually explicit material from non-sexual depictions? Bjorksten (1976) highlights its unique features and claims that the uniqueness is due to the way sex is viewed in our society: sexual information is frequently transmitted inaccurately, and in a limited way due to moral restraints, and when people do discuss their sexual attitudes, feelings and knowledge, they often do so with anxiety, indignation, or embarrassment, if not downright avoidance of the subject; and clinical psychologists are no exception in this respect. Since the materials under consideration are explicit it provides a good opportunity for therapists and sex educators themselves to learn about sexual practices outside their own experience and/or preference.

Historically, the therapeutic application of sexually explicit material began as part of desensitisation treatment programmes for reducing anxiety in specific sexual dysfunction cases (Wolpe, 1958), and relevant material was soon adopted by therapists interested in both aversive and positive training procedures for sexual deviants. However, appropriate materials remain in poor supply, and tend to be expensive.

For those seeking an overview of the effects of exposure to sexually explicit materials in normals the reader is directed to[*] previous publications of the present author (Yaffe, 1972; 1979), but Annon and Robinson (1978) have summarised the principal con-[+]clusions as follows:
> No study has convincingly shown any long-term effects of pornography on sexual behaviour and attitudes.

---

[*] The text edited by Yaffe and Nelson (1982) is devoted to a critical discussion of this subject.

[+] These conclusions are based on the results of studies, largely on normals, where the material used was devoid of aggressive content; Nelson (1982) carefully evaluates the recent experimental literature where aggressive content material was employed, and where prior anger arousal is a factor taken into account in determining the effects of exposure to such material.

Attitudes regarding various sexual behaviours appear to be quite stable, despite exposure to erotic visual materials.

Many males and females exposed to erotic films frequently report various degrees of short-term arousal.

There tend to be increases in the frequency of coital activity (if the activity already exists in the individual's behaviour repertoire) within 24 hours after viewing pornography. However, there is still no significant increase to the overall rates of intercourse.

It is relatively rare that novel sexual activities are tried, or that low frequency sexual behaviours are increased, following exposure to erotica. The most reliable behavioural effect is an increase in masturbation during 24 hours following exposure.

The majority of individuals who increase masturbation following exposure tend to be individuals with already established masturbatory patterns.

Viewing pornography often results in a temporary increase in sexual fantasy, dreams, and conversation about sex during the first 24 hour period following exposure. (p.37)

SEX EDUCATION vs. SEX THERAPY

The principal difference between sex education and sex therapy is that in the former those to whom the material is shown do not have a specific sexual problem, either dysfunctional or paraphiliac, but rather a deficit of accurate knowledge regarding sexual matters, whereas in sex therapy a sexual disorder is present and is usually associated with anxiety and performance concerns. Although straightforward sex education in normals usually does not necessitate the discussion of sexual problems, therapy for sexual problems virtually without exception involves some sex education.

Sexually explicit material in an educational context can provide information both speedily and accurately; for instance it is much more helpful to show a man an illustration of a female's genitalia in order to teach him the location of the clitoris than to attempt to do so verbally. Such material has been demonstrated to be extremely effective in providing information to patients about their own sexual anatomy, and especially so with individuals and couples who have limited sexual experience. Visual depictions enable patients to develop an appropriate sexual vocabulary, and the very use of material by therapists endorses the view that the sexual activity shown is both permissible and enjoyable.

ASSESSMENT OF SEXUAL PROBLEMS

Assessment of preferences and responses to sexually explicit material is one of the principal ways of determining an individual's potential for sexual arousal (Stoller, 1976), and enables the clinician to accurately assess sexual problems and often the specific component of the problem behaviour. Barlow (1977) has stressed the importance of measuring three channels of response: subjective report, behavioural observation, and psycho-physiological monitoring, for a comprehensive appraisal of the situation, and Yaffe (1982) gives a full account of behavioural assessment procedures where sexual materials are involved.

THERAPY FOR SEXUAL DYSFUNCTION

The precise contribution of sexually explicit materials in the treatment of problems of sexual inadequacy is difficult to assess as most reports of their use are limited to case reports, rather than controlled trials, but it is nevertheless helpful to know how it has been used, with whom, and to what effect. Conditions that have received attention include sexual anxiety, orgasmic difficulty, and both ejaculation and erection problems, and a selection of this work is now reported.

Wincze and Caird (1976) compared video and imaginal desensitisation in the treatment of heterosexual anxiety, and found that the group shown video-taped material demonstrated greater overall positive changes compared to the imagery and a no treatment control group. These were similar to those obtained by Wishnoff (1978) whose patients were anxious, coitally-experienced women, and Nemetz, Craig and Reith (1978) where both primary and secondary orgasmically dysfunctional women were treated by relaxation training, and video-taped scenes, either individually or in groups. LoPiccolo and Lobitz (1972) in their graduated masturbatory training programme for anorgasmic women recommended the use of sexually explicit texts or pictures for purposes of arousal enhancement, and their approach has been shown to be effective in helping participants to achieve heterosexual coital orgasm.

With respect to male sexual inadequacy problems, there appear to be few reports of studies where sexually explicit material has been used as a treatment variable. Reynolds (1980) used a biofeedback paradigm in his attempt to facilitate erectile function in thirty men with psychogenic erectile problems, and although he claimed that the therapeutic value of erectile feedback was not demonstrated, the provision of feedback in response to viewing an erotic film did improve the voluntary control of his subjects' erections in the laboratory. Gillan (1978), on the other hand, has developed a "stimulation" therapy technique which involves presenting sounds and pictures of explicit heterosexual activities as an adjunct to the treatment of male erectile insufficiency and female orgasmic dysfunction. She contends that, compared to a control group who were not exposed to such material, those who were reported an increase in intercourse frequency and in the quality of sexual feelings, and an improved relationship with their partner.

THERAPY FOR SEXUAL DEVIATIONS

Adams, Tollison and Carson (1981) define sexual deviations as sexual arousal to inappropriate persons, objects or activities, but in addition they often involve deficient or absent sexual responses to appropriate partners. This means that therapy must embrace both the establishment of mutually rewarding adult sexual responses and relationships and the control of unwanted sexual behaviour where indicated. This double approach is taken into account in the review of the relevant techniques which follows.

A. Increase of Heterosexual Arousal

(i) Aversion relief. This procedure involves establishing an association between heterosexual stimuli and relief from an aversive stimulus, whereby heterosexual stimuli become paired with escape from unpleasant stimulation and acquire properties of positive re-inforcement. After establishing a level of electric shock as "very unpleasant", Feldman and McCulloch (1965) had their homosexual subjects look at slides of nude and semi-clad males, which they were to turn off as soon as they were no longer found sexually arousing. However, if they did not do this within eight seconds of exposure then they received an electric shock whose strength increased until they did. When they did so the shock terminated and a picture of a female was projected. Several individuals subjected to aversion relief appear to develop increased heterosexual interest and responsiveness following treatment.

(ii) Shaping. This is a procedure designed to facilitate the development of new behaviours by reinforcing existing behaviour in the individual's repertoire that bears some similarity to that desired. Quinn, Harbison and McAllister (1970) conducted a pilot study with a homosexual patient in their attempt to increase his penile response to heterosexual stimuli. He was deprived of water for 18 hours, but drinks were made contingent on an increased erectile response to heterosexual stimuli, measured by a penile strain gauge. Significant improvement in this ability was demon-strated along with an increase in general heterosexual interests. Herman and Prewett (1974) shaped the penile responses of a bisexual with erectile insufficiency using visual feedback, and as in the

previous study their subject demonstrated increase in these responses
which were contingent on the feedback; parallel improvements also
occurred with respect to ejaculation during masturbation and sexual
arousal outside the laboratory.

(iii) <u>Orgasmic reconditoning</u>. This technique was developed to
increase heterosexual arousal through the pairing of unarousing but
wanted heterosexual imagery with elicited sexual arousal from deviant
fantasy (Marquis, 1970). In one example of its use with a fetishist,
Bebbington (1977) employed a classical conditioning paradigm where a
vibrator-facilitated erection was paired with photographs of heterosexual activity; the author claimed his subject developed a substantial increase in heterosexual erectile responsiveness and this was
maintained at follow-up after six months.

(iv) <u>Fading</u>. The intention with fading is to change what
stimuli the subject finds sexually arousing by increasing the focus
of heterosexual stimuli while the patient is sexually aroused, and
this was the method adopted by Laws and Pawlowski (1974) in order
to strengthen responsiveness to adult stimuli in two paedophiles.
They were shown superimposed slides of children and adults, and
when erection was produced above criterion response, a slide showing
a child was faded into one of an adult; the process was reversed if
responding fell below the criterion level. Covert self-instruction
helped to facilitate the change in responding which led to high level
tumescence in relation to the adult material and decreased responding
in respect of child-content slides, and indicates that widening the
sexual repertoire of an individual with deviant sexual arousal,
rather than attempting to lower that deviant response directly, is
an effective way to modify unconventional and unwanted sexual
behaviour.

(v) <u>Exposure</u>. This procedure simply involves presenting the
subject with a steady flow of explicitly heterosexual material
without any specific instruction of how to respond, and was used
by Herman, Barlow and Agras (1974) in the treatment of two homosexuals and a paedophile. They were shown a film of a seductive
nude female over a period of several days, followed by a similar
film of a male nude, and then the first film again, and the investigators report that the men responded with increased genital arousal
to the second showing of the heterosexual film, and an increased
production of heterosexual content fantasies and behaviours outside
of the laboratory.

(vi) <u>Systematic desensitisaiton</u>. This is one of the oldest
techniques in the behavioural clinician's armamentarium and in the
present context has been employed in the alleviation of maladaptive
sexual anxiety by pairing relaxation with specific sexually explicit
depictions that make the subject anxious. The rationale is that if
he is taught to experience relaxation while viewing material

depicting desirable sexual activity, then the real-life versions of these will be less anxiety-inducing. Caird and Wincze (1977) have prepared a series of video tapes ranging from less to more explicit depictions which they use for relaxation purposes with both the sexually dysfunctional and deviant; their subjects are shown the next slide in the series when a level of relaxation is achieved to the one before it (the sequences shown to each person are different, according to the individual's needs).

B. Elimination of Deviant Arousal

The concern here is to modify a maladapted sexual response by either withdrawing the reward or by presenting an aversive stimulus with its occurrence, i.e. to establish a strong association between inappropriate sexual arousal or response and aversive reinforcement. However, for their efficacy, these procedures need to be used in conjunction with those designed specifically to promote the expression of acceptable forms of sexual arousal and response.

(i) Aversion (chemical and olfactory). In this procedure an aversive physical state, produced by nausea-inducing drugs, is paired with sexual arousal produced in response to imagery and/or photographs/films of the deviant practice. Both Maletzky (1977) in the treatment of 12 exhibitionists and Laws, Meyer and Holmen (1978) whose subject was a sexual sadist, report a substantial decline in the deviant response using this method, but acknowledge that the stimulus conditions are difficult to control. This is why preference has been expressed for electrical aversive procedures.

(ii) Electrical aversion. The typical aversive stimulus used is a mild but unpleasant electric shock, the delivery of which is contingent upon the occurrence of the unwanted response to the deviant stimulus. Sexually explicit material has been used by Marshall (1973) in his mixed deviant group where relevant fantasies and slides were paired with faradic shock, and Callahan and Leitenberg (1973) who incorporated two different aversion therapy procedures - contingent electric shock and covert sensitisation, where an aversive event was generated by imagination - in a similar mixed group with sexual deviation problems. Both studies report successful suppression of penile responses to deviant stimuli, but Callahan and Leitenberg (1973) indicate that covert sensitisation is more effective than contingent shock in suppressing subjective measures of sexual arousal.

(iii) Shame aversion. In this technique shame of humiliation is the critical aversive stimulus. Typically, the deviant patient, usually an exhibitionist, is required to engage in his deviant behaviour in the presence of a number of observers, and Wickramasekera (1972) has demonstrated that it is possible to generate the desired reaction. As far as the use of sexually explicit material in this context is concerned, Serber (1971) observed and photographed a young transvestite during cross-dressing, and reported that this produced distress and anxiety in his patient and was effective in eliminating the deviant behaviour.

(iv) Satiation. This procedure is aimed at deliberately associating boredom with a patient's deviant fantasies in order to destroy their erotic nature, and Marshall and Barbaree (1978) found it effective with an aggressive man who had multiple fetishes. He was required to masturbate in clinical sessions and at home, and to continue to do so after ejaculation. For those persons who have difficulty in fantasising, appropriate deviant content sexually explicit material makes it possible for this technique to be considered.

(v) Biofeedback. This approach involves giving patients analogue information about a specific psycho-physiological response, usually a state of tumescence, in order to facilitate or suppress erection, and Laws (1980) used a biofeedback paradigm in the treatment of a bisexual paedophile. His subject's erection response to slides of young boys and girls were displayed on a closed-circuit television monitor, and his task was to develop a strategy of self-control of his erections using the visual feedback. Although Laws reports that the man learned to control his erections in the presence of the slides of boys, he did, in addition, make use of a covert sensitisation procedure.

IMPLICATIONS FOR USE OF SEXUAL MATERIAL

From the above discussion it can be seen that sexually explicit material has a definite contribution to make in both sex education and therapy for both dysfunctional and deviant individuals. Spec- ifically, Bjorksten (1976) details the range of these applications and includes the sexual enrichment of couples who have no specific sexual problem, but he also points out that such materials are poorly tolerated and their therapeutic use therefore, contra- indicated in patients who are psychotic, particularly paranoid, severely depressed, and in those who subscribe to extremely restric- tive moral principles. On the other hand, Wilson (1978) makes out a good case that this kind of material has a definite role to play in the prevention of sexual problems, which is encouraging for the future considering that existing clinical services can never hope to deal with all the sexual problems in the community. However, it must be said that the indiscriminate use of a sexually explicit film, slide or videotape, just because it is available can never be justi- fied.

It is hoped that we can look forward over the next few years to an increased availability of appropriate material that will enable effective clinical programmes to be implemented for the alleviation of sexual distress and the elimination once and for all of sexual ignorance and misinformation.

REFERENCES

Adams, H.E., Tollison, C.D. and Carson, T.C., 1981. Behaviour therapy with sexual deviations. In: Turner, S.M., Calhoun, K.S. and Adams, H.E. (Eds.), "Handbook of Clinical Behaviour Therapy". Wiley, New York.

Annon, J.S. and Robinson, C.H., 1978. The use of vicarious learning in the treatment of sexual concerns. In: LoPiccolo, J. and LoPiccolo, L. (Eds.), "Handbook of Sex Therapy". Plenum Press, New York.

Barlow, D.H., 1977. Assessment of sexual behaviour. In: Ciminero, R.A., Calhoun, K.S. and Adams, H.E. (Eds.), "Handbook of Behavioural Assessment". Wiley, New York.

Bebbington, P.E., 1977. Treatment of male sexual deviation by use of a vibrator: Case report. Archives of Sexual Behaviour, 6: 21-24.

Bjorksten, O.J.W., 1976. Sexually graphic material in the treatment of sexual disorders. In: Meyer, J.K. (Ed.), "Clinical Management of Sexual Disorders". Williams and Wilkins, Baltimore.

Caird, W.K. and Wincze, J.P., 1977. "Sex Therapy: A Behavioural Approach". Harper and Row, Hagerstown, Md.

Callahan, E.J. and Leitenberg, H., 1973. Aversion therapy for sexual deviation: Contingent shock and covert sensitisation. J. Abnorm. Psychol., 81: 60-73.

Feldman, M.P. and MacCulloch, M.J., 1965. The application of anticipatory avoidance learning to the treatment of homosexuality: 1. Theory, technique, and preliminary results. Behaviour Research and Therapy, 2: 165-183.

Gillan, P., 1978. Therapeutic use of obscenity. In: Dhavan, R. and Davies, C. (Eds.), "Censorship and Obscenity". Martin Robertson, London.

Herman, S.H., Barlow, D.H. and Agras, W.S., 1974. An experimental analysis of classical conditioning as a method of increasing heterosexual arousal in homosexuals. Behav. Ther., 5: 33-47.

Herman, S.H. and Prewett, M., 1974. An experimental analysis of feedback to increase sexual arousal in a case of homo- and heterosexual impotence: A preliminary report. J. Behav. Ther. and Exper. Psychiat., 5: 271-274.

Laws, D.R., 1980. Treatment of bisexual paedophiles by a biofeedback assisted self-control procedure. Behav. Res. and Ther., 18: 207-211.

Laws, D.R., Meyers, J. and Holmen, M.L., Reduction of sadistic sexual arousal by olfactory aversion: A case study. Behav. Res. and

Ther., 16: 281-285.

Laws, D.R. and Pawlowski, A.V., 1974. An automated fading procedure to alter sexual responsiveness in paedophiles. J. Homosexuality, 1: 149-163.

LoPiccolo, J. and Lobitz, W.C., 1972. The role of masturbation in the treatment of orgasmic dysfunction. Arch. Sex. Behav., 2: 163-171.

Maletzky, B.M., 1977. "Booster" sessions in aversion therapy: The permanency of treatment. Behav. Ther., 8: 460-463.

Marquis, J.N., 1970. Orgasmic reconditioning: Changing sexual object choice through controlling masturbation fantasies. J. Behav. Ther. and Exp. Psychiat., 1: 263-271.

Marshall, W.L., 1973. The modification of sexual fantasies: A combined treatment approach to the reduction of deviant sexual behaviour. Behav. Res. and Ther., 11: 557-564.

Marshall, W.L. and Bardaree, H.E., 1978. The reduction of deviant arousal: Satiation treatment for sexual aggressors. Criminal Justice and Behav., 5: 294-303.

Masters, W.H. and Johnson, V.E., 1970. "Human Sexual Inadequacy". Little, Brown, Boston.

Miller, J., 1982. Censorship and the limits of permission. In: Yaffe, M. and Nelson, E.C. (Eds.), "The Influence of Pornography on Behaviour". Academic Press, London.

Nelson, E.C., 1982. Pornography and sexual aggression. In: Yaffe, M. and Nelson, E.C. (Eds.), "The Influence of Pornography on Behaviour". Academic Press, London.

Nemetz, G.H., Craig, K.D. and Reith, G., 1978. Treatment of female sexual dysfunction through symbolic modelling. J. Cons. and Clin. Psychol., 46: 62-73.

Quinn, J.T., Harbison, J.J.M. and McAllister, H., 1970. An attempt to shape human penile responses. Behav. Res. and Ther., 8: 213-216.

Reynolds, B.S., 1980. Biofeedback and facilitation of erection in men with erectile dysfunction: A critical review. Arch. Sex. Behav., 9: 101-113.

Serber, M., 1971. Shame aversion therapy. J. Behav. Ther. and Exp. Psychiat., 1: 213-215.

Stoller, R.J., 1976. Sexual excitement. Arch. Sex. Behav., 33: 889-909.

Wickramsekera, I., 1972. A technique for controlling a certain type of sexual exhibitionsim. Psychother.: Theory, Research and Practice, 9: 207-210.

Wilson, W.C., 1978. Can pornography contribute to the prevention of sexual problems? In: Qualls, A., Wincze, J.P. and Barlow, D.H. (Eds.), "The Prevention of Sexual Disorders". Plenum, New York.

Wishnoff, R., 1978. Modelling effects of explicit and non explicit sexual stimuli on the sexual anxiety and behaviour of women. Arch. Sex. Behav., 7: 455-461.

Wolpe, J., 1958. "Psychotherapy by Reciprocal Inhibition". Stanford
    University Press, Stanford, Calif.
Yaffe, M., 1972. Research survey. In: Lord Longford (Ed.),
    "Pornography: The Longford Report". Coronet, London.
Yaffe, M., 1979. Pornography: An updated review (1972-1977). In:
    Williams, B. (Chairman) "Report of the Committee on Obscenity
    and Film Censorship (Appendix 5)". HMSO, London.
Yaffe, M., 1980. Commentary on current trends in sex therapy. In:
    Tennent, T.G. (Ed.), "Current Trends in Treatment in Psychiatry".
    Pitman Medical, Tunbridge Wells, Kent.
Yaffe, M., 1982. The therapeutic uses of sexually explicit material.
    In: Yaffe, M. and Nelson, E.C. (Eds.), "The Influence of Porno-
    graphy on Behaviour". Academic Press, London.

FORENSIC PSYCHOLOGY AND THE CLINICIAN

L.R.C. Haward

Professor of Clinical Psychology
University of Surrey
Guildford, England

INTRODUCTION

Psychology and Law, as objects of man's intellectual pursuits
if not as professions, have been intertwined since recorded history.
Plato (1935), in the years before Christ, spent much of his life
applying psychological ideas to legal concepts. His most famous
book, The Republic, for example, was essentially a search for the
psychological meaning of justice.

In the English courts, the clinician as a professional did
not appear until 1290 A.D., when physicians were called in to
validate pregnancy in the case of the many women who "pleaded
their belly" when sentenced to the gallows. Six centuries were
to elapse before psychologists, now boasting their own profession,
were to appear in European courts as experts, and a further half
century before such appearances became a recognised function and
duty of the clinical psychologist. Recently at the Old Bailey,
London's premier criminal court, no less than eight psychologists
were involved in what was to become the longest and most expensive
criminal trial in the history of English law, spanning more than
a year and costing more than an estimated million pounds sterling.

Forensic Psychology has clearly come of age, and the clinical
psychologist, more than any other specialist in his profession, is
intimately involved in court proceedings, both in those which affect
his own patients, and those involving non-patient clients who seek
his professional help and expertise.

Forensic, from the Latin forensus meaning 'appertaining to
the Forum' refers to both the juridical nature of the Roman

41

Forum, and also to its use as a venue for debate on controversial
matters. Thus forensic psychology has been defined as the
application of psychology to matters in dispute in a court of
law (Haward, 1981). It should be noted that this excludes the
wide range of other activities which psychologists undertake
vis-a-vis the law, such as studies on the jury system, the jud-
iciary, and the counsel; research into criminology, victimology,
and penology; enquiries into civil and criminal compensation and
its effects; legal education and police training; specific
investigations for law reform and many others.

Other countries have expanded or contracted definitions of
forensic psychology, and the disparity in the UK between what is
meant by forensic psychology and by forensic psychiatry (which has
a specific criminological connotation) is particularly noteworthy.

FOUR FORENSIC ROLES

Clinical psychologists, in their forensic work, may have to
assume one or more different roles, of which four have been
described in detail elsewhere (Haward, 1981). Briefly, these
include the clinical role, in which the clinicians enter into a
direct clinical relationship with their client, either because
some aspect of the client's status psychologicus is in issue, or
because the interaction between psychologist and client involves
some form of clinical responsibility, as when the witness is
hypnotised at the request of the police; the experimental role, in
which the psychologists apply their expertise in experimental
psychology to examine some form of behaviour in issue, and may
never see their client personally; the actuarial role where they
bring their knowledge of probability theory and observational
research to bear on the probability of some issue before the court;
and the advisory role, where they do not actually enter the witness
box to give direct testimony, but sit in the well of the court
with the counsel for the party calling on their services, in order
to analyse and interpret the technical evidence of another expert
who may be a psychologist, neurologist, psychiatrist or other
member of the caring professions. They also provide the cross-
examining counsel with appropriate technical questions designed to
betray weaknesses in the expert testimony or in the professional
competence of the witness.

These roles all have their place in forensic psychology, and
for any particular case one role will be more important than
another. Sometimes the psychologist will be expected to adopt
more than one role, occasionally all four, but it is in the
clinical role that the clinical psychologist naturally obtains
his chief satisfaction, and indeed feels more at ease in the
court.

CLINICAL PROBLEMS

Of the many varieties of problem in the clinical field posed
by the courts, those emanating from compensation cases are the
most numerous. Such cases arise from road traffic accidents mainly,
but industrial injuries will be prevalent in those cases arising
in the industrial towns. Alleged brain damage sustained during
head injury represents the most common problem, but impairment of
manual skills or locomotor activity due to limb injuries will also
come the psychologist's way. Questions will be asked concerning
the degree of disability, the prognosis including degree of
improvement to be expected over what time base, potential earning
power generally and expected decrement in previous earning rate,
alternative vocations and possibilities for rehabilitation and
resettlement, and many more.

In second place in order of frequency come the problems of
juvenile delinquency, where the question facing the magistrates
is not so much whether or not the accused youngster is guilty but
what is to be done about it. The nature of the offender, his home
background, peer group activities, motivations and potential for
improvement all need examining by interviews, consultations and
psychometric/sociometric techniques.

Of increasing importance is the psychologist's role in court
proceedings for care and/or custody orders of children brought by
the local authority or by the parents on appeal. Following
separation or divorce or alleged child abuse by the parents, the
clinical psychologist may be asked to assess the relevant psychological aspects of the parents, and of the child, together with
his or her siblings. The courts usually accord a great deal of
weight to what the psychologist has to say in such circumstances,
for the whole future of the child's mental health and development
may depend upon the judgement of the court. Social workers, often
of considerable experience in family disputes, will make their own
recommendations, and these will usually be supported by educational
psychologists employed by the same authority. Exacting clinical
evaluations, however, will sometimes yield factors of special
relevance overlooked in a more general view of overt behaviour -
psychopathy in a presentable and plausible parent, perhaps, or a
disturbing level of aggressivity in an apparently meek but brain-
damaged father. In cases of child abuse a criminal prosecution
may well follow the custody proceedings in the Juvenile court,
and psychologists must therefore prepare and present their
evidence with an eye to both the needs of the child, and the
consequences to the parents. Since the police generally have a
commonsense and understanding point of view on child abuse - most
of them will be parents themselves - they use their discretion in
deciding whether to prosecute for child abuse, and sometimes seek
the help of the clinical psychologist at an early stage of their

investigation to tell them whether the problem is basically one of neglect by an incompetent mother or is the more serious one of uncontrolled anger and assault. Children of mothers who have poor intellectual endowment or suffer psychiatric disabilities are likely to sustain injuries by neglect rather than by deliberate conduct, what the law calls a misfeasance rather than a malfeasance, and although the future safety of the child may demand its removal from the parental home, penal sanctions directed against the parent in such cases could prove both unjust and ineffective.

Other clinical problems include the mental capacity of the client to be released from the Court of Protection to manage his/ her own affairs, to enter into a legal contract, and so on. There is also the whole range of problems concerned with mens rea or criminal responsibility. The offender can evade the legal con- sequences of his criminal conduct if he can prove that he was unable to formulate the intention to commit a crime by reason of some mental state. This will include insanity, as defined by the M'Naughten Rules, diminished responsibility as defined by the Homicide Act, amnesia, automatism (such as sleepwalking), acute alcoholism, psychopathy and severe degree of mental handicap.

LEGAL PROBLEMS

In reaching an understanding of the case, the clinical psycho- logist uses those professional skills taught in formal postgraduate training and enlarged by experience. However, it is readily seen that the forensic questions put to the psychologist are quite different to the clinical ones he is used to in his everyday work. The court is not interested in learning what treatment the person requires but in his state of mind and degree of responsibility. Diagnosis is less relevant than whether the patient had a clear sensorium at the time of the offence, his intelligence is less relevant than his level of understanding of what kind of conduct is wrong in law. The needs of the court are quite different from those of the patient or the health care professional who refers him for treatment.

In providing evidence for court, either in the form of a report or as expert testimony given from the witness box, the psychologist is thus working in a new and unfamiliar context. Moreover it is one with considerable constraints, usually unscientific in its nature, sometimes even anti-scientific. Forensic psychology thus poses its own problems for the clinical psychologist, some of which are discussed below.

LEGISLATIVE DIFFERENCES

The United Kingdom has no common law. England and Wales has its own law, primarily Saxon in origin with strong Norman influence. Scottish law is different in many respects, not only in terminology - the English plaintiff becomes the Pursuer in Scotland and court officials change their title, for example - but in substantive law as well. Thus diminished responsibility, a legal concept in Scotland long before it entered English Statute law, has much wider applications north of the border than it does in England and Wales, where its use is confined to cases of homicide. Northern Ireland also differs from the other countries of the Union, and of special interest to psychologists is the refusal to recognise psychopathy in relation to mens rea as it is in England. Other states with their own jurisdiction, legal procedures, and terminology are the Channel Islands and the Isle of Man. Thus a psychologist preparing evidence in relation to a patient who has moved to a different part of the United Kingdom may have to find a completely different set of solutions to those he would propose if the patient still lived locally.

ADVERSARY BIAS

Unlike other European countries, where the so-called inquisitorial system is aimed at arriving at the whole truth, British court procedure is based upon the adversary system, where only the truth relative to the two parties concerned is admitted, and where all facts relating to other possible suspects is kept carefully away from judge and jury. The adversary system can be seen as some atavistic residue of the old trial by battle originating in the 12th Century when knights fought in mortal combat as champions of either party, or as accused and accuser themselves. Trial by battle was not abolished in England until the last century, and those who have seen the "battle of the experts" in court, when witnesses, usually psychiatrists hotly defend contradictory opinions, will be left in little doubt that trial by battle, albeit with verbal weapons only, is still with us. The system makes bias almost inevitable. The psychologists hear their client's case in full, are commissioned (and paid) by the client's counsel, whose prime duty is to win the client's case. They enter into a personal relationship with the client, whose social, domestic and psychological status they have to evaluate in detail, and if the client is already a patient of theirs, they may already have established a caring relationship. Under such conditions to preserve complete impersonal neutrality is a psychological impossibility, and although the psychologist tries hard to be a detached scientist, some degree of bias cannot be avoided even if it is not admitted. Of course, the adversary system

works on the assumption that both sides are equally biased, and
those psychologists who lean over backwards to be unbiased may be
doing their clients a grave disservice, especially when their
evidence is so sterile it cannot be used at all. Nevertheless,
this continues to pose a moral, ethical and professional dilemma
to many experts. The situation is made more difficult where the
psychologist is actually employed by one party and expected to
support its policies and function, for example the District
Attorney's Office, the law enforcement agencies such as the
constabulary, or, as in the case cited earlier, the Local Authority.
In some legislatures provision is made for the psychologist to be
called independently by the court itself and not the adversaries.
The psychologist becomes 'a friend of court' or amicus Curia, but
since this is contrary to the principles of the adversary system
it is rarely used in the United Kingdom but is more popular in the USA.

WEIGHT OF EVIDENCE

     As Lord Rutherford once said: "To measure is to know", and the
hallmark of the scientist is measurement. Modern psychology is a
numerate discipline and justifiably claims the appellation 'science'
and the only activities of clinical psychologists which are unique
to their profession are those concerned with the measurement of
behaviour. It is therefore natural that forensic psychologists
wish to be numerate in their evidence, but this is the last thing
which the court requires.

     In a criminal trial the evidence against the accused must be
'beyond reasonable doubt' if conviction on the basis of a guilty
verdict is to take place. The concept of reasonable doubt has no
scientific criterion: like equity of old, varying with the length
of the Chancellor's foot, reasonable doubt varies with the scepticism
or otherwise of a particular jury, and what one foreman will regard
as doubtful, another may well view with certitude. The psychologist,
aware that nothing in science can be certain, uses the concept of
probability, and fixes his own levels at which he is prepared to
entertain doubts about the validity of his data. Conventionally,
if somewhat arbitrarily, these have been set at the 5% and 1%
probability levels.

     In one case (Haward, 1963) the corroborated evidence of two
police officers was repeated in an experimental situation in the
same place and under the same conditions as the alleged offence.
It was demonstrated that under the appropriate conditions of
illumination and expectancy, innocent conduct was perceived as an
illegal act by over 12% of the trained observers. The inference
was that the probability of misinterpreting the innocent conduct
as a criminal offence was 0.125, and this was offered as evidence
that the police evidence was not beyond reasonable doubt. The

court, however, was not prepared to admit such quantitative evidence, possibly because by doing so it might have created a precedent in defining doubt in absolute figures. It did accept, however, the author's general statement that the situation was one in which mistakes in observation were possible.

Again, the Homicide Act requires diminished responsibility, if proved to be present, to be "substantial" but the courts carefully avoid admitting evidence which attempts to put a figure on this adjective. In Regina v. Johnson, a murder case heard at Leeds Assizes and believed to be the first in which this new defence was pleaded, the author was able to show, by cumulative psychometric evidence obtained over a number of years, that the accused had suffered a 30% impairment of cognitive functioning compared with his original level on first testing. The judge, unwilling to accept a quantitative estimate of 'substantial' impairment, carefully avoided the whole issue by moving the defence plea from the statutory one to the M'Naughten Rules of Insanity, saying to the author in the witness box, in a very pointed manner: "what you mean is that he suffers disease of the mind". To which the author, taking the hint, concurred.

In civil actions, the party with the preponderance of evidence wins the case. This means that success may be achieved with the probability of chance at anything less than 49%. To insist on entering only that evidence which conforms to the established scientific criteria of 1% is like insisting on trial by battle using a scalpel when the other side takes full advantage of foil, epee and sabre. To be over-meticulous in such circumstances does an injustice to the party requesting one's services: better to provide evidence, with its limitations on validity carefully explained, than to provide no evidence at all. At worst, the opinion of the clinical psychologist in such matters, whatever its psychometric or behavioural basis, is likely to be better informed than that of the lay public.

Of course, the consideration of quantitative evidence pre-supposes that scientific evidence is accorded due weight in the first place. Such is not the case. The jury is sometimes advised to disregard the scientific evidence and rely rather on their commonsense. In one paternity case, for example, an expert testi-fied that the alleged father had the same blood group as the child. Another expert, appearing for the father, then testified that although the alleged father matched the child on the ABO series, the two were incompatible on the MN series detected by more refined analysis, and that paternity by the defendant was impossible. The plaintiff's counsel, despite this apparent coup de grace to his case, parried this logically mortal blow by pointing out to the jury that since the two experts disagreed (which was untrue) they should ignore the blood test results since they were incompatible (which was also untrue) and pay heed to the fact that the putative father had had intercourse with the plaintiff, and that the child bore a resemblance to the defendant. The jury then found for the mother on the basis of this 'commonsense' evidence, despite the unchallenged scientific evidence to the contrary, and the defendant was left with an expensive paternity order and a strong feeling of injustice. If blood grouping, a highly sophisticated technique with almost perfect delineation when all the series are analysed, can be treated in such a cavalier manner, what hope is there for the psychologist's data?

TERMINOLOGY

The language of law differs from that of science, and always takes precedence in court. Like a computer programmed to work only in a given digital language, the law rejects any evidence which does not fit its own special vocabulary. The psychologist, in providing evidence in relation to the M'Naughten Rules, is not expected to talk in terms of a psychosis, but of insanity. The court is not interested in diagnoses which comply with international labels, but with its own labels, such as disease of the mind. It will not entertain arguments that such a concept consists of two logically incompatible concepts. Neither can the psychologist ask for an operational definition. Like the philosopher's "given", legal terms are deemed to be self evident and immediately knowable. Since the legal terms, such as insanity, are actually psychological, and not medical or psychiatric, the psychologist is perhaps better placed to give evidence on them than members of other professions, but lamentably there is no consensus of opinion within the professions on such matters. Most clinicians would regard disease of the mind as including psychosis, but Laingians refute this interpretation. Eysenck argues that a neurosis is maladaptive learning, but Neustatter happily testifies that a neurosis is a mental disease. And where does one put psychopathy?

HEARSAY EVIDENCE

Although some liberalisation of the Rules of Hearsay has taken place in the higher courts, the rigid approach of earlier times is still extant in most of the courts in which psychologists testify. Two particular problems have bedevilled much testimony in recent years. One concerns the admission of experimental evidence, which usually relies on data obtained from a relatively large sample. In a number of cases, the court has ruled that the psychologist's report of the experimental subjects' responses was hearsay and not admissible unless all the people concerned were available to testify direct to the court as to what they said and did in the experimental conditions. When large samples have been used, such a requirement is quite impracticable. Fortunately, a number of precedents admitting data from the field of social surveys, has opened the door to group data and group statistics without the whole population having to enter the witness box to validate the findings, and psychologists are already finding experimental data easier to present in court than formerly.

The other problem concerns evidence obtained from a hypnotised witness. Although a recent article argued that as the law stands there is no statutory impediment to the admission of hypnotic evidence (Haward and Ashworth, 1980), nevertheless, the courts have not yet accepted such evidence. Since hypnosis is most effective in those cases of traumatic amnesia following the shock of rape or other forms of serious assault, it follows that if the evidence finally recalled under hypnosis by the victim is to be tendered as testimony, the psychologist is prevented from restoring the defensive amnesia which protects the victim from the full effects of the crime. Clinicians may well find themselves in an ethical and moral dilemma here, when to help the police they must retain the victim's awareness of events, but in doing so they leave her vulnerable to the psychic trauma from which she had been protected by her natural mental mechanisms. Few clinicians would agree to leaving their 'patient' in such a distressed and abreacting condition, and yet their testimony, supported if necessary by police officers or independent court officials present at the hypnotic investigation, is not admissible to save the victim from this undeserved extra distress.

This also raises the additional problem of whether police officers should be trained as investigative forensic hypnotists, as they are in California, when they have no clinical skills for dealing with the abreactions and other psychiatric manifestations which can occur during hypnotic episodes.

ELECTRODERMAL TECHNIQUES

Electrophysiological techniques, widely used in biofeedback therapy, are also used in forensic investigations by psychologists. Objective and autonomous, they cannot easily be falsified deliberately, and some of them are extremely sensitive to associations with both repressed and suppressed information. The courts, however, have not been able to decide on the admissibility of evidence obtained in this way. Electrodermal GSR data obtained by the writer was rejected by one court in a case of attempted murder, yet not only admitted, but formed the central defence evidence in a later case of wilful murder. Its validity in lie detection, within closely circumscribed applications, has been shown to be remarkably high (Gudjonsson, 1981) yet lie detection data is not normally admissible in the English courts, despite the fact that

evidence under the effects of the so-called 'truth drug' have been
admitted for that purpose.   Five defendants accused of murder have
taken electrodermal lie tests with the writer, who has not been
allowed to present the results in court and to qualify them with
the necessary caveats, yet the accused individuals themselves have
been allowed to present the results - usually embellished - in their
favour.   Of course, lie detection itself, while useful to the forensic
psychologist in reaching an understanding of his client's conscious
involvement in the crime in question, is really only a small part
of the overall use of electrodermal recording.   There are many
interesting forensic problems brought to the psychologist by the
police, which can be solved by the painstaking and imaginative use
of electrodermal techniques, such as the identification of amnesics
found wandering in the streets from time to time, Gudjonsson and
Haward (1982).

PSYCHOMETRIC EVIDENCE

     Perhaps the most acute problem facing the psychologist in court
today is the misuse of test material.   On occasion, the psychologist
will be required to bring to court all the tests and associated
forms used in his evaluation, and these will be subjected to
detailed discussion in open court.   In several cases the whole
Wechsler Adult Intelligence Scale has been examined item by item,
complete with scorings and sample responses, so that the court
record, which may be purchased by anyone, becomes an immediate
'Give yourself a 150 IQ' kit.   This makes nonsense of the confidentiality of the test, and the elaborate precautions undertaken by
the test agencies such as the NFER to protect test information
and keep it out of unqualified hands.   Tests which even a qualified
practitioner cannot purchase now become available for the cost of
a short transcript of the appropriate evidence.

     More importantly, the parties who completed the tests sit in
court hearing their every response made public, their failures
derided, and their successes ridiculed.   They hear how their
responses were scored, and what they should have said to gain
perfect scores.   The tests thus become no longer valid for these
individuals, should retesting be required.   Since this is likely in
compensation cases, and occasionally necessary for criminal appeals
or retrial, the course of justice is impaired by this cavalier
approach to test confidentiality on the part of the legal profession.

SUMMARY

     The clinical psychologists providing expert testimony in a
court of law function on different principles and under special
restraints which do not obtain in their normal clinical practice.

They may be asked to fill one or more of four different roles, each of which calls upon aspects of their psychological training which are not necessarily used in their day to day routine work. These roles have already been fully described; in this section the problems which derive from the differences between court and clinic requirements are discussed. These include the logical and semantic incompatibility of relevant legal and scientific concepts, the loss of protection of the patient's most confidential communications to the psychologist; the misuse of NFER classified test material in court and its effect upon the nature of testing for forensic purposes; the distortion of scientific truth in the interests of advocacy; the nature of probabilistic significance in court judgements; and the status of data derived from experimental populations. For the clinical psychologist court work is challenging, frustrating, salutory, time-wasting and sometimes addictive. But it is never dull!

REFERENCES

Gudjonsson, G.H., 1980. "Psychological Aspects of Detection". Ph.D. Thesis, University of Surrey.

Gudjonsson, G.H. and Haward, L.R.C., 1982. Case report - hysterical amnesia as an alternative to suicide. Medicine, Science, Law, 22: 68-72.

Haward, L.R.C., 1963. Reliability of corroborated police evidence in a case flagrante delicto. Journal of Forensic Science Society, 3: 71-78.

Haward, L.R.C , 1981. "Forensic Psychology". Batsford, London.

Plato, 1935. "The Republic". Trans. A.D. Lindsay. Dent, London.

CURRENT THEORIES OF CRIME

H.J. Eysenck

Institute of Psychiatry
University of London

Crime, it is often said, is not a scientific concept because its definition is idiosyncratic, differing from country to country, and from person to person. To a small extent this objection is true, but for the major part it is certainly not applicable to the major groups of crimes, such as theft, burglary, murder, rape, etc., which have always, and in all societies, been held to be objectionable and destructive of social cohesion. Certain activities, such as homosexuality, adultery, prostitution, smoking, and drinking of alcohol during the days of prohibition, etc., are at some times and in some countries labelled as "crimes", but freely allowed in other countries, or at other times. However, these "victimless crimes" are merely projections of religious and moral objections to "sinful" conduct which have for a short period of time gained the status of being subject to enforcable rules; it is usually found that these are in fact unenforcable, that the majority of people regard them as ridiculous, and efforts to enforce them are soon abandoned. In what shall be called "crimes" in this chapter, we will refer only to those crimes which are regarded as such in practically all societies that have ever existed.

Theories of criminality are required to account for two facts. The first of these is that criminal activity changes in a given society from one year to another. Thus in England there has been a considerable increase from 1970 to 1980, an increase which began at the end of the Second World War and shows no sign of stopping. Figure 1 shows the increasing rate of serious crime in England during the past decade; similar figures are available for many other Western countries, and although criminal statistics are not on the whole very reliable, there is no doubt about the fact that an alarming increase has taken place during the past thirty or forty years.

Figure 1:   Increase over past 10 years in robberies and violence
against the person; English figures.

        The second fact requiring explanation is why some people, but
not others, engage in criminal activity. (The problem of individual
differences.)   Theories accounting for one of these facts may or may
not be able to account for the other also; clearly it would be highly
desirable if a single set of theoretical conceptions were satisfactory in explaining both. At the moment there are three major theories
which attempt to explain the occurrence of crime; these are the
sociological and economic theories, psychoanalytic theories, and
conditioning and social learning theories. We will look at these
in turn.

        1. Sociological and Economic Theories. As an example of the
kind of theory which is too poorly articulated to be properly testable, but which achieves popularity by being all things to all men,
we may perhaps quote the widespread belief that criminal behaviour
is caused by such socio-economic factors as poverty, inequality,
poor housing, and other similar conditions. This belief is so widespread, and seems to be so self-evident to many sociologists and
economists that it is hardly ever tested. Yet certain consequences
would seem to follow from it which are testable, and which should
be looked at in more detail than they have been in the past. One
obvious consequence would be that if there is a change in a given
population in the direction of less poverty, greater equality, and

general improvement in living conditions, then there should be a
reduction in criminality. Is this in fact so? In England, over
the past 80 years or so, there has been a tremendous reduction in
the inequality of possessions, and a great deal of equalisation of
wealth. At the beginning of the century, the top 10% of the population owned over 80% of the total wealth of the country; by 1974
this figure had been reduced to something like 40%. At the beginning
of the century, the top 1% of the population owned about 70% of the
total wealth of the country; by 1974 this had been reduced to just
over 10%. Figure 2 shows the decline in the wealth of the rich, and
by inference an increase in the wealth of the poor. These figures
suggest that there should be a considerable decrease in the amount
of crime; yet the evidence is exactly in the opposite direction.
There has been a considerable increase in crime, and every year shows
not only a further decline in inequality, but also a further increase
in criminality. This is counter to prediction, and therefore would
seem to invalidate the hypothesis.

Other figures are even more impressive. In 1956 two million
people took holidays abroad; in 1981 twelve million people did so.
Four million people owned cars in 1956; seventeen million do so now.
Six million occupied houses they owned themselves in 1956; the number

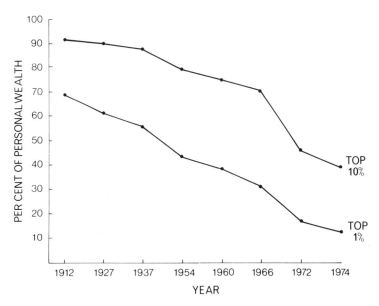

Figure 2: Decrease in percent of personal wealth owned by the
           top 10% and top 1% of the population, in England,
           during years 1912 to 1974.

now is eleven and a half million. Seven million owned telephones in 1956; the number now is eighteen and a half million. Five million owned TV sets in 1956; the number now is nineteen million. There is no question whatsoever that during the time that criminality has been increasing rapidly, so has been the well-being and the economic status of the population.

There are of course difficulties with this kind of evidence, particularly when it relies on official statistics which are known to be untrustworthy. There are changes in the public's willingness to report certain types of crime to the authorities; there are actual changes in the law, such as the anonymity given to victims of rape in court reporting since 1976, which has probably encouraged more women to go to the police, thus altering the figures; there is plea bargaining, which may alter the type of crime set down in the figures; and many more disturbing features of the official statistics which makes them rather untrustworthy. However, it is unlikely that these faults are entirely responsible for the ever increasing crime rate; when we look only at the crimes which are practically always reported, such as attacks on policemen, we find a similar increase.

A proper investigation of deductions to be made from this general theory would require the following steps. In the first place, we need a separate evaluation of the many hypothetical socio-economic factors that have been implicated. General level of well-being, degree of social inequality, housing conditions, etc., are undoubtedly all correlated, but the correlations will be far from perfect, and hence each should be quantified separately. Indeed, it it is possible for positive or negative correlations to occur between different countries. For example, in Switzerland there is a very high standard of living, but a great degree of inequality. Thus one should look at statistics within and between countries, trying to isolate what are the important variables from the socio-economic point of view.

On the other side of the coin, an effort should be made to obtain better statistics for the actual amount of crime, in the hope that the "grey area" of unreported crime could be reduced by choosing suitable types of criminal behaviour, and that a more detailed analysis of police proceedings, etc., might enable one to obtain a better estimate of the actual amount of criminality in a given area. Admittedly all this is much more difficult than simply to take pub- lished figures, but unless something of the kind is done, we will never be able to evaluate the validity of this particular type of hypothesis. It would of course also be necessary to consider rele- vant variables which might modify conclusions, such as changing numbers of police, changing probabilities of discovery, changing sentencing procedures, etc. It is safe to say that no existing study has come anywhere near to considering all these factors, and

until that is done we have no way of evaluating this particular
hypothesis. As far as existing figures are concerned, it seems
unlikely to be verified, but the data may give rise to curvilinear
relationships which have not hitherto been examined or even hypo-
thesised by many investigators. This too is an urgent task which
requires to be undertaken in a comprehensive fashion.

2. The Psychoanalytic Hypothesis. Psychoanalysts have worked
out theories linking criminal and antisocial behaviour with traumatic
events in the child's infantile sexual history, and these theories
too have become very popular. Unfortunately the theories in question
are not usually of a kind which can be tested experimentally at all,
and consequently, as Popper and other philosophers of science have
pointed out, they are not scientific theories in any meaningful
sense. The first task awaiting psychoanalysts, therefore, would be
to put these theories into such a form that they can be objectively
tested, i.e. so that falsification is possible. Until that is done
very little can be said about this type of theory.

However, there are certain data which clearly are of relevance
and interest. Thus for example a whole prison has been built in
England (Grendon Underwood) in an attempt to use psychoanalytic
principles to treat offenders and to facilitate their rehabilitation.
This is a very time-consuming and labour-intensive task, involving
great public expenditure, and it is obviously of interest to see
whether prisoners so treated do in fact show a better rate of rehabilitation (i.e. less recidivism) than do prisoners going to an
ordinary, old-fashioned type of prison, without any special psychiatric intervention.

Figure 3 shows the results of such a comparison, giving
recidivism figures for Grendon Underwood inmates and for inmates
for the old-fashioned Oxford prison. It will be seen that there is
in fact no difference at any stage between the figures for these
two prisons, and the results can hardly be said to encourage belief
in the psychoanalytic hypotheses, or the methods of treatment based
on them (Eysenck, 1977). Of course there are difficulties involved
in this comparison. Prisoners are not allocated at random to the
two prisons, but more neurotic prisoners are more likely to be sent
to Grendon Underwood than to Oxford, and vice versa. However, this
should lead to a greater success rate in Grendon Underwood, as
neuroses tend to remit spontaneously (Rachman and Wilson, 1981),
and insofar as neurotic disorders lead to criminal activity, prisoners more seriously neurotic should show an improvement in their
crime rate.

What should be noted, in any case, is that the comparison was
ad hoc and not arranged as an experimental paradigm with proper
controls. Grendon Underwood has been functioning for many years
now, but we still await a properly conducted experimental trial to

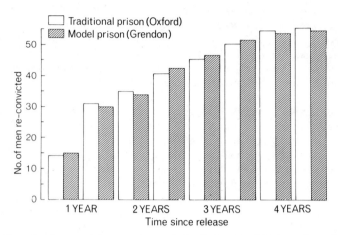

Figure 3:   Number of men reconvicted in traditional prison and
            Grendon Model Prison.

demonstrate its effectiveness, if any. Typically, such innovations
are introduced on the basis of some theoretical hopes, but are not
properly assessed because there is too much official involvement in
the success of the enterprise to make objective scrutiny, with
possibly negative results, feasible.

    More ·interesting, because more of an experimental study, is the
famous Cambridge-Somerville Youth Study (McCord, 1978). In 1935,
this study was instigated by R.C. Cabot. Several hundred boys from
densely populated, factory-dominated areas of Eastern Massachusetts
were included in the project, with schools, welfare agencies,
churches, and the police recommending both "difficult" and "average"
youngsters to the programme. These boys and their families were
given physical examinations and were interviewed by social workers
who then rated each boy in such a way as to allow a selection
committee to designate delinquency-prediction scores. In addition
to giving delinquency-prediction scores, the selection committee
studied each boy's record in order to identify pairs who were
similar in age, delinquency-prone histories, family background,
and home environment. By the toss of a coin, one member of each
pair was assigned to the group that would receive treatment. The
treatment programme began in 1935, when the boys had a median age
of 10.5 years. Treatment continued for an average of five years,
and counsellors assigned to each family visited on the average
twice a month. They encouraged families to call on the programme
for assistance. Family problems became the focus of attention for

approximately one third of the treatment group. Over half of the boys were tutored in academic subjects, over 100 received medical or psychiatric attention; one fourth were sent to summer camps; and most were brought into contact with the Boy Scouts, the YMCA, and other community programmes. The whole programme was based on a combination of psychoanalytic principles and social philosophies of a family-centred kind. The control group participated only through providing information about themselves, and of course both groups contained boys referred as "average" and boys considered "difficult" in equal proportions.

McCord conducted a 30-year follow-up of treatment effects, comparing 253 men who had been in the treatment programme after 1942 with the 253 matched mates assigned to the control group.

The results of the study were most disappointing. Almost equal numbers in the treatment and control groups had committed crimes as juveniles - whether measured by official or unofficial records. As adults, equal numbers had been convicted for some crime. Among men who had been in the treatment group 119 committed only relatively minor crimes (against ordinances or orders), but 49 had committed serious crimes against property (including burglary, larceny, and auto theft) or against persons (including assault, rape, and attempted homicide). Among men from the control group 126 had committed only relatively minor crimes; 42 had committed serious property crimes or crimes against persons. Twenty nine men from the treatment and 25 men from the control group committed serious crimes after the age of 25. None of the differences were significant; however, a higher proportion of criminals from the treatment group than of criminals from the control group committed more than one crime!

Many other comparisons were about family, work and leisure time, beliefs and attitudes and other factors. As McCord concludes: "The objective evidence presents a disturbing picture. The programme seems not only to have failed to prevent its clients from committing crimes - thus corroborating studies of other projects (see e.g. Craig and Furst, 1965; Empey and Ericson, 1972; Hackler, 1966; Miller, 1962; Robin, 1969) - but also to have produced negative side-effects. As compared with the control group,
1. Men who had been in the treatment programme were more likely to commit (at least) a second crime.
2. Men who had been in the treatment programme were more likely to evidence signs of alcoholism.
3. Men from the treatment group more commonly manifested signs of serious mental illness.
4. Among men who had died, those from the treatment group died younger.
5. Men from the treatment group were more likely to report having had at least one stress-related disease; in particular, they were

more likely to have experienced high blood pressure or heart trouble.
6. Men from the treatment group tended to have occupations with
lower prestige.
7. Men from the treatment group tended more often to report their
work as not satisfying."

It should be noted that the side-effects that seem to have
resulted from treatment were subtle. There is no reason to believe
that treatment increased the probability of committing a first crime,
although treatment may have increased the likelihood that those who
committed a first crime would commit additional crimes. Although
treatment may have increased the likelihood of alcoholism, the
treatment group was not more likely to have appeared in clinical
hospitals. There was no difference between the groups in the number
of men who died before the age of 50, although men from the treatment
group had been younger at the age of death. Almost equal proportions
of the two groups of men had remained at the lowest rungs of the
occupational structure, although men from the treatment group were
less likely to be satisfied with their jobs and fewer men from the
treatment group had become white collar workers. The profoundly
discouraging effects of this study, and those other studies mentioned
in our quotation from McCord, do not seem to have penetrated the
public consciousness of the effects of psychoanalytic, psychiatric,
and social intervention, even at an early stage. Programmes are
still being instituted which differ only in minor ways from those
found not only unhelpful, but actively likely to worsen the future
status of the child.

Clearly for practical purposes the results should be taken very
seriously, but from the research point of view there are many unsatisfactory features. In the first place, the programme combined
a number of different methods of intervention, from psychoanalysis
and psychiatry generally, to social interventions of various kinds.
It might have been more satisfactory to have concentrated on one
form of intervention; as it stands, the results, although certainly
not favourable to psychoanalysis, cannot be taken to disprove it
completely, as it might always be argued that not all the children
were subjected to proper psychoanalytic treatment. From this one
would argue that for future work a more specific type of treatment
would have to be used in order to derive generalisable conclusions
about that particular form of treatment; hold-all combinations of
treatment are probably more likely to appeal to public bodies, grant
giving bodies, and others, but they do not throw much light on the
processes involved, or the value of the individual components.
However, our conclusion must be that the study certainly does not
support psychoanalytic hypotheses, and that these are still in a
state where no favourable conclusions concerning them can be
reached.

3. Conditioning and social learning theories. The last group

of theories suggests that socialised behaviour has to be learned,
or becomes conditioned, so that we introject a social "conscience"
which leads us to behave in a socialised manner. This may occur
through modelling (imitation); through instruction by parents,
teachers, priests, etc., or through a simple process of Pavlovian
conditioning. According to the last of these theories, the child
throughout childhood is punished for wrongdoing by parents, teachers,
and peers; the antisocial act which is being punished is the conditioned stimulus, the punishment the unconditioned stimulus, and the
resulting pain, anxiety and shame are the unconditioned responses.
Through repeated pairings the child becomes conditioned to experiencing feelings of pain, anxiety and shame in response to wrongdoing,
and these conditioned responses thus constitute his "conscience"
and powerfully dissuade him from wrongdoing. This theory has been
discussed in great detail by Eysenck (1977), who quotes much
supporting evidence from both animal and human studies.

The conditioning theory has been elaborated to take account of
two facts. The first of these is the presence of genetic factors
in causing criminal behaviour. It has been found that monozygotic
twins are over four times as frequently concordant for criminal
behaviour as are dizygotic twins; this finding, replicated by many
investigators in several different countries, is powerful support
for the genetic hypothesis. Equally strong support are the findings
from adoption studies (Schulsinger, 1972; Crowe, 1972) in which it
was found that adopted children behave in a socialised or antisocial
manner depending on the criminality or otherwise of their true
parents, regardless of the behaviour of their adoptive parents.
These are important findings which are completely neglected by
psychoanalytic and socio-economic theorists.

They link up, however, with another finding, to wit that
personality factors, themselves strongly inherited, correlate with
antisocial behaviour in children, juveniles and adults (Eysenck,
1977). It is noteworthy, and in accordance with theory, that the
personality features which have been found to correlate with antisocial and criminal behaviour are those which have been found in
laboratory investigations to correlate with poor conditionability.
In other words, it is precisely those persons who are difficult to
condition who tend to behave in an antisocial manner. This is in
good accord with the theory. It should further be noted that
these personality-criminality correlations are found not only in
Western society, but also in Communist, and Third World Countries,
suggesting the cross-cultural validity of the hypotheses in question.

One proviso must be made here, namely the inclusion of the
content of the conditioning programme in the general theory. A
child who conditions well will be more likely to introject the
stimulus-response contingencies to which he is subjected, and if
these are in the right direction, he will be more readily socialised

than the child who is slow to form conditioned responses. However, if a child is brought up in a bad environment which reinforces antisocial conduct, such as fighting, stealing, etc., then according to the theory it is precisely the child that is easily conditioned who would incorporate these conditioned responses in his repertoire.

A special study to test this hypothesis has been reported by Raine and Venables (1981), and their main results are shown in Figure 4. Using GSR conditioning they found that under-socialisation was indeed correlated with poor conditionability in children coming from high-class homes, but this relationship was reversed in low-class homes. This study thus supported the hypothesis that in more criminogenic environments superior conditionability facilitates antisocial behaviour.

The conditioning theory can thus explain why certain individuals act in a socialised, others in a non-socialised manner; can it also explain the changes that have taken place in the amount of criminal activity over the past thirty years? Eysenck (1977) has suggested the following hypothesis. If socialised behaviour is mediated by Pavlovian conditioning, then two factors are implicated: one is the actual <u>conditionability</u> of the child, the other is the <u>amount of conditioning</u> that takes place, i.e. the number of contingencies (wrongdoing-punishment) presented to the child. The permissive atmosphere which has permeated society during the past thirty years has significantly reduced the number of such contingencies to which most children are exposed, both in the home, in school and in society, and as a consequence we would expect that while there has been no change in the genetic constitution of the population, the number of conditioning trials has been drastically reduced, producing also a reduction in the "conscience" of the children involved, and hence

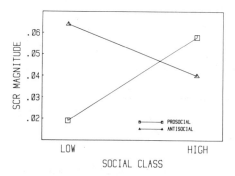

Figure 4:   Prosocial and antisocial behaviour of children coming
             from low and high social class homes, as related to
             SCR conditioning. (From Raine and Venables, 1981).

an increase in the amount of antisocial conduct and criminality. Thus we find an answer to both our problems in the conditioning model of criminality.

This all too short discussion of various theories of criminality cannot, of course, lead to a convincing and universally acceptable answer. The problem is multifaceted, and many different causal factors must be responsible for the observed phenomena. Nevertheless it does seem that at the moment psychological theories of social learning and conditioning, linked with facts relating to personality involvement and genetic determinants, are more adapted to what is known about the phenomena of criminality than are either psycho-analytic or socio-economic theories. There is at present no final answer available to these complex and difficult problems, but further research along the lines here suggested may enhance our understanding of these phenomena.

REFERENCES

Craig, M.M. and Furst, P.W., 1965. What happens after treatment? A study of potentially delinquent boys. Social Service Review, 39: 165-171.
Crowe, R.R., 1972. The adopted offspring of women criminal offenders: A study of their arrest records. Arch. Gen. Psychiat., 27: 600-603.
Empey, L.T. and Ericson, M.L., 1972. "The Provo Experiment: Evaluating Community-Control of Delinquency". Lexington Books, Lexington, Mass.
Eysenck, H.J., 1977. "Crime and Personality". (3rd ed.). Routledge and Kegan Paul, London.
Hackler, J.C., 1966. Boys, blisters, and behaviour: The impact of a work program in an urban area. J. Res. Crime and Delinqu., 12: 155-164.
McCord, J., 1978. A thirty-year follow-up of treatment effects. Amer. Psychol., 33: 284-289.
Miller, W.B., 1962. The impact of a "total community" delinquency control project. Soc. Problems, 10: 168-191.
Rachman, S.J. and Wilson, G.T., 1981. "The Effects of Psychological Therapy". Pergamon, London.
Raine, A. and Venables, P.H., 1981. Classical conditioning and socialisation - a biosocial interaction. Person. individ. Diff., 2: 273-283.
Robin, G.R., 1969. Anti-poverty programs and delinquency. J. Crimin. Law, Criminol. and Police Sci., 60: 323-331.
Schulzinger, F., 1972. Psychopathy, heredity and environment. Internat. J. Ment. Health, 1: 190-206.

ANOREXIA NERVOSA: COUNSELLING AND SELF HELP GROUPS

ANOREXIA NERVOSA: COUNSELLING AND SELF-HELP GROUPS - AN

INTRODUCTION

Eric Bromley

Liverpool Psychology Service
Liverpool Health Authority

Anorexia presents two main problems, how to understand or explain the phenomenon and how best to help people who are displaying anorexic behaviour. To many people anorexia is a complete enigma. The idea of people starving themselves to emaciation, even to death, seems a phenomenon utterly devoid of meaning and an almost alien challenge to even primitive joy, and to life itself.

This symposium, although its individual papers address themselves on occasion to aspects of the theoretical articulation of explanatory concepts in relation to "anorexia", had as its main emphasis the practical issue of how best to help people labelled "anorexic".

A major contribution to the symposium, not recorded among the following papers, was the presentation by Dr. Jill Welbourne (Medical Advisor in Student Health at the University of Bristol) of the film "Sharon". This excellently made film recounted the story of the experience, and eventual cure, of just one anorexic patient. We were fortunate to have with us, for the discussion section of the symposium the subject of the film, Sharon. Another contributor "from the platform" to the discussion was Nina Buckley, the founder of the Merseyside "Anorexic Aid" group, and herself a recovered anorexic.

The first paper, that of Peter Slade, has as its main theme the presentation of a locally organised piece of empirical "consumer" research. The research shows the importance of less "formal" resources available to the anorexic and leads Dr. Slade to propose a model for the optimal utilisation of the total resources available.

Gill Edwards' paper is perhaps rather more theoretical in content. In it she reviews and rejects some of the traditional treatment procedures and the three underlying myths on which these procedures are based. She argues very forcibly for a "socio-dynamic" formulation of the problem of anorexia and a counselling approach to its alleviation. Pat Hartley's paper concentrates on a description of the history and nature of Anorexic Aid, a self-help organisation of which she is one of the founder members. She argues that anorexic behaviour represents the outcome of underlying problems relating to autonomy and that, therefore, it is particularly important to emphasise self-help as being reinforcing to feelings of autonomy, of control over one's own behaviour.

The discussion section of the symposium was important and inevitably, perhaps, was largely theoretical in character.

One question raised was in what sense anorexic behaviour could, or should, be labelled as abnormal or as an "illness". There was general agreement on the impossibility of defining normal eating. It was suggested that in practical, clinical terms abnormal eating behaviour was that which gave rise to significant anxiety in either the person concerned or people in contact with them. Another suggestion was that normal eating could only be defined by excluding the abnormal. Examples of such abnormality would include for instance a diet consisting, for significant periods of time, of little more than a cup of black coffee per day at one extreme, to the regular ingestion of 6,000+ calories per day at the other. The related aspect of whether anorexia nervosa could be construed as an illness seemed by most of the discussants to be answered affirmatively. One suggestion (from Jill Welbourne) was that the defining characteristic was an overwhelming pre-occupation with food intake and that where this was present a "quite recognisable psychiatric illness" was present. At least one contributor from the audience disagreed, suggesting anorexia should be seen more as a phase in growing up, possibly overly extended but nevertheless a phase which could presumably be "worked through" rather than cured.

Two related themes emerged towards the end of the session and are worthy of more detailed comment than was possible then.

Firstly, why should anorexia be treated at all and, in traditional terminology and as a sub-set of this question, is "no treatment control" significantly poorer in outcome than other regimes? Jill Welbourne, in responding to this question, suggested that there was initially a two stage selling job to be done to the potential "customer" of anorexic help. The first job is to persuade the customer that there is a problem and the second is to convince the customer that there is a need to do something about the problem. The client had to be converted from "slimmer" to "patient" and Jill quoted figures that, of approximately 120 clients she had dealt

with, only one had come as a result of perceiving the situation as
being a problem, the rest presumably being under varying degrees of
pressure and coercion from relatives and/or friends. Many of her
clients have undergone this conversion which is seen as necessary
to prevent the alternatives of death by starvation or chronic, un-
ending, anorexia. Clearly such an approach brings into sharp focus
the basically moral dilemma of "treating" people who do not see
themselves as "ill" (or in less medical terms "helping" people who
do not see themselves as having a "problem"). This general issue
within psychiatry is of particular relevance to anorexia given the
common finding that a large proportion of such people do not seek
help, and that another large proportion seek help only following
the urgings of others. There would appear to be no published studies
comparing treatment with "no treatment"controls" - perhaps not surprisingly in view of the potentially fatal outcome of no treatment.
But if it is true that no such studies exist (the only possibly
relevant one would seem to be that of Cremerius (1965), quoted in
Bruche (1974)), then the question of the appropriateness of "radical
non-intervention" as a form of treatment would seem to be an open
one even on empirical grounds.

A similar, though perhaps not such an extreme "shaking of the
foundations" question raised in the discussion was whether anorexics
should be construed, and treated, as an identifiable group different
from other individuals (with or without "problems"). All the contributors seem to assume the answer is yes (albeit from different
viewpoints). Again, though, there seems to be very little, if any,
evidence showing that anorexics treated as members of an anorexic
group fare any better than if treated as a member of a more general
group.

It might be interesting to argue this case a little more fully.
Let us describe anorexia as "pathological fasting" without defining
that term. Let us look at forms of (arguably) non-pathological
fasting. Three types spring to mind:-

1. Religious fasting. This would seem to have one main function -
    an act of self-renunciation either to assuage guilt, as an act
    of identification with a religious figure or to free (usually
    symbolically) the faster from too great an attachment to the
    needs of the body. (Another function in more prolonged fasting
    can be to help achieve some altered state of consciousness
    presumably via the biochemical changes produced by prolonged
    fasting).

2. Hunger striking. Here fasting essentially serves the function
    of protest - usually of a political nature. Often this form of
    fasting is undertaken by people who perceive themselves as being
    in the circumstances of powerlessness. Their action usually is

designed to achieve some aim, to exert some power over circumstances.

3. Dieting. Here "fasting" - or perhaps more accurately - reduction
    in food intake is related to achieving some change in body dim-
    ensions for either supposedly aesthetic or supposedly health-
    giving reasons.

There would thus seem to be at least three logically distinct
functions of normal fasting. To discuss the function of, or the
motivation behind, religious fasting as though it were necessarily
the same as dieting or hunger striking would be quite illogical and
unnecessary. To put it another way the important factors in analysis
of religious fasting would be religious, in hunger striking political
and in dieting aesthetic and/or health.

There is a respectable argument that similar considerations
apply to the pathological fasting labelled anorexia. It is not
necessary to accept that the three categories of normal fasting can
by a process of analogy be applied to pathological fasting (although
aspects of the three categories figure under various guises in most
discussion of anorexia). The argument is more that what is important
in the individual anorexic patient is not the symptom of anorexia
but the function, or the underlying motivation, represented by that
symptom in that particular individual. That individual may be batt-
ling with underlying problems which have far more similarity to the
underlying problems of patients with different symptomatology or,
for that matter with the problems of non-patients displaying no
obvious symptomatology at all. This might be true both conceptually
(self-control issues for instance are often the substrata of obsess-
ive/compulsive symptomatology and "normal" people in groups often
struggle with autonomy/powerlessness problems). More importantly it
might have considerable bearing not just on the conceptual problems
but on the nature of treatment approaches used.

In terms of treatment there are dangers about treating "symptomatically". All the contributors to this symposium might agree with
this statement - in terms of concentrating on, and attempting to
analyse, the dynamics of anorexia rather than viewing it purely
symptomatically. Yet all seem to accept the advisability of treating
anorexics by defining them, as a group, in terms of those symptoms.
"An identity as an anorexic was felt preferable to no identity at
all", to quote from Pat Hartley. But whilst this might be felt to
be preferable it is not necessarily true that it is preferable. One
danger, in these terms, is that this false or partial identity becomes
hard to relinquish. Groups of "people" or "women" searching for
identity might be better than groups of "anorexics" identifying
themselves as such and seeking a solution to their anorexia.

Of course, this debate about person-oriented rather than symptom-oriented approaches is much wider than a discussion about anorexia. But it does seem of particular relevance to anorexia for the following reasons:-

1. The apparent dearth of empirical evidence comparing non-treatment or treatment not specifically related to anorexic symptomatology (e.g. heterogeneous psychotherapy groups or women's groups or individual counselling) with treatment focussing on anorexic symptomatology.

2. The likelihood that quite essentially different mechanisms underlie anorexic symptoms in different individuals. Attempts to explain anorexia as a single entity are bedevilled by the perceived necessity to incorporate many different functions as explanatory concepts in synthetic ways. Synthesis might not be necessary if we cease to construe anorexia as a disease entity (implicitly or explicitly) and instead see it as a possibly convenient symptomatic label for a large group of individuals representing different patterns of underlying dynamics or different functional analyses of behaviour.

3. The experience of anorexics themselves. The majority see no need for help. The remaining minority emphasise the more general, less specifically anorexic, aspects of the help they received or needed. Thus Pat Hartley states: "What the patient described as recovery ... rarely had much connection with weight gain alone." Thus the role for, and emphasis on, non-specific help such as 'friends' or 'the church' referred to in Peter Slade's paper. Thus the emphasis in Gill Edward's paper on concepts such as autonomy, sex roles, control, and self-esteem - all being the common currency of psychotherapy in general, indeed of humanity itself.

I was struck, in the discussion following this symposium by the comments of both Sharon and Nina Buckley. Sharon talked about the need for "somebody (the therapist) to subtly care for you" and Nina the need to "find one's being". Both express in epigramatic form what psychotherapy, in a very general sense, is all about. So perhaps any emphasis on "anorexia", analytically, conceptually or in terms of treatment is counter-productive. In terms of treatment the assumed specific needs of anorexics may be nothing more than, or a sub-set of, the general needs of people seeking psychotherapy. The sadness is not that relatively few seek such help but that to obtain help so often they have to self-affix the label. They have to have "pathological" anorexic problems rather than the virtually universal problems of coping, or coming to terms with, problems of autonomy, self-control etc.

Any practical implications of this alternative approach might be difficult to think through and certainly difficult to attain. Presumably Anorexic Clinics, Anorexic Aid, Anorexic Counselling, etc., would end. Given the fact that most "anorexics" are women and that most of the analysis emphasises the alleged specifically female nature of the underlying dynamics, then the alternative might be "Women's Groups" - women meeting to discuss and work through the universal problems shared by women whether anorexic or not. Such a proposal would, naturally, be "political" for the major location of the problem would cease to be the individual but would lie in the social matrix of power relationships which determine, or help to shape, woman's view of herself. Perhaps an even more revolutionary and/or ludicrously impractical suggestion (depending on one's point of view) would be to move on to people's groups. For then even the generality of problems of women would be seen to be transcended. The focus of attention would shift to the universal human problem of powerlessness, of alienation, which each of us in his or her own individual way react to, work out, fight against or come to terms with. The intra-individual battleground of anorexia would become a microcosm of much greater conflicts.

REFERENCES

Bruche, H., 1974. "Eating Disorders: Obesity, Anorexia Nervosa
     and the Person Within". Routledge, Kegan Paul, London.
Cremerius, J., 1965. Zur prognose der anorexia nervosa. Arch.
     Psychiat. Nervenkr., 207: 378-393.

THE ROLE OF COUNSELLING AND SELF-HELP GROUPS IN THE MANAGEMENT OF

ANOREXIA NERVOSA

Peter Slade

Senior Lecturer in Clinical Psychology

Liverpool University Medical School

INTRODUCTION

The term 'anorexia nervosa', literally translated, means 'loss of appetite of nervous origin'. This is a misleading and inadequate term for a complicated psychosomatic condition which continues to pose problems of diagnosis, aetiology, treatment, management, and prognosis and, at a more basic level, problems in simply under-standing what motivates the anorectic to behave in the way she/he does. The central thesis of this paper is that anorexia nervosa, unlike most other medical or even psychosomatic complaints, involves multifaceted and multilevel problems which both impinge upon and derive their energising force from every aspect of the individual's makeup, environment, and the interaction between these. It follows from this thesis that treatment (or help) cannot be restricted to one aspect of the problem, of the person, of the person's environment, or to one setting in which the afflicted anorectic is placed or finds herself/himself.

DIAGNOSTIC CRITERIA

Although the diagnostic criteria of Feighner et al. (1972) are now generally accepted as setting the standard for research purposes, the three-fold essential criteria of Russell (1970) seem more appropriate (less restrictive) for clinical purposes. These are: (1) severe loss of weight due to self-imposed food restriction, (2) amenorrhea (loss of periods) in females who would otherwise be normally menstrual or an equivalent endocrine disturbance in males, and (3) a specific psychopathology involving abnormal attitudes to body size and shape, weight, food and the eating function.

More recently Russell (1979) has proposed a separate category
for what he terms 'bulimia nervosa', a category which he has distinguished symptomatologically from 'anorexia nervosa'. Once again
the criteria are threefold, namely: (1) an irresistable urge to
overeat (binge-eating) which may alternate with periods of starvation,
(2) morbid fear of weight gain/becoming fat, and (3) attempted
avoidance of weight gain by means of self-induced vomiting and/or
purgatives. The relationship between these two categories is as yet
poorly understood. However the writer has recently proposed a
functional model relating one type of 'bulimia nervosa' to 'anorexia
nervosa' (Slade, 1982).

For current purposes this paper will concentrate on the category
of anorexia nervosa as defined diagnostically by Russell (1970).

LONG-TERM OUTCOME IN ANOREXIA NERVOSA

Over the past twenty-five years a sizeable number of follow-up
studies of anorectic patients have been reported in the literature
(for recent reviews see Bemis, 1978; Hsu, 1980). However, as the
latter reviewer has pointed out, many of these studies have had
methodological weaknesses for one reason or another. For current
purposes it was decided to concentrate on just two such studies
(i.e. those of Morgan and Russell, 1975 and Hsu et al., 1979) which
have the following characteristics:
1. a follow-up period of at least four years.
2. a sample size of at least forty patients.
3. a follow-up rate approaching/attaining the maximum.
4. the use of multidimensional adjustment criteria (in fact similar
    criteria).
5. involvement of apparently similar patient groups (both studies
    were conducted on anorectic patients admitted to inpatient
    specialised units in London Teaching Hospitals).
6. inpatient treatment programmes involving, among other things,
    clearly defined refeeding programmes.
7. although the inpatient treatment programmes differ in many other
    respects, the outcome findings show a remarkably consistent
    picture across the two studies.

The detailed findings are reproduced in Table 1. In column one
are the variables/criteria investigated; column two shows the findings from the Morgan and Russell (1975) study; column three shows
the findings from the Hsu et al. (1979) study; while the totals
and/or means are presented in column four for the two studies
combined.

TABLE 1.   Outcome of Anorexia Nervosa: Findings from two British
          studies

Variable	A) Morgan and Russell, 1975	B) Hsu et al, 1979	Total A) and B)
Length of follow-up	4 - 10 years	4 - 8 years	
No. of cases	41	105	146
No. followed-up	41 (100%)	102 (97%)	143 (98%)
No. of deaths	2 (5%)	2 (2%)	4 (3%)
A) Weight Status			
1. Normal weight (±15%)	22 (55%)	65 (62%)	87 (60%)
2. Normal but fluctuated	6 (15%)	13 (12%)	19 (13%)
3. Intermediate (75% - 85%)	3 (7%)	6 (6%)	9 (6%)
4. Underweight (< 75%)	8 (20%)	16 (15%)	24 (16%)
5. Overweight (16% +)	2 (5%)	2 (2%)	4 (3%)
B) Eating Problems			
1. Normal	14 (33%)	37 (35%)	51 (35%)
2. Dietary restriction	20 (50%)	48 (46%)	68 (47%)
3. Bulimia	22 (54%)	20 (19%)	42 (29%)
4. Vomiting	10 (25%)	22 (21%)	32 (22%)
5. Purgative abuse	13 (33%)	36 (34%)	49 (34%)
6. Anxiety on eating with others	21 (51%)	33 (31%)	54 (37%)
C) Menstrual Status			
1. Regular	18 (47%)	54 (51%)	72 (49%)
2. Sporadic	3 (8%)	17 (16%)	20 (14%)
3. Amenorrhea	15 (39%)	29 (28%)	44 (30%)

.../Contd.

TABLE 1.   Contd.

Variable	A) Morgan and Russell, 1975	B) Hsu et al, 1979	Total A) and B)
D) Psychosexual Adjustment			
1. Normal attitudes and behaviour	24 (60%)	60 (57%)	84 (57%)
2. Clearly abnormal	9 (23%)	21 (20%)	30 (21%)
E) Psychosocial			
1. Difficulties with family	22 (55%)	39 (37%)	61 (42%)
2. Social phobia	18 (45%)	25 (24%)	43 (29%)
F) Vocational			
Full-time employment	29 (73%)	82 (78%)	111 (76%)
G) Other Symptoms			
1. Symptom-free	16 (40%)	47 (45%)	63 (43%)
2. Depression	14 (45%)	40 (38%)	54 (37%)
3. Obssessive-compulsive	9 (23%)	22 (21%)	31 (21%)
4. Social phobia	18 (45%)	25 (24%)	43 (29%)

The first point of note is that mortality rates across the two studies are fairly low (3%) and rank very favourably by comparison with some of the other follow-up studies reported in the literature (c.f. review of Bemis, 1978). In terms of weight status both samples also did well, 60% maintaining a normal weight and a further 13% fluctuating around a normal weight. By contrast only 35% were judged to have 'normal' eating patterns, sizeable numbers still indulging in dietary restriction (47%), bulimia or binge-eating (29%), vomiting (22%) and purgative abuse (22%). More of the Morgan and Russell sample continued with the former two abnormal patterns than the Hsu et al. sample.

Turning to the findings on menstrual status and psychosexual adjustment, the combined results demonstrate an intermediate outcome.

Approximately half of the patients (49%) were having regular periods
and another 14% were menstruating sporadically, while over half
(57%) were adjudged at follow-up interview to have normal attitudes
to sex and to show normal sexual behaviour. Similarly psychosocial
adjustment represented an intermediate outcome, 42% still having
clear family problems and 29% exhibiting social phobia. The final
two categories in Table 1 show a marked contrast. Seventy-six
percent were involved in full-time employment (including housewives)
but only 43% were completely symptom-free. The commonest symptoms
reported were depression (37%), obsessive-compulsive problems (21%)
and social phobia (29%).

The above outcome findings are summarised in Table 2, using a
three-fold classification of good, moderate and poor. Given the
consistency of the findings presented in Table 1 and summarised in
Table 2, a number of tentative conclusions can be drawn. First that
the outcome in anorexia nervosa is extremely variable. Not only do
individuals vary but outcome varies according to the adjustment
criterion involved. Moreover the latter type of variability shows
a remarkably consistent pattern over comparable studies.

Secondly, weight status which is the most commonly used yard-
stick for recovery, both clinically and in research studies, is in
fact a relatively poor indicator of overall adjustment; particularly
with respect to the normality of eating patterns and the absence of
other forms of psychopathological symptoms. The above consistent
discrepancy between adjustment findings could be due to one or more
of several reasons. It could be that the restoration and maintenance of a normal weight is easier to achieve therapeutically than
changes in eating patterns or other forms of accompanying psychopathology. Or it could be that therapeutically more time and
emphasis is placed on the former than on the latter. Or it may
reflect a mixture of both. Whatever the truth of the matter the
unmistakeable conclusion from these two follow-up studies (which
are typical if not better than most) is one of variable success
with anorectic patients. In simple terms, specialised inpatient
treatment units are effective in keeping such patients alive, in
restoring a normal weight and ensuring the maintenance of such, but
far less effective in dealing with other problem areas presented by
anorectic patients, including the normalisation of eating patterns.
Thus while hospital treatment seems to have an important role to
play, particularly when the anorectic is in a critically poor
physical and nutritional state, it does not currently seem to
provide all the answers to the problem. There appears to be both
a need and scope for additional forms of help.

Table 2:   Summary of Outcome Findings from Two British Studies
           (Morgan and Russell, 1975; Hsu et al., 1979)

Criterion	Total %	Evaluation
Vocational adjustment	76%	
Normal weight (inc. fluctuations)	73%	Good
Psychosocial adjustment	58 - 71%	
Psychosexual adjustment	57%	Moderate
Menstrual function	49%	
Symptom-free	43%	
Normal eating patterns	35%	Poor

CONSUMER RESEARCH

     Another way of evaluating the contribution of hospital treat-
ment (and at the same time exploring the possible value of additional
forms of help) in the management of this difficult problem is by
consumer research. Consequently a small survey was conducted
through a recently formed branch of Anorexic Aid, a self-help and
advice organisation now registered in the UK as a national charity.
In conjunction with Miss Nina Butler, the local Anorexic Aid
contact, a simple questionnaire was devised and circulated to 154
members of this local branch, of whom 103 were sufferers or ex-
sufferers and 51 were parents of sufferers. In addition to
eliciting information on age and sex, nature of problem and its
duration, respondents were presented with a list of 14 services/
potential forms of help and asked to indicate which ones they had
had contact with and in addition to rate the degree of helpfulness
on a three-point scale: not at all helpful (1), fairly helpful
(2) and very helpful (3). Unfortunately there was a disappointing
return rate from sufferers and ex-sufferers, only 37 (36%) returning
completed questionnaires. The findings therefore need to be treated
cautiously.

     Of the 37 respondents all but one was female, 28 describing
themselves as sufferers and 9 as ex-sufferers. Their mean age was
22.97 years (S.D. 5.54) and the mean duration of the problem was
6.16 years (S.D. 5.00). The findings for this sample are presented

in Table 3. The first five categories are concerned with different
types of medical treatment. As can be seen from Table 3 three-
quarters of the sample had received treatment from their general
practitioners, of whom only 41% reported such treatment as being
fairly or very helpful. By comparison psychiatric treatment fared
somewhat better, 61% reporting inpatient and 52% outpatient treatment
as helpful. Only a quarter had received inpatient medical (as
opposed to psychiatric) treatment but a similar proportion (62%)
reported this as helpful. None of the five individuals who had
received outpatient medical treatment reported this as helpful.
Thus inpatient psychiatric and medical treatment was reported to
be the most helpful, outpatient medical treatment the least, with
outpatient psychiatric and general practioner treatments being
intermediate.

The next two categories involve alternative procedures to
conventional medicine: hypnosis and acupuncture. Less than a
quarter of the sample had had contact with either, but of those
who had only one quarter to one third rated them as being fairly or
very helpful.

The next three categories involve community services/potential
supports. Only 19% had received formal help from the Social Services,
of whom 57% described it as helpful (approximately comparable to
outpatient psychiatric treatment). By contrast, larger numbers
had received help from 'friends' and the 'church', the overwhelming
majority of whom reported favourably on these two kinds of community
help. Finally, the last two categories are those of Anorexic Aid
and anorexic counsellors. Only a half and a quarter of the sample
respectively, had had regular contact with these, but once again
the overwhelming majority reported favourably on the help received.

While the data reported in Table 3 should be treated with
caution, they do suggest at the level of the lowest common denomin-
ator the possibility that diverse agencies may prove helpful to the
anorexic patient. Among medical services formal inpatient treatment
was rated the most useful, while among community services the less
formal help provided by friends and the church were rated the most
highly. It is unlikely that these two very different services/
groups are helping with the same problem; much more likely that
they are acting in some complementary fashion. In conclusion,
consumer research suggests the possibility that groups other than
the medical profession may be able to contribute to the management
and treatment of anorexia nervosa in some form which complements
that of medical treatment.

Table 3:   Preliminary Results of A.N. Survey

N = 37 sufferers and ex-sufferers

Type of service	No. % Having had contact		Ratings of Helpfulness			
			Not at all helpful		Fairly or very helpful	
1. GP treatment	27	(73%)	16	(59%)	11	(41%)
2. In-patient psychiatric	23	(62%)	9	(39%)	14	(61%)
3. Out-patient psychiatric	29	(78%)	14	(48%)	15	(52%)
4. In-patient medical	8	(24%)	3	(38%)	5	(62%)
5. Out-patient medical	5	(15%)	5	(100%)	0	(0%)
6. Hypnotists	9	(24%)	6	(67%)	3	(33%)
7. Acupuncturists	4	(11%)	3	(75%)	1	(25%)
8. Social services	7	(19%)	3	(43%)	4	(57%)
9. The church	16	(43%)	1	(6%)	15	(94%)
10. Friends	25	(68%)	4	(16%)	21	(84%)
11. Anorexic Aid	18	(49%)	1	(6%)	17	(94%)
12. Anorexic counsellors	10	(27%)	0	(0%)	10	(100%)

SUGGESTED FRAMEWORK FOR HOSPITAL/COMMUNITY MANAGEMENT

The general conclusion which emerges from both long-term outcome studies and more limited consumer research is that medical services do not currently have the complete answer to the problem. It is therefore of some import to consider how other professional/volunteer/community services can contribute.

In line with the theoretical model recently put forward by the writer (Slade, 1982) the anorectic is viewed as passing through a number of different stages. Early on the anorectic discovers weight-control as a satisfying <u>pursuit</u>; then it becomes a defensible and acceptable <u>obsession</u>; and finally it emerges, after a number of tortuous years, as a tormenting <u>addiction</u>. The pattern of help required, and the possibility of a favourable response, vary arguably according to the stage reached. At a very early stage, the problem may be averted, given early identification and appropriate advice and support in the community; during the intermediate stage specialist medical treatment will probably be necessary, on a recurrent basis, to keep the anorectic alive; and finally, once the anorectic has reached the final stage of wanting and seeking real help, specialist advice and support in the community may enable her/him to kick the habit for good.

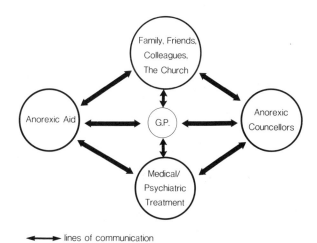

Figure 1:   Suggested Framework for Hospital/Community Management of Anorexia Nervosa.

In the consumer survey described above one of the common views
put forward by anorectics/ex-anorectics was that there is currently
a dearth of services available in the UK to meet their needs. The
view of the present writer is that there are more sources of help
available (professional, volunteer and community) than are currently
being capitalised upon and that what is urgently required is a manpower study to identify such resources and, perhaps more importantly,
to establish a viable framework for the acute and long-term
management of such problems within a hospital/community framework.
A possible framework is presented in Fig. 1. in which a central role
is accorded the general practitioner. The latter is viewed as the
professional capable of bridging the gap between community management, on the one hand, and referral for specialist help and advice,
on the other. However, in order for such a management model to
become viable, it is clear that general practitioners will require
more knowledge and training in the problems posed by anorexia
nervosa.

The following chapters are concerned with the potential, and
real, contributions that can be made by both Anorexia Counsellors
and Anorexic Aid.

REFERENCES

Bemis, K., 1978. Current approaches to the etiology and treatment
     of anorexia nervosa. Psych. Bull., 85: 593-617.
Feighner, J.P., Robins, E., Guze, S.B., Woodruff, R.A., Winokur, G.,
     and Munoz, R., 1972. Diagnostic criteria for use in psychiatric
     research. Arch. Gen. Psychiat., 26: 57-63.
Hsu, L.K.G., Crisp, A.H. and Harding, B., 1979. Outcome of anorexia
     nervosa. Lancet. 1: 61-65.
Morgan, M.G. and Russell, G.F.M., 1975. Value of family background
     and clinical features as predictors of long-term outcome in
     anorexia nervosa four-year follow-up study of 41 patients.
     Psychol. Med., 5: 355-371.
Russell, G.F.M., 1970. Anorexia nervosa: its identity as an illness
     and its treatment. In: Price J.H. (Ed.), "Modern Trends in
     Psychological Medicine". Butterworths, London.
Russell, G.F.M., 1979. Bulimia nervosa: an ominous variant of
     anorexia nervosa. Psychol. Med., 9: 429-448.
Slade, P.D., 1982. Towards a functional analysis of anorexia
     nervosa and bulimia nervosa. Brit. J. Clin. Psychol.,
     21: 167-169.

COUNSELLING FOR CLIENTS WITH ANOREXIA NERVOSA

Gill Edwards

University of Liverpool

Corinne, aged fourteen, scurries in for her first appointment, behind her small, rotund and concerned mother. "She eats like a sparrow", the mother says, "And last week I caught her hiding food in the dustbin. I'm sure she's got that 'slimming disease' that you read about. Is there anything you can do about it?" Corinne, meanwhile, is endeavouring to merge symbiotically with the wallpaper, lest her mother might notice her presence. "So how do you feel about it, Corinne?" asks the therapist, gently. "Do you think you have some sort of problem?" "Oh, no", the mother breaks in. "She seems to think it's quite normal to exist on black coffee and green salad. And she used to have such a good appetite." Corinne shrinks still further into the chair, until her skeletal frame threatens to disappear into its womb-like depths. Her mother glances at her anxiously, then continues to speak.....

Although somewhat caricatured, many who have worked with anorexic clients will recognise the above exchange. It illustrates two major problems one may encounter in an initial session: firstly, the use of the medical model by the client and/or her family, which provides a "treatment barrier" (Scott, 1972) right from the start; and secondly, the possibility of an unwilling client, dragged along by a concerned and often voluble parent.

To start at the beginning, the recognition of "anorexia nervosa" dates back to Sir William Gull, in 1873, who described the problem as "a peculiar form of disease characterised by extreme emaciation... (affecting) mostly the female sex, and chiefly between the ages of sixteen and twenty-three." Gull suggested that the most suitable treatment for this "peculiar disease" was bedrest and plenty of food.

Despite the fact that our understanding of anorexia nervosa
has advanced considerably over the past ten or fifteen years, the
new perspective is slow to spread, and three misleading views about
anorexia continue to be widely held: firstly, that it is a puzzling,
mysterious "disease" which causes strange behaviour which cannot be
understood; secondly, that sufferers resist any form of help; and
thirdly, that the appropriate treatment is restoration of normal
weight, by some method of refeeding. I shall therefore begin by
suggesting that each of these three views is a myth, and then move
on to discuss counselling clients who are anorexic.

To deal with the first view first - the idea that anorexic
behaviour is incomprehensible. Over the last decade, several
writers - such as Hilde Bruch (1974, 1978), Mara Selvini Palazzoli
(1974), Marlene Boskind-Lodahl (1976), Marilyn Lawrence (1979) and
Sheila MacLeod (1981) - have all suggested that anorexia can be
understood. Most of these writers agree that anorexia represents
a way of coping with an autonomy or identity crisis. Hilde Bruch
(1978) suggests that the central feature of anorexia is a "para-
lysing sense of ineffectiveness". Somehow, says Bruch, an anorexic
young woman has grown up to be over-submissive, lacking in self-
esteem and deficient in a sense of autonomy; she has lost touch with
her own feelings and desires, and constantly struggles to fulfil
others' expectations; she may even feel that she has to be "special"
in order to live up to a privileged family background.

Given this framework, self-starvation begins to make some sense:
the potential anorexic feels she has no control over her life or
other people, sees herself as inadequate and worthless, and is
alienated from her own body. The "control struggle" then becomes
internalised, so that she strives for a sense of autonomy and self-
esteem via an increasingly desperate attempt to control her own
body weight and food intake. Such a perspective also explains other
aspects of anorexic behaviour: notably the tendency towards sub-
jugation of all bodily needs. Anorexics do not only starve themselves, but often deny themselves warmth, sleep and physical rest;
they may exercise daily to the point of exhaustion, and often work
compulsively. Their ideal is thus not an aesthetic one, not the
slim fashion model, but an ascetic ideal - the saint or martyr.
(One client told me that she would never eat strawberries, in spite
of their low calorie content, since they are a luxury food which
she had done nothing to deserve.)

Anorexic behaviour, then, may serve several functions for the
person involved. First it gives her a much-needed sense of control
and effectiveness; secondly, it helps her to maintain her fragile
self-esteem (since both slimness and self-control are highly valued
in our society); thirdly, it both expresses, and is an attempt to
resolve, her basic conflicts over autonomy and self-image; and
lastly, the obsession with food and body weight enables her to

avoid facing the more important issues in her life, at least for the time being. In individual cases, of course, anorexia may serve other functions as well. Sheila MacLeod (1981) suggests that the main issues involved are introjection and projection, separation and loss, helplessness and hopelessness, identity and autonomy - and that anorexia nervosa "is a last stand against being engulfed by such emotional disasters". So, in answer to the view that anorexia cannot be understood, I have briefly outlined a perspective which suggests that anorexic behaviour is fully comprehensible, if seen within its social and psychological context.

The second view under discussion is that people who are anorexic resist any attempts to help them. As with many myths, there is some truth in this, in that most anorexics will at some stage deny that there is anything wrong, and even believe this themselves. However, one need not listen to anorexic clients for very long to realise that being anorexic is a black, nightmarish existence, dominated by constant and interminable conflicts over eating, which interfere with every aspect of daily life. So why do so many anorexics deny that there is any problem? The operation of defence mechanisms is only a partial explanation. Many seem to refuse help because they guess, or are aware, that the only "help" on offer is hospitalisation and (to quote an ex-client of mine) "being fed up like livestock". Needless to say, the prospect of having little or no control over food intake is quite horrifying to most anorexics. As Sheila MacLeod (1981) points out: "To the anorexic, hospital must seem like a prison where she is being punished for seeking autonomy by being deprived of what little autonomy she has managed to find."

There is therefore a considerable gulf between prevailing medical methods of treating anorexia nervosa, and socio-psychodynamic formulations of the problem. It was in recognition of this gulf that the Anorexia Counselling Service was founded, in 1978, by Marilyn Lawrence and myself. In the first year, despite limited publicity, we received about four hundred letters (and as many telephone enquiries), of which 55 percent were from anorexics them-selves - most of whom desperately wanted any information, advice or counselling which we had to offer. Many of them had been hospital-ised, some repeatedly, but all felt that the treatment had left their real problems untouched. The following brief quotes are fairly typical of the letters we received:-

"I feel very desperate at the psychiatric approach to my daughter. She is refusing any solid food while in hospital, saying she will resume her former rigid diet when she returns home. The psychiatrist accuses her of "playing games", and says she is not fighting this "thing" that won't let her eat..... My daughter has said that the inner turmoil is so bad that life is not worth living." (Mother of fourteen year old.).

"I am twenty-seven, and have suffered from anorexia nervosa since I
was fourteen. I have been in hospital many times, and last year even
had a leucotomy - all without ultimate avail."
"I have not been able to obtain any help for our daughter, or ourselves, in coping with her illness. She sees her doctor every three
weeks for a chat, but has no specific treatment at all. Her doctor
says she will grow out of it in time, and that I must ignore it -
something I find almost impossible to do." (Mother of seventeen
year old.)
"Please help! I have been anorexic for four years, including two
spells in hospital. I'm desperate, feeling ill and being a great
worry to all the family .... The mental strain is enormous, with
part of me wanting to put on weight and the other half saying No!
Please help me. I am really desperate." (Male, aged twenty.)

It was soon clear, therefore, that there was a great demand
both for counselling and for information which might help sufferers
and their families to understand the problem - which leads us on to
the third and final myth: the idea that the most appropriate treatment for anorexia is the restoration of normal weight via a refeeding
programme. Although hospitalisation and refeeding will be necessary
in some cases, as a short-term life-saving measure, it should in no
way be regarded as "treatment". Indeed, there is a considerable
risk that such a procedure may compound the very problems which
underlie anorexia. It may even increase the specific eating problems;
many anorexics report learning to binge and vomit, or to abuse
laxatives, while in hospital. Many more are discharged with a
renewed determination to lose weight, in an urgent attempt to regain
their fragment of autonomy and self-respect.

The main alternative to refeeding and/or drugs is some form of
counselling or psychotherapy. But what can one offer to an anorexic
client, as a potential counsellor? Firstly, I think it is useful to
have some theoretical formulation of anorexia, such as that which I
briefly outlined above. It is essential, at least, to believe that
anorexia can be understood - that it is not symptomatic of some
strange "illness", but is instead a desperate way of coping with
certain problems-in-living. Given this basic assumption, what does
counselling someone who is anorexic involve?

It is often helpful to convey, in the first session, one's
belief that the client's problems do not revolve around food, eating
and body weight, but rather around more basic issues such as her
feelings about herself and her life. This is one way of conveying
the fact that you are interested in her as a person, rather than in
her body weight or eating habits. Personally, I have never asked
an anorexic client how much she weighs (although the information
is often offered spontaneously). I believe it to be therapeutic to
state, from the beginning, that a client's body is her own responsibility, and that one is not particularly interested in how much

she weighs, <u>unless</u> her weight falls so low as to endanger her health.
At the Anorexia Counselling Service, our policy was to warn clients
that we should have to discontinue counselling if a client allowed
her weight to fall so low that we became anxious about her; in
practice, we never had to exercise this sanction. If a counsellor
does decide to make regular enquiries about a client's weight, there
is the danger of reinforcing the anorexic assumption that body weight
is all-important, and that all the counsellor is <u>really</u> interested
in is restoring her weight to normal. (One client told me, in our
final session, "I used to think you were crazy, never asking about
my weight. Sometimes I thought you'd forgotten that I was anorexic.
Then I came to realise that I felt quite good about that, because
it was your way of saying that it was <u>me</u> you wanted to hear about.")

One common mistake in counselling anorexics is to appeal only
to the sensible, rational part of the person, and to encourage her
to overcome or reject the 'anorexic' part of herself. This only
serves to reinforce a neurotic split within the client which is
already well-established. Marilyn Lawrence (1979), who explored
the "control paradox" of anorexia, noted that (despite appearances
to the contrary) anorexics experience themselves as very much <u>out</u>
of control. Thus, for a counsellor to suggest that the "anorexic"
part of the self is "sick", or must be battled against, only
increases a client's feelings of helplessness. It is therefore
crucial to therapy that the client is encouraged to re-own her
experience of anorexia, and not to split it off as "sick" or "crazy".
Both the anorexic and the rational parts of the client must be
acknowledged and accepted before the conflict between them can
begin to be resolved.

Given that anorexics tend to feel helpless and out of control,
a counsellor often needs to give hope that it <u>is</u> possible to escape
from what Hilde Bruch (1978) calls "the golden cage" of anorexia.
Firstly, one can impress upon a client that, although anorexia is
her current way of coping with life, the underlying problems are
ordinary problems-in-living, which can be resolved in other ways.
Secondly, one can refer to former anorexic clients who are now
leading happy, fulfilling lives, and who no longer use eating or
starvation in an attempt to cope with life's difficulties.

Much has been written in an attempt to explain why roughly
95 per cent of anorexics are female. There is little doubt that
there are many contradictory pressures upon, and irreconcilable
roles for, the young educated woman of today; and it is still more
difficult for a woman to become autonomous and gain a self-
respecting identity than it is for a man. In my paper "Is there
an anorexic family?" (1979), I argued that the pathological characteristics of families with anorexic members - summarised by Minuchin
(1978) as enmeshment, rigidity, over-protectiveness and avoidance
of conflict - may be seen as an exaggerated form of patriarchal

"normality". Sheila MacLeod (1981) suggests that, to the anorexic, autonomy and femininity seem antithetical; and Susie Orbach (1978) argues that anorexia symbolises a simultaneous rejection and exaggeration of the female stereotype. (Susie Orbach also explores the complex relationship between eating disorders and the pressures and politics of the slimming industry.) It is therefore worth examining one's own preconceptions about appropriate behaviour and lifestyle for the sexes, before embarking upon a counselling relationship with someone who is anorexic. (Male anorexics, although relatively few in number, seem to have similar conflicts over autonomy, identity and self-esteem; as with female anorexics, sensitivity to sex stereotypes may be an important element of therapy.)

Perhaps the most important component of counselling is careful and patient listening - letting the client tell her own story, and helping her to explore and unravel her own feelings, thoughts and behaviour. Carl Rogers' "therapeutic triad" of accurate empathy, non-possessive warmth and genuineness, is particularly important in working with anorexics. It is essential that the client feels that her emotions and experiences are taken seriously, and not invalidated as mere "symptoms" of anorexia. The first priority, then, is to help the client realise that she is an individual capable of thinking, feeling and judging for herself, that she is able to make her own decisions and lead her own life. (cf. Palazzoli, 1974.) Counselling also involves considering what functions are being served for the client by being anorexic, and helping her to find alternative ways of fulfilling her needs. Naturally, conflicts over autonomy will emerge during therapy, and must be worked through - either by explicitly working through dependency issues via the transference, or by the less explicit method of gradually encouraging the client to break away from the counselling relationship. Hilde Bruch (1978) summarises therapy as follows: "The task of psychotherapy in anorexia is to help a patient in her search for autonomy and self-directed identity by evoking an awareness of impulses, feelings and needs that originate within her....Therapy represents an attempt to repair the conceptual defects and distortions, the deep-seated sense of dissatisfaction and isolation, and the conviction of incompetence.

The overall aim of counselling, then, should be to develop a warm, trusting relationship between equals, and not to become an all-knowing parental figure who informs the client what her problems are and how she should deal with them. All too often, distressed and unhappy anorexics have been treated as either rebellious, defiant children who do not know what is best for them, or as sick young people who are not responsible for their own behaviour. Needless to say, neither approach is conducive to the development of autonomy and self-respect. Hilde Bruch (1978) recommends a fact-finding, non-interpretative approach; traditional psycho-analytic or naive behavioural methods certainly carry dangers for anorexic clients. The client must be very much an active participant in therapy, and not a passive recipient of interpretations or advice, which may serve only to reinforce her sense of helplessness and ineffectiveness. In many ways, an existential approach seems most appropriate; in existential terminology, the aim of therapy is to help the client find her "being-in-the-world". Since most anorexics are afraid of having conformity thrust upon them, it is important that counselling is seen, by both counsellor and client, as leading towards personal growth rather than adjustment. An anorexic client is someone who is grappling with the vital issues of autonomy, identity and self-esteem, someone who wants to be autonomous and to live at peace with herself. She is also someone who is deeply afraid of being forced into a certain mould by others - and the therapist must be highly sensitive to this issue.

The content of sessions will, of course, depend very much on the individual client. Lawrence and Edwards (1978) point out that: "Since everyone is different, counselling sessions involve piecing together a different jigsaw puzzle for each person, of how they came to think and feel as they do about themselves, eating, body weight and life in general.... We feel that one can be most help by listening to someone who is anorexic; validating her feelings and experiences rather than telling her she feels that way because she is "ill"; helping her to explore her present and past relationships; unravelling contradictions and false assumptions; and forming a trusting, one-to-one relationship as a basis for her personal growth.... Gradually, eating and body weight become less important, as the underlying problems are resolved."

One ex-client of mine, sixteen year old Karen, had been hospitalised on three occasions for re-feeding, earning "privileges" such as a book or radio by putting on weight; each time she had quickly lost the regained weight after discharge. Karen's mother - like many mothers of anorexics - seemed caring and concerned, but was at a loss to understand her daughter's self-starvation. Karen's father - a university professor - presented as forceful, rather obsessional, and ambitious for both of his daughters. Both parents, though well-meaning, had strongly-felt and irreconcilable expectations of Karen, leaving her little space in which to discover and fulfil her own needs and desires. In addition, Karen felt overshadowed by her musically talented and attractive elder sister; she was torn between competing with her sister, and accepting and valuing her own resources and limitations. Much of our time together - weekly sessions over fourteen months - was spent in clarifying Karen's needs, beliefs and attitudes, and in working through her anger towards her parents, along with the associated guilt. At one point, both her anger and developing self-assertion were acted out in a session in which Karen did not speak for forty minutes; she later revealed that she had been testing out my "one expectation" that she should speak during our sessions; my passive acceptance of her silence (after one or two probes) had apparently reassured and

satisfied her. When I finally said goodbye to Karen, she had
changed from a pale, frail-looking girl into a lively, attractive
young woman. A year later, she wrote to say she was fit and happy,
and reading biochemistry at university.

Of course, not all encounters with anorexic clients are
"successful". Extrinsic factors - such as a family leaving the area -
may intervene; or a client may decide, after one or more sessions,
that she is not ready to explore her problems; or, for various
reasons, the therapeutic relationship may not "gel", so that little
progress is made, or the client drops out. Also, some qualities of
the therapist which may be valuable with other clients may impede or
block progress with anorexic clients. The therapist must beware of
becoming a "too-good mother" to an anorexic: excessive warmth, over-
concern and intense involvement may be perceived as intrusive and
frightening by a client who is unsure of her own identity and
boundaries, and who may have felt overwhelmed by her own mother.
Letting an anorexic client "unfold" in therapy requires patience,
perseverance and non-intrusive warmth and respect.

The countertransference may include experiencing the client's
own feelings of being overwhelmed, powerless and out of control. In
such cases, it is essential to recognise such feelings as countertransference, and not to allow oneself to become submerged in one's
clients' helplessness and impotence. One must also be on the look-
out for the unexpected. While there is no room for complacency
with any clients, with anorexics there may be a particular danger
of retreating into the safety of known commonalities between
anorexics, and missing some of the unique problems and dynamics of
the individual client. Similarly, a presenting problem of anorexia
does not preclude other major "symptoms" of emotional disturbance,
with their associated dynamics. For instance, after three months of
therapy with one client, I discovered that she had a serious drinking
problem; another anorexic client more quickly revealed that she was
agoraphobic. Flexibility in one's approach is also essential; for
example, although I have focussed here on individual therapy, family
therapy might well be more appropriate with younger clients (cf.
Minuchin, 1978) - or a combination of individual and family sessions.

In several cases, I have found the concepts of Transactional
Analysis (cf. Berne, 1964) to be useful. In anorexic clients, the
Critical Parent - the moralistic, authoritarian part of the self,
which favours words such as 'should', 'must' and 'ought to' - tends
to be overactive; so too its counterpart, the Adapted Child (or
Frightened Child), which whiningly yields to every demand of the
superego. It is the Critical Parent which restricts food intake,
and compels the Adapted Child to undertake ascetic and obsessional
thoughts and actions. If and when a client "binges", it is Rebellious Child which has taken over; Critical Parent may then either
force her to vomit, or subject her to guilt and self-recrimination

over the excessive food intake.

Therapy might be seen as strengthening the more healthy parts of the self; namely, the Adult (or ego, which is in touch with internal and external reality, and makes decisions), the Natural Child (the spontaneous, fun-loving part of the self, with its healthy, self-regulating appetite), and the Nurturing Parent (which cares lovingly for itself and others). In "successful" cases, a client seems to experience the control of her food intake shifting from Critical Parent towards Nurturing Parent and Adult, and finally (ideally) to Natural Child. (It is worth noting that, in our culture, the food intake of many people, especially women, is often dictated by Critical Parent. The advertisement of cream cakes, for example, as "naughty but nice" implies an overruling of Critical Parent by Rebellious Child, rather than any contact with one's natural appetite. The observation that many anorexics become "health food addicts" for a time, may be understood in terms of their Critical Parent becoming moralistic about eating "healthy foods" as it once was about restriction of food intake.)

Giving labels to these different "ego states" which a client experiences in herself helps her to transcend her own subjectivity, and makes her inner world seem a little less chaotic and incomprehensible, thus strengthening her Adult. It also aids her in contacting the more passive parts of her personality, and in beginning to overrule the Critical Parent (with the therapist's support). Perhaps most important of all, it teaches her that her "craziness" can be understood, in terms of parts of the self which we all experience in our daily lives, and that being anorexic is merely descriptive of a functional imbalance between these different "ego states".

With some clients, the concepts of Topdog and Underdog - borrowed from Gestalt therapy - seem more appropriate than Transactional Analysis terminology. The techniques of Gestalt therapy can also be used effectively - such as enacting a conversation between Topdog and Underdog, with the proviso that Underdog must eventually stand up for itself and win the argument. Dreams which clients bring along to sessions often provide suitable material for such a technique. For example, a client who was experiencing severe guilt associated with episodes of binge eating, dreamt she was in a courtroom being sentenced for what the judge called "disgusting and self-indulgent behaviour". Since the dream clearly lent itself to such an analysis, I suggested that my client take the parts of the judge and defendant, and let the two speak to each other (using the "two chairs technique", in which the client swaps chairs as she changes parts). The conversation went something like this:-

JUDGE: You know, we really can't allow this sort of behaviour. It's quite disgusting.

DEFENDANT: (whining) Yes, I know. But I really can't help it. You see, I just sort of lose control.

JUDGE: (mocking) "Sort of lose control!" That's no kind of an excuse! You have a responsibility to control yourself. Do you think I would let myself behave like that?

DEFENDANT: No, of course not. I know - I really am a pathetic little creature, aren't I? I deserve to be punished.

JUDGE: Indeed. Most severely punished. You should be setting an example.

(At this point, the client is urged to force Underdog to stand up for itself.)

DEFENDANT: No, hang on a minute. What am I saying here? I really don't mean what I just said. I'm perfectly entitled to behave as I did. After all, I didn't harm anyone else, or break any laws - so what's all the fuss about?

JUDGE: (Getting angry) What sort of talk is this? You ought to be ashamed of yourself! Do you seriously imagine that moral behaviour requires only that no-one is harmed, and no laws are broken? What kind of world would we live in....

DEFENDANT: (breaking in) You're twisting my words. I wasn't talking of moral behaviour....

JUDGE: Well, that's perfectly clear....

DEFENDANT: I'm not listening to any more of this. I've been starving myself, at your command, for nearly two years now, and I've had enough. And I'm perfectly entitled to overeat as much as I like while I'm sorting myself out.....

There is a common misconception that anorexics make difficult or unrewarding clients. I believe this to be the case only when either the client has not reached the stage of wanting help, or the counsellor has little understanding of what it means to be anorexic. For many clients, anorexia is little more than a problematic and distressing phase in their personal development. With a helping hand to assist them over the hurdle, many clients emerge on the other side with a strong sense of maturity and self-acceptance. In many cases, the crucial catalyst to this metamorphosis is a warm, accepting, trusting relationship within which the client can explore herself and her life, and slowly develop a more effective and fulfilling way of life.

In summary, then: the main problems underlying anorexia nervosa seem to be those of autonomy, identity and self-esteem. Any form of therapy which does not tackle these issues is unlikely to be effective in the long-term (unless, of course, the client concurrently establishes an informal "therapeutic" relationship). The major components of counselling may be seen as: a) taking the focus off food and body weight; b) acknowledging and accepting both the anorexic and rational parts of the person; c) listening to her, taking her seriously as a person, and trying to understand her experience; d) establishing a warm, empathic, trusting relationship with her; e) working through her conflicts over autonomy and dependency; f) helping her to find a self-respecting identity and fulfilling lifestyle.

REFERENCES

Berne, E., 1964. "Games People Play". Grove Press, New York.
Boskind-Lodahl, M., 1976. Cinderella's stepsisters: a feminist perspective on anorexia and bulimia. Signs 2, Winter: 342.
Bruch, H., 1974. "Eating Disorders: Obesity, Anorexia Nervosa and the Person Within". Routledge and Kegan Paul, London.
Bruch, H., 1978. "The Golden Cage: The Enigma of Anorexia Nervosa". Open Books, London.
Edwards, G., 1979. Is there an anorexic family? Paper presented at first annual conference of the Anorexia Counselling Service, Leeds.
Lawrence, M., 1979. Anorexia nervosa: the control paradox. Women's Studies Int. Quart. , 2: 93.
Lawrence, M. and Edwards, G., 1978. Information sheet prepared for the Anorexia Counselling Service, Leeds.
MacLeod, S., 1981. "The Art of Self-Starvation". Virago, London.
Minuchin, S., 1978. "Psychosomatic Families: Anorexia Nervosa in Context". Harvard University Press, New York.
Orbach, S., 1978. "Fat Is A Feminist Issue". Paddington, London.
Palazzoli, M.S., 1974. "Self-starvation: From the Intrapsychic to the Interpersonal Approach". Chaucer, London.
Perls, F., 1972. "Gestalt Therapy Verbatim". Bantam, New York.
Rogers, C.R., 1961. "On Becoming a Person". Constable, London.
Scott, R.D., 1972. The treatment barrier. Br. J. Med. Psychol., 46: 45.

THE VALUE OF SELF-HELP GROUPS IN ANOREXIA NERVOSA

Dr. Patricia M. Hartley

Founder of Anorexic Aid

Anorexic Aid came into existence as the result of an article
in the Observer newspaper of 24th February, 1974. It was written by
Monica Wilson whose adolescent daughter had eventually been diagnosed
anorexic. The article described her difficulties in obtaining an
initial diagnosis and the time this took. During this time Mrs.
Wilson had herself been diagnosed - as a neurotic, over-protective
mother. Once her daughter's problems had been accepted as truly
existing other difficulties arose in terms of the various approaches
to treatment which were encountered. Mrs. Wilson described the
years during which her daughter struggled with the condition and
with doctors and family who were trying to help her. The strain
placed on the family was also described. Mrs. Wilson explained how,
as a mother, she felt totally helpless. She could not understand
her daughter's behaviour, any more than it seemed could the various
professionals to whom she turned for help. What she did experience
was a growing sense of anger and frustration which presumably led
in part to the writing of the article.

Readers' comments were invited and a selection of the two
hundred plus letters was published. These included not only letters
from patients and relatives but also from teachers and friends -
all of whom had in some way experienced the problems of anorexia
nervosa.

Several core themes were revealed in these letters, mostly
reiterating those expressed in Mrs. Wilson's article. These themes
included difficulty in persuading the individual that she was
behaving abnormally - a classic feature, the agonies of coercing
the "patient" to visit a doctor, especially those girls or boys who
were over eighteen and perhaps living away from home, the somewhat

95

unsympathetic attitude of some members of the caring profession, which included advice like "For God's sake, pull yourself together and go home and eat a square meal" or "Stop behaving like a spoilt child". Many parents and patients described how the initial GP reaction often included fear and an open confession that they had no idea how to cope with the illness.

These experiences tended to increase the fear of both patient and relatives, and at the same time increased the sense of isolation they were already undergoing. Feelings of guilt were described over and over again - guilt by the patient when she allowed herself to eat or when she upset her family by refusing to eat, when she lied about eating or hid the food she had been given and most of all when, having eaten, she would dispose of the food by vomiting or purging in secret.

The parent's guilt, especially that of the mother, hinged on a sense of blame and remorse - many parents felt directly responsible for their daughter's illness whereas some felt ashamed that they had produced a child who could behave in this bizarre way. Rejection of the patient by one parent at least was not uncommon.

This article and the letters described occurred at a time when a relative of mine was also experiencing all the problems discussed. I was involved in psychology at undergraduate level and had read as much of the available literature as possible. It seemed to me that the missing link in treatment was involving the patient in her own recovery in a fairly structured way - in short through a self-help or mutual aid group. Groups of this type were growing daily and I discovered as much as possible about the aims and objectives of groups like Alcoholics Anonymous, the Phobic Society and the Samaritans. I felt that an organisation which involved features of both self-help groups and support or counselling would be useful. After discussion with my professor at Manchester I wrote to the Observer saying that I would be prepared to organise such a group provided sufficient demand existed. In response to a brief paragraph in the next edition of the paper I received five hundred and thirty-five letters - all within a fortnight. It was then abundantly clear that some form of support group was very much needed. The inaugural meeting of Anorexic Aid was held in the Department of Psychology, the University of Manchester in May 1974. Within a matter of weeks at least twelve groups had been set up and a contact register, of those members who were willing to publicise their names, was circulated to every person who had written or telephoned. Before twelve months had elapsed we had over 1,000 members, some as far afield as the USA.

In the early meetings the most frequent talking point was in fact relief at being given the opportunity to talk. This was certainly expressed by parents, most of whom had not met any other

parents in their position and had felt too ashamed and guilty to
discuss their daughter's difficulties as they felt that no-one
would understand. Rejection of food is often seen by the mother as
rejection of love - most mothers would want to know the reasons
for this. Parents were mystified seeing their child bent on self-
destruction and felt that this was a failure on their part. The
anger and frustration experienced led to enormous problems in
family relationships and many respectable, caring parents felt that
they could not disclose these tensions to their doctor. Many said
that they had not been encouraged to do so. Anorexic Aid provided
the opportunity then for parents to release some tensions and also
to learn that they were by no means alone.

Individual patients maintained that being a member of a group
helped them in a similar way. Many had felt greatly ashamed of
their bizarre eating habits, their swings from stuffing to starving,
their force-vomiting and excessive use of laxatives. They had
many private worries about their future. Listening to other group
members expressing the same worries and tensions was a relief -
maybe only temporary - but in fact served to reduce the hateful
feeling of being completely different from everyone else.

Patients had tended to withdraw from social contacts as they
became more and more involved in anorexia nervosa. They felt that
too many social occasions involved eating or drinking and that the
safest way to cope was not to join in. The illness itself is a
very private one and the effects of starvation do seem to include
withdrawal from relationships, especially those involving the
opposite sex. The degree of self-hate described by the patients
had also intensified withdrawal - if no attempt at interaction were
made, failure - on the grounds that other people would not want
this relationship - was avoided. Anorexic Aid gave members the
opportunity to meet other people with the same "faults" and
therefore group acceptance was guaranteed. Many individual members
soon became firm friends.

Recovered anorexics were especially valuable at meetings and
also as postal contacts. So often, after years of struggling,
patients and parents alike had given up hope. Members who had
conquered the illness were invaluable in terms of offering advice
and giving hope to those in the early stages of the condition.
The information-sharing aspect of the group's activity supports
the notion that giving the patient at least some information about
her illness and treatment methods tends to reduce anxiety and
therefore increase recovery rate. Currently there is much emphasis
on "peer-group education" in health education. It became increasingly obvious during early meetings that the anorexic patient was
more likely to accept help and advice from a member of her own
"group" rather than from family or professionals involved.

Anorexics and their families found relief through displacing their anxiety from the private and personal aspects of the illness and sharing their experiences with other members. Contemporary counselling techniques stress the advantages of merely stating the problem - the patient often clarifies her own situation by putting her private feelings into words. Being able to "admit" to being anorexic is very similar to "admitting" to being alcoholic. This statement may be seen as a starting point for change. If the statement is made with the support of the group this reinforces the notion of acceptance and the guarantee of help from group members. In some cases, the strength to make this admission took time to develop but often telephone and postal contacts encouraged individuals to come along to group meetings.

Anorexic Aid in fact gave parents and patients the chance to operate a variety of defence mechanisms, all reducing anxiety. Displacement from the "private" aspect of the situation has already been mentioned. Many members also used "intellectualisation" - channelling tremendous energy into discovering as much information as possible about anorexia nervosa and available treatment. Relief was expressed by parents who felt at last that they were able to do something positive about their child's situation. Through these joint activities the cohesiveness of the group increased and anorexics had become an identifiable section of the population. An identity as an anorexic was felt preferable to no identity at all!

Group discussions included information sharing on various treatments experienced. It became clear that many anorexics had co-operated with treatment merely in order to gain discharge from hospital after which the patients could return to their former regime. This hypothesis was supported by information obtained by a questionnaire in 1975. These discussions promoted insight both in the patient and the family - again helping to clarify the problem and to increase understanding of the processes at work within the family. Parents learned much from other parents and often began to view the situation from a totally different per- spective.

Anorexic Aid meetings provided several starting points for further research. It gave the ideal opportunity to investigate anorexia nervosa from the patient's point of view - one which Kelly (1955) suggests is often ignored in treatment. Shortly after the inaugural meeting a questionnaire was devised in an attempt to quantify some of the information gleaned from meetings being held throughout Great Britain. Questions ranged from "Age at onset" - which proves very difficult to isolate - to "Treatment methods found successful". There were 21 questions in all.

The results indicated that much of the treatment experienced was of little advantage to the patient. The initial difficulty of persuading the individual to accept the label "patient" was repeatedly stressed. Why should an individual who, when she looks in the mirror sees a "fat" body do anything other than diet? "Fat" in our society is bad. We are constantly bombarded with information on how to lose weight. Dieting is very "positively reinforced". Dieting must therefore be "good behaviour" and eating "bad". One would accept then that the anorexic's reaction to being forced to accept food would be highly resistant.

Attitudes to treatment were found to be fairly constant throughout the groups. "Reward" treatment seemed to be the most common method and was in fact almost universally detested - seen as punishment rather than reward. The punitive aspect as far as anorexics could see involved having to behave in the way most feared by them (i.e. eating) in order to regain those things of which they had been deprived. It is seen as punitive also because it increases body size which in turn increases self-hatred and disgust - the very basis of the condition itself. This explanation of anorexia nervosa was often given in group discussions and forms the basis of my own study.

Bed-rest and high calorie, high carbohydrate diet were viewed in a similar way. Members suggested that this treatment denied the patient the opportunity to exercise any control over her life (her body). The need to impose control over one's own existence has been stressed by Bruch (1974) and others, as one of the motivating factors underlying anorexia nervosa. This type of treatment was also described as increasing self-disgust. It was also suggested that it contributed to "bingeing" - over-eating in fact was being positively reinforced.

Tube-feeding was described by all patients as a violation of the body and the individual's rights. All control was here forcibly removed. Many members at this stage in the life of Anorexic Aid drew attention to the public sympathy expressed when two "freedom fighters" were being force-fed to avert death during a hunger strike. One patient stated "no-one asks the anorexic if she wants to be tube-fed". It is interesting that since this episode both these terrorists have been diagnosed as suffering from anorexia nervosa. This type of treatment was felt to be both physically and psychologically damaging.

From the questionnaire results it seemed that acceptable treatment involved those which catered for the psychological as well as the physical needs of the patient. For example, behaviour modification, coupled with psycho-therapy gradually became acceptable to many patients. Some forms of hypnotherapy were also acceptable and useful. It would seem that any treatment which aimed to improve the patient's self-image, and therefore resulting in a more positive body image, would eventually achieve the patient's co-operation and a higher degree of recovery.

One of the main functions then of Anorexic Aid was to provide the opportunity to assess treatment from the point of view of the patient. It also gave the opportunity to investigate the duration of the illness and discover exactly what the patient described as recovery. This recovery rarely had much connection with weight gain alone.

"Self-help" is a rather idealistic term, especially when applied to patients. In some respects it is quite paradoxical - had the individual been capable of helping herself presumably she would not have become ill.

Self-help with group support is quite different. If Bruch and others involved in the treatment of anorexics are correct in their view that the illness involves a struggle for control and a fight for independence it seems logical that patients should need to be involved in their own treatment. Patients who have recovered describe how they felt the need "to grow through their illness". Their attitudes to independence had been ambivalent. They had found that personal growth was impossible to achieve on their own or even with the support of their families. In some cases the family itself prevented this growth taking place. Anorexic Aid seems to have provided a suitable matrix for the necessary growth process. Within twelve to eighteen months of inauguration many branches of Anorexic Aid sprang up. Some of these were formed and organised by recovered anorexics.

One of the difficulties encountered in the field of self-help is the tendency for the group members to become dependent on the group leader. The need for decision-making is removed from individual members who are often quite happy to allow someone else to take over this responsibility. It is essential therefore to encourage the group members to be actively involved - as chair-person, secretary, treasurer or publicity agent.

A further difficulty experienced is that many individuals come to the meetings with unrealistic expectations. At no time is "treatment" offered. Anorexic Aid has always emphasised that the aim of the group is mutual support and self-help. Anorexics whose expectations were not met would either accept the supportive aspect of the society or decide not to join.

Although meetings are held at varying intervals in different groups, the support offered is fairly constant. Initially a register was circulated to each member, enabling her to contact any member at any time. Members were advised to write or telephone

each other especially at those times when despair at over-eating
was overwhelming or when the obsession with food was making ordinary
life virtually impossible. Simply being able to talk over the
experience was found to be helpful. More than one member has maintained that this facility has averted a suicide attempt. Many
members meet informally between group sessions in some cases going
out for a meal.

It has been suggested that Anorexic Aid may encourage competi-
tion, i.e. each member would strive to be the thinnest. From my
own experience, the converse applied. Sometimes girls at meetings
expressed horror and distaste at the emaciation of fellow-members,
causing them to take a fresh look at themselves.

As a society cannot function without financial support, some
groups have diverted some energy into fund-raising. This fulfils a
dual need. Members are publicly active, thus removing some of the
stigma resulting from the label "anorexic". The attention of the
public is also, through this activity, focussed on the anorexic's
situation. Since the association was formed, far more information,
of mixed quality, has been available through the media. Self-help
groups act as pressure groups within society, hopefully bringing
about a change in the attitude of the public to their members, and,
ideally, gaining Government support for the group aims. There is
always a danger, however, that self-help groups may seem to absolve
the Government from their share of the responsibility involved.

A further aim of the self-help group is to enable the individual
to come to terms with her own body and in so doing achieve independence from it. It has been obvious from discussions at meetings
that the anorexic's behaviour is determined by her perception of
her body. This view is constantly reinforced by the growing
literature on the subject.

Western society places great emphasis on the "ideal figure" -
typically female - but the need to conform is also stressed in
males who are confronted with a "masculine ideal". The pattern is
similar, the essential feature being "slimness". Fat in our society
is "bad" - almost sinful. To be accepted as a person requires
conformity to the cultural ideal. Much of the available literature
suggests that a single bodily imperfection may be generalised to
dissatisfaction with the self - the whole person. Evidence from
interviews with patients and from their written accounts suggests
that a similar mechanism is operating within the anorexic - but in
reverse. That the anorexic's body image is distorted has been
clearly shown. Russell (1977) states that "Food intake in anorexia
nervosa is unduly dependent on the patient's awareness of her body
size; as this awareness is a distorted one in the direction of
seeing herself as unduly large, it follows that the patient will
starve herself in an attempt to return to what she considers to be

more normal proportions". A pilot study carried out by the author
in 1975 suggested that the delusional body image found in anorexia
nervosa may result from the projection of a "bad" self-image on to
the body. This is felt to be a function of faulty development and
leads the anorexic to believe that by changing the body she will
bring about a corresponding change in the self. The logical
behaviour accordingly is to reduce the body size by dieting - hence
the apparently stubborn denial by the patient that her behaviour is
inappropriate.

If this view is correct it follows that the perceptual distortion will be subjective, confined only to the patient's view of
her own body. Data from tests carried out to determine the nature
of this perceptual distortion supported the hypothesis. Evidence
also supported the further hypothesis that in the anorexic a
distorted body image and poor self-image are inter-dependent.

Body image is seen as a function of development and is in many
ways related to the development of the self. One explanation of
the growth of self is expressed by Sullivan (1956). He suggests
that "We are the sum of the reflected appraisals of others". If body
image develops along with self-image it is suggested that the
anorexic may be helped towards recovery by enabling her to change
her self-image through the support of her group. If this is possible
the patient will begin to develop a more realistic sense of self-
worth. Most Anorexic Aid members are high-achievers in society's
terms, but perceive themselves as inadequate. If the self-image
were to improve the patient may well develop correspondingly a more
realistic body image. Within the illness the way in which the
anorexic perceives both herself and her body is unrealistic. Kelly
(1955) states that even if a person misrepresents a real phenomenon,
this misrepresentation for him will itself be real. This is so
with the badly deluded patient. What he perceives does not exist
but his perception does. Similar concepts have been discussed by
McGhie (1969).

Self-help, then in the matrix of the support group, aims to
reduce the feeling of isolation, experienced both by anorexics
and their families, to increase the amount of information available,
thereby relieving tension and allaying anxiety, to focus the
patient's energy on to the more positive areas of helping others
in a similar situation and to encourage self-growth and self-
acceptance. In this way it is hoped to enable the anorexic to gain
independence from the body and to become an individual in her own
right. The sense of achievement resulting from being instrumental
in one's own recovery is bound to increase self-esteem and self-
confidence. As one girl explained "I am now in control of my
body - instead of my body controlling me".

REFERENCES

Bruch, H., 1974. "Eating Disorders, Obesity, Anorexia Nervosa and
    the Person Within". Routledge and Kegan Paul, London.
Kelly, G., 1955. "The Psychology of Personal Constructs. Vol.
    1 and 2". Norton, New York.
McGhie, A., 1969. "The Pathology of Attention". Penguin Books.
Russell, G.F.M., 1977. The present status of anorexia nervosa.
    Psychological Medicine, 7: 363-367.
Sullivan, H.S., 1956. "Interpersonal Theory of Psychiatry".
    Tavistock, London.

COMPUTER APPLICATIONS AND BIOFEEDBACK IN CLINICAL PSYCHOLOGY

COMPUTER APPLICATIONS AND BIOFEEDBACK IN CLINICAL

PSYCHOLOGY - AN INTRODUCTION

J.B. Ashcroft   R. Glynn Owens

Moss Side Hospital   Sub-Department of Clinical
Liverpool   Psychology
                                 University of Liverpool

There can be little doubt that one of the most outstanding
characteristics of life in western countries over the past two
decades has been the growth of the influence of micro-electronic
technology. This influence, in the home, the work place, and elsewhere will undoubtedly continue to grow at a rapidly accelerating
rate. It is particularly in the hardware field that the rapid
development is taking place. Computers, for example are becoming
smaller and more powerful whilst at the same time becoming cheaper.
There is now a computer available, the size of a desktop calculator,
which, in equivalent hardware power terms would have filled a medium
sized office fifteen years ago; all this for less than £100. Perhaps
of particular interest, to those in the biological field, is the
potential for use of the so-called "biochip", still in very early
stages of development but holding out the potential of an organically-
based computer technology.

Such rapid development within the field of computer technology
has a number of implications for clinical psychology. Two of these
may be particularly noted:-

1. The social impact of the new technology such as the possibly
    over-stated effect on employment and the effects of such things
    as computer games which are virtually unexplored. There is also
    the ethical problem of ready access to mass files by police, tax
    inspectors and other government agencies, as well as commercial
    organisations.

2. The ability of clinical psychologists to use the technology.
    This problem is not specific to clinical psychology. In general,
    software developments have not kept abreast of hardware

development. Three current projects, reflecting the growing
awareness of this, may well have substantial impact.

Firstly there has been an attempt by those industrialists
involved with computers to allow school children to sample their
value, by inviting them to "come along and play with" computers
in their factories. Secondly, there is a growing investment by
government education departments in the improvement of computer
literacy. This is being done by subsidy of the cost of purchas-
ing computers by schools and the presentation of prizes of
computers. Thirdly there is a major project by the British
Broadcasting Corporation consisting of a series of computer
literacy programmes together with the production of a micro-
computer based on a proposal by Acorn. This is aimed at bringing
computers and their uses to the public at large.

Whilst the use of computers by psychologists is by no means universal,
psychologists have been involved with computers from the early days
of computer technology. Bush and Mosteller (1955) for example
employed computer simulation procedures to explore theoretical
aspects of avoidance behaviour, an approach later developed in some
detail by other workers (see e.g. Hoffman, 1966). Clinicians appear
to have been rather slower at developing computer applications, but
even so there is now over a decade's work on clinical applications.
(For a discussion of some early work see e.g. Lang, 1969). Computers
however still remain alien to many clinicians and of those who
actually use the machines a disturbingly high number appear to have
adopted what may be described as a "quill pen" mentality, using
computers to store data with little or no analysis.

The papers in the present symposium provide excellent illus-
trations of the wider use of computers by psychologists. The use
of computers as clinicians, despite optimistic early efforts in
this field, e.g. Colby and Enea (1967) is still not a prospect for
the foreseeable future. However it is clear that certain of the
tasks of the therapist can potentially be delegated to the machine.
Dr. Elithorn's paper in the present symposium demonstrates the use
of computer technology in the field of psychological testing,
pointing out that in some circumstances such procedures, far from
being a second-rate cheap alternative, may actually have advantages
over more conventional test procedures. It is notable that the
main source of psychological test materials in the United Kingdom,
the National Federation for Educational Research, is now supplying
tests for use with popular microcomputers like Commodore's PET.
Rather less pleasing is the appearance on the open market of computer
programmes for domestic machines claiming to test intelligence,
personality etc. Such "Know your intelligence" programmes unfortunately tend to rely on unspecified or non-standard tests on which
there is little if any standardisation data or information regarding
psychometric properties. Whilst the cynical observer might assume

that the motivation for such items is purely commercial, the notion of increasing a person's awareness of their own potential and characteristics may be commendable. It is ironic however that other psychologists have put considerable effort into preventing such information becoming widely available, pointing out the dangers of misinterpretation of such data by unqualified individuals. Leaving aside such "fringe" elements, however, it does seem clear that the future holds great potential for computerised assessment.

A further application of computers in the clinical field is illustrated by Dr. McAllister's paper on the use of computers in biofeedback of heart-rate. Such experiments have come to rely upon the ability of the computer to make rapid and frequent assessments, analyses and decisions. Not only are such procedures of potential therapeutic benefit, it is clear from the present paper that their use permits the extension of theoretical considerations, both in the clinical and the more general psychological field.

The possibilities for a wide range of psychological applications make the appearance of Mr. Dewey's paper a useful complement to the specific applications described by Drs. Elithorn and McAllister. The notion of using the computer as an aid to decision making has a number of aspects outlined by Mr. Dewey. In particular it is important to note that the use of rational procedures, particularly the Bayesian model described, generally agreed to lead to more effective decisions. The problem is that the effort involved in such procedures may be so great as to reduce their value, a point that has led one writer to refer to "two types of rationality". Good (1967) distinguishes between type 1 rationality, Bayesian decision-making, and type 2 rationality, which involves including an allowance for the cost of theorising. The use of computers as decision aids implies that the "cost of theorising" can be reduced thus making type 2 rationality, "superior rationality", easier to achieve.

With the realisation that the application of computers to clinical problems is bound to spread, Dr. Lovie's paper is particularly timely. Not only does he provide a useful introduction to the basic units of microcomputing, he also highlights a number of ethical issues implicit in clinical computer use. The relationship between an "expert system" and its user may be fraught with difficulties. It would be tempting to suggest a Luddite approach discarding the new technology, but this would only avoid (postpone?) the problem, not solve it. Dr. Lovie's solution, that the user make efforts to understand the system - "gain access to intellectual technology", suggests a more positive and progressive approach to a solution.

REFERENCES

Bush, R.R. and Mosteller, F., 1955. "Stochastic Models for Learning".
    Wiley, New York.
Colby, K.M. and Enea, H., 1967. Heuristic methods for computer
    understanding of natural language in the context-restricted
    on-line dialogue. Mathematical Biosciences, 1: 1-25.
Good, I.J., 1967. The probabilistic explication of information,
    evidence, surprise, causality, explanation and utility. In:
    Godambe, V.P. and Sprott, D.A. (Eds.), "Foundations of Stat-
    istical Inference". Holt, Reinhart and Winston, Toronto.
Hoffman, H.S., 1966. The analysis of discriminated avoidance. In:
    Honig, W.K. (Ed.), "Operant Behaviour: Areas of Research and
    Application". Appleton Century Crofts, New York.
Lang, P.J., 1969. The on-line computer is behaviour therapy
    research. Amer. Psychol., 24: 236-239.

THE MICROPROCESSOR IN CLINICAL PSYCHOLOGY - TECHNICAL AND

ETHICAL ASPECTS

Sandy Lovie

Lecturer in Psychology

University of Liverpool

"And thick and fast they came at last,
And more, and more, and more - "

The Walrus and the Carpenter

INTRODUCTION

It was recently reported in the home hackers journal, Personal
Computer World (June 1981, hereafter PCW), that the pioneer American
computer ENIAC had been pitted against a TRS80 microprocessor, the
chosen task being to square all the integers from 1 to 10,000.
ENIAC (short for Electronic Numerical Integrator and Computer) was
completed in 1945, weighed over 30 tons, occupied some 3,000 cubic
feet of space, consumed 140 kilowatts of power and cost (at 1945
prices) $500,000. The TRS80 (short for Tandy Radio Shack, the number
80 is a code for the processor type) appeared about 1978, weighs
about 15 lbs., sits on your desk and costs about £400 (at 1981
prices). Of course, the TRS80 beat the ENIAC hands down, performing
the task some eighteen times faster!

One of the major points that I would like to convey therefore,
is that microprocessors are becoming more sophisticated and cheaper
each day. They are also becoming smaller.

Another anecdote illustrating my point is that it has recently
been suggested (Practical Computing, September 1981) that the only
barrier to zero or even negative cost computing by the turn of the
century is the price of the case!

111

My first purpose, therefore, is to introduce you to the rapidly
expanding world of microcomputing, mainly through a discussion of
hardware developments, but also providing some coverage of software.
In general, hardware improvements take place faster and are more
visible than software ones, hence it is easier to fall behind hardware than software developments.

A Word in your Ear

On the assumption, doubtless rather insulting, that you know
little about microprocessors, I will start by defining one or two
important terms. First, microprocessor: this is a device (usually
very small, and mounted on a wafer of silicon) that handles information. Since most information in computers is digital in form, so
the information is represented by a stream of binary digits or bits.
Not only does the machine add and subtract bits (in fact that is
usually the only arithmetic that it can do), it also conveys
information to and from a variety of storage media: my second and
subsequent terms therefore refer to these storage devices.

RAM stands for random access memory, that is, memory whose
contents can be interrogated and altered by the microprocessor,
hence RAM acts as a working store. Other forms of what are called
semiconductor memories (that is, transistor based and mounted on a
silicon chip) are ROM (read only memory), which is a more or less
permanent memory store (hence read only), whose contents, unlike
RAM, do not dissipate when the power is turned off. Such storage
is useful for holding often accessed programmes or languages such
as BASIC or PASCAL. Variants on ROM are PROM (programmable read
only memory) and EPROM (erasable programmable read only memory). I
hope that the meaning of these buzz words is fairly clear from the
earlier definitions, but if they are not, then here's a clue: the
EPROM's memory contents can be erased using ultra-violet light and
then reprogrammed.

There are other forms of mass or backing store including audio
cassette tape and various forms of disk, for example, floppies and
Winchester technology hard-disks. There is even a form of cheap
storage called stringy floppies. These are sophisticated tape
systems whose performance and reliability, it is claimed, are
comparable with floppy disks. Bubble memory systems are also not
to be discounted. But more on these a little later.

To those of you who know something about more conventional
computing on large mainframes or midi- or mini-computers little of
the above, except for the funny names, will be unfamiliar. And it
is true that microprocessors receive, store and manipulate data in
comparable ways to the larger machines, while programmes and data
are usually entered via the keyboards, usually with an associated

visual display unit (VDU). Further, these latter devices, with conventional printers, also act as output devices. However, what I would now like to argue is that recent and forthcoming developments in microcomputer hardware (and to an increasing extent software as well) are generating a revolution from below, which will rapidly replace these older systems.

The following are just a few of the signs of the profound changes to come: the increasing processor power now becoming available to users, the falling prices of mass storage, the large number of cheap additions available and lastly the increasing number of multi-user systems. All are dealt with below.

Longer and Longer

In the last section I pointed out that microcomputers handle and store binary digits or bits. Now the traditional way of defining a computer is in terms of the size of the minimum piece of information that the machine could process and remember. This quantity is called word size and is given as a number of binary digits. Most of the popular machines use processors with words that are eight bits in length. Interestingly eight bits is also called a byte, hence the memory capacities of such machines are given as so many bytes, for example, 16k bytes of RAM means sixteen thousand eight-bit bytes of random access memory. Clearly, word length determines the size and precision of any of the numbers stored and operated on by the machine. Less clearly, it also limits the number of memory addresses that can be directly interrogated (most popular 8-bit micros can only address up to 64k bytes of storage, either ROM or RAM). Word length also limits the sophistication of the software: few of the 8-bit micros really have the fuller BASIC or PASCAL implementations that are available on most 16-bit minis, for example.

However, although today's micros are limited to 8 bits (PET, Apples, TRS80, Sharp MZ80k, etc., etc.), machines with 16-bit words are just around the corner, while Intel, one of the giants of Silicon Valley, have recently sent out examples of 32-bit micros for evaluation. Now 16-bit word lengths are the usual size for mini computers like DG NOVA 2 or the PDP11 range from DEC. Hence the challenge to the existing medium size machines is very clear. Equally, too, the newer 32-bit machines will eventually challenge the mainframe market. Let me repeat that the current price of 8-bit microprocessors such as the 6502 in the PET and Apple and the Z80 in the Superbrain is very low indeed, often well below £10. Consequently, although the current cost of 16- and 32-bit micros and store is and will remain high for some time (perhaps 4 to 5 years), eventually the price will plummet and even very powerful machines will be within everyone's pocket. Of course the various

forms of semiconductor memory, mainly RAM and ROM, will also be
developed to match the processors.

A further wrinkle here, possible because of today's low prices
for 8-bit micros, is to use several processors within the same
package to speed up the various processing chores. For example,
many output printers now have a micro and ROM or RAM in them so as
to reduce the arithmetic unit's processing overheads. Equally,
certain packages use a separate micro to handle input from keyboards
and VDU's, and transfers to and from disk files. Although conventional multi-processing micro systems are rare, at least at the
small computer end, there are now multi-tasking software systems
for certain larger micros, while, as will be seen later, there is
an increasing development in multi-user micro systems.

Bigger and Bigger

Most of today's micros' backing stores, for example, cassette
or floppy disk, although of larger capacity than RAM working store,
are still small compared to even mini-computer disk storage. For
example 5" diameter floppy disks typically hold about 250k bytes
per diskette. Audio cassette tapes usually have much less capacity,
with stringy floppies somewhere between, for example, 120k bytes
per wafer. The price too tends to vary somewhat, with £50 or so
for specially modified cassettes to about £300-£400 per drive for
floppies, with stringies about £200 per drive.

An alternative form of storage that has emerged over the last
two years is the so-called Winchester hard-disk system which offers
multiples of the number of stored bytes on say floppy disks
(typically 5 to 20 megabytes, that is 5 to 20 million bytes), but
at a correspondingly high cost (£3,000 plus for the lowest paid
system). However, there are now (PCW, September 1981) a range of
low cost hard-disks, viz. 16 megabytes for £1,206, 10.7 megabytes
for £1,013 and 5.3 megabytes for £825, the latter challenging dual
drive floppies. This also seems to represent the cheapest cost per
byte yet.

Yet another form of storage, although not perhaps as successful
as its advance publicity might suggest, is called bubble memory.
This is a semiconductor wafer containing a vast number of magnetised
bubbles which act as a storage medium when powered up (see Peter
Large's 1980 paperback for a nice description of these and other
microbits). Unfortunately, bubble memories have so far proved to
be uncompetitive on a pence per byte and write/access times when
compared with hard-disks. However, they are more portable than such
devices and are much more rugged and environment indifferent.
However, with mass production and a few more technical developments
the bubble memory system will I think take over. (Intel has recently

announced a plug-in bubble memory system for about $3,500 for 128k bytes per memory cartridge).

More and More

The burgeoning home, school and business market for microsystems has meant that most of the fancy add-ons and extra facilities for larger machines have now trickled down to the personal computer. All that I can do in this section is to mention some of the more juicy items, leaving the most exciting to the last.

The number of printers for micros now on the market is stagger-ing. If you want printers that offer graphics, digital plotting, daisywheel quality, 40 or 80 column width or more and up to 300 cps line-printer speed then the market can satisfy you. Regular surveys or printers in the home hacker journals usually cover over 50 firms offering over 100 machines (Practical Computing, June 1981). More specialised outputs are fewer in number, for example, there are only one or two good graph plotters and analogue to digital and digital to analogue conversion systems, while as yet micros do not produce microfilm/fiche, but these will surely come.

There are now at least eight machines that produce colour graphics on an ordinary unmodified home colour TV set. The prize for the highest quality colour graphics so far goes to the Ingersoll Atari 800 (PCW rated the simulated view from the Starship's windows during a game of Galaxy Invaders run on an Atari as the most con-vincing yet! - prices around £600 and falling). The number of truly high resolution graphics machines is also slowly rising, with even the Apples able to plot some 190 by 200 points. A recent machine from Sharp, however, the MZ-80B, allows a graphics display of 320 x 200 points to be overlaid by a further one of the same size while the recently announced British Broadcasting Corporation machine claims a 640 x 256 2-colour graphics display (more on this machine later). Some machines, for example PETs and TRS80s, are now offering animated graphics packages; although not yet in the Tom and Jerry league, they can generate some interesting effects. Finally, it is possible to add graphics terminals to micros, although these tend to be expensive now. However, the increasing demand for such devices will inevitably drive down the price, so if you have an interest in good quality graphics, then it is worth hanging on for a little while longer.

Input devices have not gone through the same hectic developments as output ones but many computer firms now routinely offer light-pen hardware and software and there has recently been a touch screen VDU where any of 32 commands can be sent to the micro by merely touching a zone on the TV display (Practical Computing, September 1981). Certain machines will also accept digitiser information,

for example, graphs and maps. Again these are relatively expensive
but increasing demand should do its usual magic job (micro technologies are usually energy cheap to use and construct!).

The most interesting developments I feel, however, are in the
provision of teletext and viewdata (Prestel) interfaces for your
home computer. Currently only one Prestel interface, the Tangerine
New Tantel, is available, although there are more teletext ones.
The problem with the Tantel, however, is that it communicates
through the computer's cassette interface and hence is rather slow
when transferring data (1.3 kilobaud, compared to 9.6 kilobaud with
many floppies). There is also the question of software protocol
since the Tantel's output satisfies only the Kansas City CUTS system.
However, even with the Tantel there now exists the possibility of
interactive computing either with British Telecom's large Prestel
computer or with other users via this large mainframe. In addition,
the Prestel and teletext links could allow what is called the down-
loading of software from Prestel or teletext "pages". The newly
announced BBC computer, which is to be manufactured by Acorn
computers, will offer such TV interfaces as well as an enhanced
BASIC and high resolution graphics. This single TV interface will,
I believe, prove to be the most important development in home
computing in the last few years.

More Chairs Round the Table

Other developments where micros are now emulating bigger
machines are multiuser systems whereby anyone with a cheap micro,
say a PET, can get together with his or her equally indigent PET
owning friends to share an expensive item like a floppy disk and/or
printer. There are now multiuser systems for such PETs (so-called
MUPET), while Apples have the Nestar system, and the Acorn Atom
offers the cheapest multiuser system of all (called the Econet).
The secret of good multiuser systems lies as much in the provision
of good software as it does with matching hardware - Econet is
unfortunately not only the cheapest but also the least software
developed (see PCW, July 1981 for a Benchmark test of Econet).

Of course, yer pays yer money and yer takes yer choice: there
is available a hard-disk based multiuser system that sends the
reviewers into polysyllabic ecstacy (PCW and Practical Computing,
both April 1981). This is the Onyx system running the multiuser
Unix system. Basic prices for a four user system start at £11,800
and for an eight user one at nearly £15,000. Contrast this with the
Acorn Econet's prices of £4,200 for a four user system and £7,200
for an eight user system. Since there are now several multiuser
systems on the market, I am unlikely to saw off the branch behind
me by predicting that the prices will quickly tumble and the software and sophistication of these increasingly cheap computer systems

will soar.

My final word of advice is to read the personal computer press for the hot news: notice for example, that all my examples have been culled from this year's issues.

Expert Systems and Ethics

My second major purpose is to discuss the ethical and political implications of one recent aspect of applied cognition/computing, that is, the development of so-called "expert systems". Expert systems are usually computer emulations/simulations of the experts in a particular professional,scientific or academic area. Some systems consist of an enormous database holding highly complex information about, say, chess moves or chemical structures. Other systems simulate important decision-making tasks, for example, medical diagnosis. In all cases, the purpose of the system is to answer questions and to advise the human expert (see Smith and Green, 1980, for a recent series of articles on relevant aspects of man-computer interactions; see especially Taylor's paper in the collection; see also Forester, 1980 and Weizenbaum, 1976).

I do not intend to describe the range of such systems, this I will leave to Alick Elithorn in his paper (this volume). However, I want to describe one well tried and long developed expert system for clinical diagnosis in psychology whose form and ethical implications are typical of other systems. Further, such a system is reasonably easy to implement on a large micro with floppy disk storage.

In a series of studies from 1960 to the present a small group of psychologists based at the Oregon Research Institute, principally Hoffman (1960), Goldberg (1970) and Dawes (1979) have been testing a linear regression model for handling MMPI profiles and other psychometric instruments (see also Lovie, forthcoming). The one major finding of the work is that various forms of the linear diagnostic models derived from a large number of expert judges outperform these same judges! This phenomenon has been termed bootstrapping by Dawes who has been responsible for the most recent developments in the area. He has, for example, divided such models into proper linear models and improper ones.

Conventional linear regression equations with predictor weights estimated by least squares and hence optimally correlated with the criterion variable are examples of the former class, while ones with non-optimal weights such as random (normal deviate) or unit (equal) ones belong to the class of improper linear models. Dawes and others have shown that unit weight linear models even outperform proper or random weight models! In Dawes' view (see, for example,

1979) the role of the clinician with such models is to choose what predictor variables are to be fed into the regression equation and also to scale them monotonically with respect to the criterion.

This illustrates three major features of expert systems: first that the experts provide the raw material for the systems, second, that the systems outperform the experts mainly because of their greater reliability and higher information processing capabilities and, third, that the necessary calculations are carried out on a computer.

A major class of ethical, psychological and political question with such bootstrapped systems is concerned with the relationship between people and the system. For example, given that the total system outperforms the judges, does this mean that the system is more powerful and more important than the judge? In other words, is the vital end job of diagnosis now the system's concern and not the clinician's? Also is such a finding so immutable that people could never learn to outperform their models? Can the clinician have a richer and more satisfying role in the relationship? Can the relationship reflect changes in knowledge since the output of the system is always calibrated against the judge's current state of knowledge and performance?

In earlier papers (Lovie, 1978, 1980) I have argued that the problems of relating to such "intellectual technology" as boot- strapped linear models can be restated as problems of access to intellectual technology. In other words, the problems of who has the power in the relationship can be solved in people's favour provided that we can gain a deeper and more profound intuitive insight into how these expert systems work and what we should reasonably expect from them.

Recent important work in cognition (see, for example, Hogarth, 1980) has painted a gloomy picture of our limited ability to adopt reasonable procedures of thought, inference and decision-making. We should not allow these shortcomings to be used as a form of intellectual oppression, whereby the important and vital decisions of our life are made by systems and procedures of whom we have no knowledge or understanding. We must use as wide a variety of devices to learn and to appreciate how such systems work and hence how to control them.

Donald Michie has recently suggested that all expert systems should include a window so that human experts (and non-experts) could peer inside and see just what was going on. We could help in providing this window. We could also help in training people to monitor the results of the system since, of course, we provide the raw input (and garbage in, garbage out is still true). Apprec- iation of the system's working would also allow us to modify its operations as new knowledge came along.

There is an old adage increasingly quoted to characterise our new post-industrial society, which is that knowledge is power. Expert systems are a part of this new kind of knowledge whose importance, because of their real value, will grow over the years. If we would control them then we need to spread information about expert systems as widely as we can, since only then will their use produce the greatest benefit to the largest number of people.

REFERENCES

Dawes, R.M., 1979. The robust beauty of improper linear models.
    Amer. Psychol., 34: 571-582.
Forester, I. (ed.), 1980. "The Microelectronics Revolution".
    Blackwell, Oxford. (Reprints the famous 1979 exchange between
    Bell and Weizenbaum on what computers can and should do.)
Goldberg, L.R., 1970. Man versus model of man: A rationale, plus
    some evidence, for a method of improving on clinical inference.
    Psychol. Bull., 73: 422-432.
Hoffman, P.J., 1960. The paramorphic representation of clinical
    judgement. Psychol. Bull., 57: 116-131.
Hogarth, R.M., 1980. "Judgement and Choice". Wiley, New York.
Large, P., 1980. "The Micro Revolution". Fontana Paperbacks.
Lovie, A.D., 1979. Applied psychology in the post-industrial society.
    Bull. Br. Psychol. Soc., 31: 281-184.
Lovie, A.D., 1980. The computer - universal helpmate or technological
    Black Hole? Paper given at the Annual Meeting of the British
    Psychological Society.
Lovie, A.D.,   . Multiple cue person perception. In Cook, M.
    (ed.) "Aspects of Person Perception". Methuen, London.
    Forthcoming.
Smith, H.T. and Green, T.R.G., (eds.) 1980. "Human Interaction
    with Computers". Academic Press, London.
Weizenbaum, J. 1976. "Computer Power and Human Reason". Freeman,
    San Francisco.

PSYCHOLOGICAL TESTING: THE WAY AHEAD

Alick Elithorn

Institute of Neurology and Royal Free Hospital
London

INTRODUCTION

Psychometrics and psychological tests are topics which often
meet with considerable adverse social and scientific criticism and
the contribution which such tests can make to clinical work is
undervalued. Indeed some clinical psychologists with some reason
regard testing as often an unrewarding chore.

In spite of the criticisms made, psychological tests are widely
used in educational and vocational guidance and personnel selection.
Within the health services they are used mainly for assessment in
neurology, neurosurgery and psychiatry. In industry and education
group testing is often adequate but in the clinical field and for
some aspects of education individual testing is frequently essential.
Individual testing is labour intensive and involves highly skilled
professionals in a considerable degree of mindless clerical work.
For this reason the simple automation of a range of existing psychological tests would be cost effective in terms of manpower saving
alone. Much greater advantages, however, will accrue from the
development of automated psychological test systems if we exploit
to the full the available computer technology. Testing will not
only become less tedious and less expensive but automated testing
will provide psychologists with new and powerful tools.

To take one example, psychological medicine today has available
a wide range of powerful treatments, which aim either to depress
mental functions which are over active or alternatively to stimulate
functions that are pathologically depressed. Many of these treatments carry unwanted and sometimes dangerous side effects and their
use can only be justified if the degree of improvement brought about

justifies the risks and side effects involved. No physician would
dream of treating hypertension without measuring the effect of the
treatment on the patient's blood pressure. It is equally desirable
that in treating mental illness the psychologist should measure and
record the effect that treatment has on his patient's mental competence.

With the tools currently available this, except in research
trials, is impracticable. Thus a review (Elithorn et al., 1975) of
a number of psychological studies on the effects of Leva-Dopa on the
mental status of patients suffering from Parkinsonism showed that
results from several different studies were contradictory. Some
workers found that Leva-Dopa produced no effect on mental functions,
others reported an improvement. A third group claimed that Leva-Dopa
produced intellectual deterioration. While existing psychological
tests may be effective in assessing gross differences between individuals and the relatively large intra-individual changes which
accompany maturation and education, they are insensitive to small
changes in individual competence and unsuited to the repeated testing
of the same individual. As Lishmann (1977) has emphasised, research
in clinical psychology should give a high priority to developing
tests which are sensitive to change. Certain computer techniques
make this possible. Using computer item generation, randomised item
selection and process control we can develop criterion referenced
tests which are suitable for repeated testing and which have the
sensitivity needed. Thus in a pilot study, John Weinmann and I,
using a small battery of tests based on a PDP8 system, were able to
show (Elithorn et al., 1975) that the main changes in intellectual
functions produced by Leva-Dopa could be related to its arousal or
alerting effect and its stimulating action on mood.

AUTOMATED PSYCHOLOGICAL TESTS

Automated psychological test procedures require a moderately
complex graphic display in which the duration of each stimulus and
the timing of each stimulus can be accurately controlled. They also
require that the subject's responses be timed accurately, in some
instances to the nearest millisecond. It is also important that
the system responds rapidly whenever subject-system interaction is
required. During the test the terminal must respond instantly to
the subject, but a slight delay of up to five or even thirty seconds,
is tolerable between tests. Such a system would be used not infrequently by clinical psychologists with a primary interest in
psychotherapy rather than in experimental psychology and should also
be capable of being operated by nursing staff, receptionists, or
even by the patients themselves. The system therefore should not
require any technical expertise for its operation.

A key development which computer technology brings to psychological testing is the computer item generation. This combined with randomised stratified item sampling allows the psychologist to use criterion referenced tests to take full advantage of the computer's process control ability to interact with the subject and to present items determined by its analysis of the subject's performance to date. This "tailored testing" is more efficient and also becomes more acceptable to the subject in that he is presented with an "encouraging" mixture of success and failure. A small computer or microprocessor can provide these facilities and a system designed round a small inexpensive microprocessor forms a powerful tool which can collect a range of behavioural data of great value to both the clinical psychologist and the psychiatrist. Such data, for its full exploitation, needs complex analyses which are outside the capability of small laboratory computers. Moreover, psychological test data is often of comparative rather than absolute value and if the data collected is to be used effectively, sizeable data storage facilities for a reference data bank are also required. The absence of central computing facilities in hospitals and schools means that for some time stand-alone psychological test systems will be needed. With the development of institutional automation intelligent terminals connected to a central computing facility will in many applications provide a more cost effective solution (Elithorn et al., 1980).

With criterion referenced tests in contrast to norm referenced tests a subject's performance is evaluated not solely in relation to the performance of other subjects but primarily in terms of his ability to achieve objective levels of performance. With criterion referenced tests item difficulty can be determined in terms of the values taken by the variables which determine the item character-istics e.g. the span of digits a subject can recall without error or the size of a maze he can solve in a given time. It is important to remember, however, that factors other than the criterion selected may be important sources of variance. With Digit Span the actual digits and their arrangement can make a large difference to item difficulty. The series 432 1234, formerly HEA 1234 the telephone number of the headquarters of the British Post Office, is arguably more memorable than 930 4832 the number for Buckingham Palace. With the Perceptual Maze Test (PMT) (see Figure 1) the arrangement of the dots on the lattice can be equally critical. With both tests these pattern effects can be controlled by programmed filters which exclude items in which, for example, there are repetitions, sequences or, in the case of the maze, excessive runs of dots.

Many psychological tests lend themselves readily to automation and those we have so far programmed include: Digit Span, a Coding Test, the PMT, a Tracking Task, Memory Tests for Words and Nonsense-Syllables, Self-Recording Analogue Scales, a Tapping Test, Visual and Sound Reaction Time Tests, an Adjective Check List, a Stress Questionnaire, Tests of Reading Speed, a Vigilance Test and a Three-Letter Word Recognition Test which has been shown to correlate well with linguistic skill.

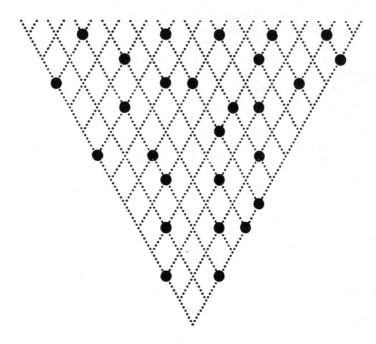

Figure 1:   The Perceptual Maze Test

In this test the subject's task is to find a pathway along the background lattice which passes through the greatest number of target dots. At each intersection the path must continue forward, i.e. the subject may fork right or left but must not double back. In general, there is more than one solution. A subject is either told the maximum score he can obtain, or this information is withheld. Conventionally, these two methods of presentation are called the 'with information condition' and the 'without information condition'.

COGNITIVE STYLE

    Psychologists have for a long time been aware that intellect and personality are not independent. Different subjects may solve the same problem in different ways. Differences in the ways subjects perform intellectually as contrasted with the differences in the levels of intellectual performance they can obtain, are considered by psychologists to be a difference in cognitive style. Because computer based tests can be analysed in greater detail and the different components of a subject's response separately timed, these tests can be used to evaluate these differences in cognitive style (Weinman et al., 1981).

The amount of time that a subject spends on different aspects of a task is one aspect of performance which reflects both the level of his ability and his cognitive style. This latter can perhaps best be visualised as the product of the interaction of his relevant skills and his personality. On any particular occasion it may also reflect his mood. Cognitive style may also be affected by treatment such as ECT, drugs or psychotherapy. We might hope, therefore, that the detailed analysis of a performance which computer techniques make practicable would provide information which correlates with personality variables and perhaps also with the subject's mental state. It is encouraging to find that this is the case.

TEST DESIGN

Any final discussion on the composition of a standard automated psychological test battery must still be some way away but there are some principles which provide important guide lines. The basic battery of tests must be relatively small. Each test should have a systematic structure which lends itself to the analysis of the skills required to solve the problems it presents and the cognitive style adopted by the individual subjects. It should sample relatively coherent skills. The interaction between tests should provide the maximum amount of information about each subject's cognitive structure. Finally the battery should lend itself to repeated administration. This latter requirement, particularly if repeated testing is to be frequent, imposes considerable restrictions on test design. Indeed in the present state of test development this latter restriction would certainly reduce the diagnostic sensitivity of the battery. It is probable therefore that for the forseeable future the versions of the tests used for repeated testing would differ significantly from those used diagnostically. In the present paper I shall limit myself to the principles and method of evaluation which should determine test development. I will illustrate these with some results from the work we have been doing with the Perceptual Maze Test.

The Perceptual Maze Test has a number of characteristics which make it particularly suitable for automation and computer development. It is a criterion referenced test with a simple binary structure which lends itself both to computer item generation, presentation on a computer driven display and also to computer analysis. The PMT is a performance test which has been identified by Butcher (1968) as one of the few tests which bridge the gap between psychometric endeavour and experimental psychology. It has been shown to be a perceptual scanning task which is a relatively pure measure of perceptual speed (Beard, 1965; De Fries et al., 1974) and which is particularly sensitive to both biochemical and physical impairment of right hemisphere functions (Carter-Saltzman, 1979; Archibald, 1978). As one of the most culture fair tests available it was selected as a recommended behavioural measure for the International Biological Programme (Biesheuval, 1969). A sample item from the Neuropsychiatric version of the PMT is presented in Figure 1.

The subject's task in the PMT is to find a pathway along the background lattice which passes through the greatest number of target dots. He must keep to the lattice or tracks and must not cut across from one path to another. At each intersection the path must continue forward, i.e. the subject may fork right or left but must not double back. In general, dependent on the arrangement of the target dots, there is more than one "best" pathway and the subject is said to have succeeded if he finds any one of these. There are two main conditions under which the PMT is presented. A subject is either told the maximum number of dots which can be obtained, or this information is withheld and he is then left to decide whether he has found a "best" solution or not. Convention-ally, these two methods of presentation are called the 'with information condition' and the 'without information condition'.

In the computer version of the test, the subject using left and right response keys fills in a pathway on a TV display. A rub-out key is provided and the subject uses additional keys to indicate when he is satisfied with his solution and when he is ready for the next item. Each key response is timed individually.

In solving the PMT most subjects scan each pattern before making any response. They may then complete a full solution path without an appreciable pause. More commonly the subject's tracking response is built up with three types of response. 'Trills' in which the subject fills in a pre-determined path as quickly as he can, 'pauses' during which the subject is looking for further information, and an intermediate type in which he appears to be looking around him while still advancing. Within an individual performance it may be difficult to isolate these components succinctly and we have found it useful to treat the fastest 10% of the response times as 'motor' times and to treat times greater than one second as pauses. The indices of performance that we are currently using are there-fore:-

1. Search time: The time until the first motor response.
2. Track time: The time from the first motor response
                    until the completion of the task.
3. Check time: The time between a subject completing
                    his tracking and his signifying that he
                    is satisfied with his solution.
4. Non Fatal Errors: Number of corrections per item.

5.	Fatal errors:	Number of items incorrect.
6.	Motor Index:	Average of fastest 10% of key responses.
7.	Refresh Index:	Number of pauses >1 sec during the tracking phase.
8.	Laterality Index:	Percentage of right preferences.

Analysing performance in this way shows that a subject who spends relatively little time on his initial search will tend during the tracking phase to spend relatively more time conducting additional searches and perhaps making and correcting more errors. Extroverts as opposed to introverts tend to behave in this way. Not unexpectedly the interaction between cognitive style and personality is affected by the information condition under which the test is presented. Extroverts are less constrained by the lack of information and for example find it easier to start the tracking part of the task while still uncertain as to whether or not they have found a solution. Interestingly both these aspects of the subject's performance on the PMT - his readiness to "have a go" - and his response to the "without information condition" may be shown to be affected by drugs which produce little or no change in the subject's overall competence at the basic task.

As mentioned earlier the PMT is particularly sensitive to organic damage to the right hemisphere. Here the variation in a subject's responses to individual items may be of diagnostic import. Thus patients with cerebral lesions even when they find a correct solution tend to choose different solutions to those chosen by normal subjects. Analysis of the individual solutions can contribute significantly to the power of the test to discriminate normal and brain damaged subjects and between subjects with lesions in the different hemispheres. Moreover, with this type of analysis it is possible to undertake simulation studies which provide alternative models for, for example, the effect of brain damage on perceptual scanning skills (Smith et al., 1978).

SINGLE PERSON TRIALS

Criterion reference tests like the PMT which lend themselves to computer item generation are suitable for repeated testing and hence to monitoring therapeutic changes. The possibilities inherent in this type of development are best illustrated by two examples from the proving studies which have guided our development programme. One study was undertaken with a 20 year old girl with severe obsessional neurosis and a mixture of depression and anxiety symptoms. This patient was at first treated with diazepam which caused excessi disinhibition. This was then discontinued and amylobarbitone substituted. Eight days later she started a therapeutic trial designed to determine whether the addition of a stimulant, amphetamine, to her sedative regimen would produce further improvement in her

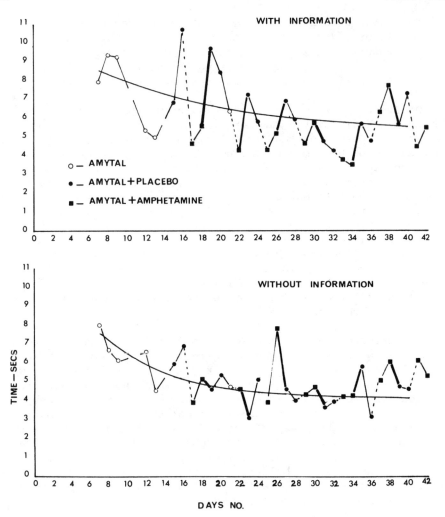

Figure 2:   Median Solution Times

Daily observations from a patient with a severe obsessional neurosis
and the points plotted are the median solution times for the Perceptual Maze Test.   The data for the two test conditions - with and
without information - have been plotted separately.   The exponential
curves have been fitted to the observations made when the patient
received amylobarbitone alone.   On the day during the trial plotted
with an open circle, the second (amphetamine-placebo) capsule was
inadvertently omitted (see text).

symptomatology or her accessibility to psychotherapy.   In this
study the patient received two treatment regimens which alternated
every second day.   For a warm-up period and during the trial, the
patient's competence on a small battery of psychological tests was

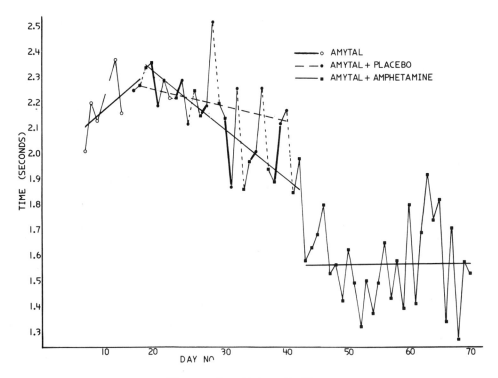

Figure 3: Motor Indices

The mean motor indices derived for the results obtained from both
the with and without information condition for the 28 days of the
trial for the same subject as in Figure 2, together with the data
for the 5 preceeding and the 28 succeeding days. Straight line
plots have been fitted to the days when she was receiving amytal
alone before the trial and during the trial, and on the days when
she was receiving amytal and amphetamine combined, both during the
trial and for the 28 days after the trial ended. It is clear that
the added stimulant has greatly improved this patient's motor speed.

assessed daily.

Figures 2 and 3 show plots of two of the indices derived from
this patient's performance on the Perceptual Maze Test. In Figure
2 we have plotted, for the period of the trial, the median search
times under the with- and without- information conditions. It is
apparent that her performance was more variable under the with-
information condition than under the without-information condition.
The diagrams and Table 1.1 show that this increase in variance
reflects the effect that under the former condition the 'search'
times are at times very much longer on the amylobarbitone days than
on the amylobarbitone plus amphetamine days. Although the number

of observations is relatively small it was possible to conclude that
this effect was most marked on the first of each pair of days. That
is to say there was evidence of habituation.

This speeding of performance was accompanied by an increase in
the number of spontaneous corrections but a marked reduction in the
number of fatal errors (Table 1.2). Thus it seems reasonable to
conclude that this patient was tackling the test more energetically
while maintaining or perhaps increasing her ability to monitor her
performance.

The detailed behavioural data which computer techniques enable
us to collect not only allow us to look separately at a perceptual
component of the subject's performance, but we can also analyse the
effect of treatment on the motor component. In Figure 3, we have
plotted for this same trial the mean motor index. Again it can be
seen that the increased variance during the trial period is due to
the fact that the mean times on the days on which the patient is
receiving amylobarbitone alone are much slower than the times recorded on the days when she also received amphetamine. It is also
clear that there is a progressive slowing of the motor times during
the pre-trial period when the subject is on amylobarbitone alone,
that the addition of amphetamine reverses the trend and that, during
the trial period, this reversal effect is reduced by the fact that
the amphetamine is being administered on only half the days. It
also appears that the perceptual effect tends to habituate fairly
rapidly, while the motor effect is initially cumulative.

On the basis of this trial it seemed reasonable to conclude
that in this patient a combination of stimulant and sedative treatment
produced a higher level of mental competence than did treatment with
a sedative alone and the combined treatment routine was therefore
adopted with clinical benefit. It is also interesting to note that
the patient's motor performance during the post-trial period remained
considerably faster, as indeed did her overall performance. This
increase in the patient's competence and self-confidence enabled her
to tackle more effectively her psychotherapeutic programme, which
included a period of intensive 'flooding'. Subsequently the amphetamine and amylobarbitone were withdrawn blind sequentially without
any subjective complaints of withdrawal and with some minor disturb-
ances of her test performance.

STATISTICAL PROBLEMS

The difficulty of specifying the degree of confidence with which
it is possible to ascribe to intervention effects in single person
studies, in which the data collected is time-dependent and auto-
regressive, is the key problem which has deterred psychologists from
developing the methodology of single person studies.

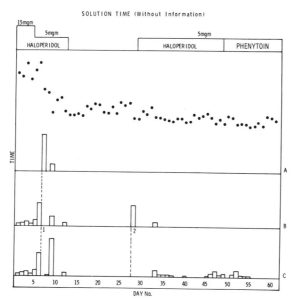

Figure 4a: Daily median solution times for the Perceptual Maze Test
under the without information condition for a 24 year
old schizophrenic patient (for description see text).

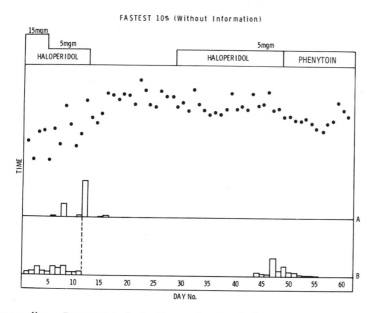

Figure 4b: Perceptual indices derived from data plotted in
Figure 4a (see text).

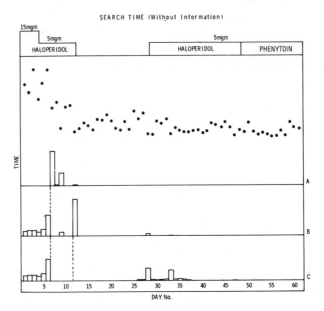

Figure 4c: Motor indices for the same data as for Figures 4a and
            4b (see text).

    Recently we have been fortunate in being able to work with
Professor Adrian Smith who has developed a Bayesian technique with
which it is possible to analyse intervention effects in time-series
data even though these may contain auto-regressive and learning
components (Smith, 1977). This technique first fits a mathematical
model to the data, then sets up the hypothesis that there is a discontinuity in the data and that this would be better represented by
two models. A likelihood analysis then calculates for each point
the probability that the discontinuity occurs at that point. If
there is a relatively high probability of a discontinuity at one
point, the data is then split at that point and the analysis is
repeated on each section. If there is little likelihood that there
is a discontinuity then these probabilities - totalling 1 - are
distributed evenly between the observations. In one study we used
this technique to look at the effects of psychotropic and anti-
convulsant medication in a 24 year old man suffering from a severe
schizo-affective illness. This patient had been changed from
Chloropramazine to Haloperidol because he had had a suspected con-
vulsive episode while on the former drug. He found the Haloperidol
depressing and decided to refuse medication. Subsequently he agreed
to undertake regular testing in order that we could better determine
dosages which did not cause unnecessary side effects. Examples of
the results obtained are given in Figures 4a, b, c.

    Figure 4a gives an analysis of the median solution times
obtained with the PMT under the no-information condition over a

period of 62 days. The first analysis indicates that there is a
high probability that a break in the underlying processes occurred
during the period when the patient was coming off Haloperidol. In
the next analysis a second break in the series appears when the
patient restarts Haloperidol.

In Figures 4b and 4c similar analyses for the perceptual and
motor components of the test performance are presented. It is clear
that the perceptual component of the subject's performance - his
search time - was affected by the reintroduction of Haloperidol,
but not by the addition of Phenytoin (Epanutin). However, the
motor component (fastest 10%) was not affected by the reintroduction
of Haloperidol but was affected by the addition of Phenytoin. This
was an unexpected finding. In general the literature on Phenytoin
suggests that pharmacologically this has little effect on mental and
motor skills. In this case, however, EEG studies revealed that this
patient had a large area of abnormal electrical activity just anter-
ior to his left motor area. The finding that Phenytoin affected his
motor performance can therefore be explained and this is a strong
confirming instance for both the validity of the statistical analysis
and for this technique of computer fragmentation of test performance.

REFERENCES

Archibald, Y.M., 1978. Time as a variable in the performance of
    hemisphere damaged patients on the Elithorn Perceptual Maze
    Test. Cortex, Vol. XIV No. 1: 22-31.
Beard, R., 1965. The structure of perception: a factorial study.
    Brit. J. Educ. Psychol., 35,2: 210-222.
Biesheuval, S., 1969. Methods for measurement of psychological
    performance. In: Biesheuval, S. (Ed.), "International Bio-
    logical Programme Handbook". Blackwells, Oxford.
Butcher, H.G., 1968. "Human Intelligence: Its Nature and Assess-
    ment". Methuen and Co., London.
Carter-Saltzman, L., 1979. Patterns of cognitive functioning in
    relation to handedness and sex-related differences. In:
    Wittig, M.A. and Petersen, A.C. (Eds.), "Sex-Related Differences
    in Cognitive Functioning". Academic Press, New York.
De Fries, J.C., Vandenberg, S.G., McClearn, G.E., Ashton, G.C. and
    Johnson, R.C., 1974. Near identity of cognitive structure in
    two ethnic groups. Science, 183: 338-339.
Elithorn, A., Jagoe, J.R. and Lee, D.N., 1966. The simulation of
    a perceptual problem solving skill. Nature, 211: 1029.
Elithorn, A., Lunzer, M. and Weinman, J.J., 1975. Cognitive deficits
    associated with chronic hepatic encephalopathy and their res-
    ponse to Leva-Dopa. Neurol. Neurosurg. and Psychiat., 38,8:
    794-798.
Elithorn, A., Powell, J., Telford, A. and Cooper, R., 1980. An
    intelligent terminal for automated psychological testing and

remedial practice. In: Grimsdale, R.L. and Hankins, H.C.A.
(Eds.), "Human Factors and Interactive Displays". Network,
Buckingham.
Lishmann, W.A., 1977. "Senile and Presenile Dementias". Medical
Research Council, London.
Smith, A.F.M., 1977. A Bayesian analysis of some time-varying
models. In: Barra, J.R. (Ed.), "Recent Developments in
Statistics". North-Holland, Amsterdam.
Weinman, J., Elithorn, A. and Farag, S., 1981. Test structure and
cognitive style. In: Friedman, M., O'Connor, N. and Das, J.P.,
(Eds.), "Intelligence and Learning". Plenum Press, New York.

COMPUTERS: DECISION-MAKING: CLINICAL PSYCHOLOGY

M. Dewey

Department of Psychiatry
University of Liverpool

This paper reviews the ways in which computers have been used
in medical practice, with particular emphasis on decision making and
mental health. First we consider two areas in which the role of the
computer has primarily been to provide better data on which decisions
can be made. These are psychiatric databases, psychological testing
and psychological assessment. After a brief interlude in which the
use of computers in modelling is considered, we move on to the second
major area where computers have been used to actually make decisions.
The simplest decision tree approach is considered, then the more
powerful Bayesian approaches are presented, and finally work on
expert systems is discussed. The final section consists of an
evaluation of all the methods discussed, and of likely progress
over the next few years.

The reader is assumed to have some knowledge of the functions
of electronic digital computers, although no detailed knowledge of
either hardware or software is required. Similarly some familiarity
with the notions of probability and statistics will be helpful,
although detailed references are provided as needed. For each area
only one or two key examples are given, usually a recent research
paper. These will provide a source of further examples and references. No attempt has been made to translate job titles and currency
from one side of the Atlantic to the other.

PSYCHIATRIC DATABASES

Anyone who has tried to use medical records for research or
treatment will testify that considerable problems of accuracy and
legibility arise. The advent of large-scale computer systems has

135

given rise to the idea that the records might well be held on a
computer system and accessed by program rather than manually. A
well known example of this type is described in Hedlund et al. (1977).
This is a mature system which holds the records of tens of thousands
of patients.

These systems have been used as adjuncts to decision-making.
They provide the possibility of searching the database for records
of patients similar to the current admission, and then providing
information to the clinician on what had happened to them.

Cho and his co-workers (Cho et al., 1981) provide a description
of such a system. They use the Missouri Actuarial Report System
(MARS) which contains data on more than 300,000 cases (and occupies
more than 500 megabytes of disc space). The actual database is
described more fully in other references, but Cho et al.'s paper is
of interest to us because it combines the database with a decision-
making system. Data on a patient can be combined with information
from the case register, mental state and emergency room check-list
data already stored, to yield predictions of the diagnostic category,
probable prescription of medication, likelihood of absconding, and
length of stay in hospital. The first three of these are calculated
using a linear discriminant analysis, and the length of stay is predicted using linear multiple regression. The reader who is unfamiliar
with these techniques should consult any good text on multivariate
methods (e.g. Morrison, 1976). Discriminant analysis and regression
analysis are parallel statistical techniques, the former for qualitative response variables, the latter for quantitative. In both cases
the explanatory variables are combined in an optimum way for predicting the response variable.

TESTING

The computer may act as an adjunct to decision-making simply
by providing data. It may be useful here to review some of the
ways in which this has been done.

One technique uses the computer to present test material to the
patient, who gives a response on a keyboard. The keyboard may either
be a standard computer terminal, or a special purpose device which
has a key for each possible response, and is labelled with the
responses. The material presented may either be specially written
for the application, or it may be an adaptation of existing paper
and pencil tests.

These techniques have the advantages that they are more systematic than manual presentation, can be used with patients who cannot
write, and in general have been shown to give good correlations with
more conventional techniques without being less acceptable to the
patient.

One comprehensive system interviews the patient for between 4 and 8 hours (Angle et al., 1977). This system uses a time-shared PDP11/40 and presents the questions to the patient on a VDU screen. The database consists of more than 3,000 questions, not all of which are posed to any given patient. If he/she evinces any sexual arousal problems a further section of 1,000 questions on sexual arousal may be asked. The authors do not report any numerical data, but the diagrams in their paper indicate that a majority of the patients held positive feelings about the computer after the interaction. They also preferred it to human interviewing, felt that the interview length was "about right", and were usually prepared to be re-interviewed. They were also happy about being asked personal questions by the machine. These findings are fairly typical of the response of patients to this sort of system, although few other authors have had the patience to think of 3,000 questions (to say nothing of 1,000 about sexual matters) let alone dared to ask people to be interviewed for 8 hours.

A smaller scale system based around a PDP11/03 (Johnson and Williams, 1978) which will simultaneously interview five patients shows that cost need not be a major obstacle in this field. They estimate the cost at 1978 prices at $26,000 with annual maintenance of $4,000. Their system imposes some limitations of speed, but these are apparently acceptable to the interviewees.

These fixed response systems have disadvantages, of course. Although it is possible to build in a certain degree of "branching", so that questions are only asked if replies to earlier items indicate that they may be relevant, the programs are still inflexible, compared to a human interviewer.

Other workers have therefore adopted a more naturalistic app-roach. They have devised programs which analysed natural language text (Colby) and allowed the patient to type in free format material. This approach has not so far been very productive, recent advances in parsing techniques may lead to a resurgence of interest, but the techniques have also been criticised on other grounds. Weizenbaum, who devised one of the earliest systems which responded to the interviewee in a natural way, has been particularly critical of this approach on ethical grounds.

Even quite simple systems of the ELIZA type (Weizenbaum, 1967) appear to exhibit understanding of the text typed in. (ELIZA is a pattern matching system, which analyses the input, and by applying a few simple transformations to it produces replies. A program DOCTOR uses ELIZA to mimic a non-directive therapist. Weizenbaum notes that his secretary asked to use the program, and so strong was the illusion of understanding, that she asked him (Weizenbaum)

to leave the room while she communicated with the machine. The fact
that this is possible tells us nothing more than that much human
interaction is content-free (in the sense that acceptable replies
can be produced by a machine which has no understanding or model of
the world which it seems to describe), but it has seemed that the
comfort which people draw from talking to a machine who appears to
understand their problems might point the way to the use of computers
as therapists. The question left then would be who should take the
responsibility for the therapy. This has led some workers to argue
that there are activities which are inherently human, and which we
should not delegate to machines. Further discussion would convert
this into a paper on medical ethics, which it did not set out to be,
so the reader is left with the moral problem.

MODELLING

    Although it is slightly peripheral to the main theme, mention
should be made of work on modelling processes in psychiatric patients,
particularly that of Colby and his associates. Here the computer
simulates the processes which are claimed to form a particular
illness. A good description of this is given in Colby et al.,(1971).
This presents examples of the dialogue between the interviewer and
the computer model. The model is one of a patient with a paranoid
illness. The program analyses the natural language input looking
for key words and phrases which are relevant to its internal model.
It also keeps track of its own internal state, so that the occurrence
of appropriate stimuli will increase its feelings of fear, anger
and mistrust.

    The examples are too long to include here, but some idea of
their verisimilitude may be gained from the statement that of 25
psychiatrists who interviewed the model 23 thought it paranoid.
(The other 2 felt that it was brain damaged, because of its limited
linguistic functioning.) A sort of Turing test is applied (Turing,
1950), and an example of a "real" dialogue between a patient and an
interviewer is included in the paper for comparison. (The Turing
test named after Alan Turing the philosopher and artificial intelligence pioneer, consists of interviewing the computer model and a
human being down communication lines. If the observer cannot tell
which is which, the program is deemed to simulate human behaviour.)

DIAGNOSTIC SYSTEMS

    Under this heading we will only consider the simpler systems
which have been developed. The more complex methods are dealt with
in the next two sections. One method of providing a computerised
diagnostic system involves the use of a decision tree. In this
system a series of choices are made, and at the end of the process

a diagnosis is produced. For instance one choice might be "Does the patient have depressed mood?" and the answer to this would affect what further questions would be asked, and ultimately the diagnosis. This is the use of computers as a professional assistant, rather than as a device for interacting with the patient.

A straightforward example of such a system (Greist et al., 1976) makes diagnoses according to a set of research criteria. The authors note that difficulty is encountered with such systems because of the lack of generally agreed operational definitions of the disease entities. This means that such a system can only be evaluated against the judgement of clinicians, unlike a system in internal medicine, where surgical or post-mortem evidence can confirm or falsify the diagnosis.

This problem is of course endemic to all psychiatric diagnostic projects, it may diminish with the use of DMA-III, time will tell.

BAYESIAN APPROACHES

The theorem of Bayes provides us with a method for updating estimates of probabilities. This is not the place to provide a detailed account of the theorem, for which any good introductory text on probability may be consulted. (E.g. Feller, 1968, where it is called the Rule of Bayes.) However the following may serve as a reminder. We know the probabilities of each diagnosis, these are the "prior" probabilities, call these $p(D1)$, $p(D2)$ ... $p(DN)$. We also know the conditional probability of each sign or symptom given each diagnosis, for symptom S these will be $p(S1D1)$, $p(S1D2)$ ... $p(S1DN)$. These are read "the probability of S given D1" and so on. We can compute the probability of the hypothesis given a particular symptom. Let this be $p(Di|S)$.

$$p(Di|S) = \frac{p(Di)p(S|Di)}{p(D1)p(S|D1) + \dots + p(DN)p(S|DN)}$$

These "posterior" probabilities will now become the prior probabilities for the next round of updating.

Note that this approach relies on having suitable estimates of the probabilities, and assumes that they will be stationary throughout the series. We are also assuming that the diagnoses are mutually exclusive and together exhaustive. It is not difficult to include an "unspecified" category to take care of the latter requirement, but the first may prove troublesome in practice. A further assumption is that the symptoms are conditionally independent across diseases. This means that the probability of a symptom should not depend on whether another symptom is present or absent. In the fullest form of the theorem such an assumption is unnecessary, as the conditional probabilities can be included, but in practice they are not.

Note that the theorem is a consequence of the axioms of probability theory, (Kolmogorov, 1933, 1956) and is the optimum way of updating probabilities under the assumptions mentioned. Some of the misapplications of the theorem (see Feller, 1968) have suggested that its truth might be questioned, but this is absurd. The empirical questions are related to the accuracy with which we can specify the probabilities, and the extent to which the assumptions in fact hold in the world.

The work of Gustafson and his colleagues provides two interesting examples. In the first study they show that Bayesian techniques can be used for predicting the probability of attempting suicide, and in an extension of this work they try to predict the lethality of such attempts.

In the first study (Gustafson et al., 1977) estimates of the necessary probabilities were collected from experienced clinicians. The patients were interviewed by the computer, although this is irrelevant to the decision-making part of the system. In a trial using the estimates in a Bayesian model the computer predicted whether 20 cases would attempt to commit suicide (10 cases attempted). Its performance was compared with that of 10 residents and 8 psychiatrists who used the same data. The Bayesian model predicted 70% of the attempters, the residents 33% and the psychiatrists 38%. All were more successful with the non-attempters (90%, 97% and 93% respectively). In addition the computer assigned higher probabilities to the successful predictions than the humans (0.85, 0.61 and 0.63) and also assigned higher probabilities to the correct outcome in the cases when it made the wrong prediction (0.31, 0.22 and 0.20).

In the second paper Gustafson and his colleagues (Gustafson et al., 1981) compared two methods of predicting whether a suicide attempt would result in the death of the attempter. Using various features of the patient and his/her surroundings they obtained ratings from clinicians of their seriousness, and the probability that such a feature would be present in a successful attempt. They then used a linear regression model, and a Bayesian approach to predict outcome of a series of 32 attempts. The two models were at least as successful as the clinicians with whom they were compared, particularly for the successful attempts, although there was a slight tendency for the Bayesian system to over-estimate the probability of death among the group who in fact lived.

It would be fair to point out that other workers have found the use of subjective estimates unsatisfactory. For instance, De Dombal has built a system with an impressive skill at diagnosing acute abdominal pain. This is perhaps the best known Bayesian medical

diagnostic system. He found (Leaper et al., 1972) that when the
clinicians were asked for their estimates of probabilities, and
these were used in the same model as estimates obtained from a survey
the performance of the computer was much worse. The clinicians
successfully diagnosed 79.7% of the 472 cases, the computer using
their estimates was correct in 82.2% of cases but using estimates
from a survey of 600 cases it obtained a 91.1% success rate. The
authors comment that the error primarily springs from the poor
probability estimates, rather than from a failure to combine the
evidence in an optimal fashion.

EXPERT SYSTEMS

The problem of the representation of knowledge is one which has
exercised many workers in the field of artificial intelligence (AI).
It is natural that workers dissatisfied with the progress made by
other types of diagnostic system would turn to AI techniques as an
alternative.

The reader who feels that a quick refresher course in AI would
be helpful should try either Winston (1977) which is perhaps the
best straightforward guide to the area, or for a more exotic experience Hofstadter (1979) which is perhaps more interesting for the
general reader. Both of them discuss some of the systems mentioned
in this paper, and give examples of the output produced.

The technique which has been most successful is that of the
"production system". In this the knowledge about the problem domain
is embodied in a series of rules (called productions for reasons
which do not concern us here). These rules are of the form "If
condition then consequence". The knowledge of the program is then
embodied in a number of these rules. The program itself contains
an interpreter which decides which rule to try next in order to
reach the goal. If the rule which it chooses has a condition which
is known to be true, then the consequence can now be considered to
be true too, and is added to the list of things which are known to
be true.

The best-known example of this type is not psychiatric in nature
but selects antibiotics for infections (Davis et al., 1977). MYCIN,
as it is known, has a series of rules about the nature of bacterial
infection, the sterility of culture methods and collection sites and
so on. There are about 200 rules, which are stored in a form which
can be expanded into a natural language form relatively easily,
although of course for the program's use they are stored more
compactly. This means that the user can interrogate the system
about its rules, and about the inferences it made. Examples are
given in the reference of how the system will say why it decided
something, by referring to rules and facts which it already knew.

These facts can in turn be queried, and the evidence for them will
be produced.

This method of representing knowledge has the advantage that
new rules can be added very easily, and old ones can be changed if
errors are detected, or advances made in medical science. All the
rules carry with them numerical values reflecting the degree of
certainty they carry. These values are combined by the program to
yield a value for each inference. The performance of this system
is impressive, although no formal testing has been reported yet.

Other systems have been developed for larger and smaller problem
domains. Mention should perhaps be made of the program INTERNIST
which assists in the diagnosis of all diseases in internal medicine.
The system has a fairly limited human interface, and is not yet used
in clinical practice.

Some critics of AI have accused it of only tackling "toy"
problems. Whether this is fair or not, it is not a criticism which
can be levelled at INTERNIST.

EVALUATION

This section reviews the six sections which precede it, and
attempts for each to answer the questions: whether more progress
is to be expected in this area over the next two or three years,
and whether much useful work can and will be done using micro-
computer facilities of the type that individual departments in the
mental health field might expect to possess or purchase.

In the database area little progress can be expected. Most of
the concepts in database technology have already been the subject
of intensive study, and the problems are primarily computing science
rather than psychological in nature. We can expect that systems
will become more powerful, and easier to use, but they will still
do the same things.

As far as micro-computer database systems are concerned we can
foresee the possibility of larger systems being mounted on small
machines. Obviously the MARS example mentioned above will not be a
micro-computer application for years to come, the use of half a
gigabyte of disc rules that out, but we must remember that it is a
particularly large system. It is already possible to obtain systems
using Winchester technology which can support tens of megabytes of
disc storage, and such a system would support a database package to
handle more than a thousand patients fairly easily.

In the testing field we can look for some progress on several fronts. Increasingly workers are becoming dissatisfied with the idea of mechanising tests which already exist. Although this has obvious cost benefits, and we should be grateful that we do now know that such a thing is possible, and also acceptable to patients and clinicians alike, we would also feel that there must be better things to do with the power of the computer than setting it to repeat the tests of our forefathers. In particular, the control over timing and measurement which the machine allows means that we can develop tests of entirely new types.

We can also expect that advances will be made in the development of software for analysing free-form input. It seems unlikely that this will ever replace the more restricted methods, if only because most people cannot type, but perhaps that is not an immutable law either.

This is perhaps the area which is most suitable for micro-computer applications. Indeed it is hardly an exaggeration to say that it is impossible to achieve some of these effects on anything except a micro-system. Automated testing demands a degree of control over timing, a guarantee of quick response, and the ability to address parts of the screen directly. These are features which are not found in most main-frame operating systems, and it is unlikely that they could be provided as cheaply thus, as in a smaller dedicated system.

Modelling was not one of our major concerns, but for completeness it should be mentioned here. Some progress may well be seen here, notably following on from work in AI on representation of knowledge, and the simulation of psychological processes in general. Most people in this field use large main-frame systems, or at least large mini-systems, and there seems little reason for this situation to change. This is likely to continue to be a research, rather than a service, tool.

Decision-making applications have so far made relatively little headway in the mental health field. We can expect progress here, even though the bottleneck of inadequate criteria will remain with us for some time.

If computers are going to make an impact on clinical decision-making it is clear that micro-systems will be used. It may be possible to integrate them into the sort of small database system discussed above. The processing demands of the simple decision-making systems are small, and the only stumbling block is providing the system with a good model of the decision system, and a good human interface.

Much the same points apply to Bayesian approaches to decision-making. One difficult problem remains obtaining adequate information about the probabilities in the model. Despite the success of Gustaf-son's work we should remain cautious about the use of subjective estimates, and the collection of objective estimates is a difficult task. The advantages of having a micro-system by the clinician's desk, mentioned above, apply to these systems as well of course.

The major growth area in decision-making seems likely to be expert systems. The main obstacle to the widespread use of such systems in the past has always been the need to use specialised software only available at a few research institutions, and then run the programs on a very large main-frame until steam was coming out of it. All this has changed dramatically over the past few years, and AI software which will run non-trivial problems on micro-systems is widely available.

OTHER PSYCHOLOGICAL CONSIDERATIONS

One area which has received little real attention so far in the literature is the ergonomic design of computer systems for decision-making (or indeed the design of systems for any purpose). Although it is not difficult to provide long lists of research systems which show good performance at decision-making it is difficult to point to cases where substantial clinical use is made of these. It can hardly be said that the medical profession is slow to take up the use of computing when we consider the use of CAT scanning which is at least as expensive as 90% of the systems mentioned here, and performs a task which is not as conceptually complex as the task of decision-making.

Fox (1977) provides an account of the issues involved here. Many of the systems have poor interfaces, and demand that the human behaves like a computer, rather than vice versa. (This is of course endemic to all computer systems, not just medical ones.) Many of the decision-making systems have taken the approach that if an optimum decision rule is applied, then users will follow the computer's recommendation. This is a naive view. The user, who ultimately takes the moral and legal responsibility for the decision, must be convinced that it is indeed optimum. In this regard MYCIN, with its ability to justify its decision in a way which humans can understand, has been a step forward, but there is still far to go.

The systems which have achieved the greatest acceptance appear to be those which enable the user to do something he or she could not do before without the machine. Systems which automate the tasks of the professional's assistant also seem to have good chances. Where the greatest resistance has come is with systems which purport to replace those activities which professionals see as lying at the core of their role, in our subject area, diagnosis and therapy. Only time will tell if that resistance can be overcome by improved programs.

REFERENCES

Angle, H.V., Ellinwood, E.H., Hay, W.M., Johnsen, T.and Hay, L.R. 1977. Computer aided interviewing in comprehensive behavioural assessment. Behav. Ther., 8: 747-754,

Cho, D.W., Hsu, Y. and Monroe, E.J. 1981. A computerised mental patient classification system. Computer programs in biomedicine, 13: 139-147.

Colby, K.M., Weber, S. and Hilf, F.D., 1971. Artificial paranoia, Artificial intelligence, 2: 1-25

Davis, R., Buchanan, B. and Shortliffe, E., 1977. Production rules as a representation for a knowledge based consultation program. Artificial intelligence, 8: 15-46.

Feller, W., 1968. "An introduction to probability theory and its applications. Volume One". Wiley, New York.

Fox, J., 1977. Medical computing and the user. International Journal of man-machine studies, 9:669-686.

Greist, J.H., Klein, M.H. and Erdman, H.P., 1976. Routine on-line psychiatric diagnosis by computer. Amer. J. Psychiat., 133: 1405-1408.

Gustafson, D.H., Greist, J.H., Strauss, F.F., Erdman, H. and Laughren, T., 1977. A probabilistic system for identifying suicide attemptors. Computers and biomedical research, 10: 83-89.

Gustafson, D.H., Tianen, B. and Griest, J.H., 1981. A computer-based system for identifying suicide attemptors, Computers and biomedical research, 14: 144-157.

Hedlund, J.L., Sletten, I.W., Evenson, R.C., Altman, H. and Cho, D.W., 1977. Automated psychiatric information systems: a critical review of Missouri's standard system of psychiatry (SSOP), J. Oper. Psychiat., 8: 5-26.

Hofstadter, D.R., 1979. "Godel, Escher, Bach: an eternal golden braid", Basic Books Inc.

Johnson, J.A., Williams, T.A., 1978. Using a micro-computer for on-line psychiatric assessment, Behaviour research methods and instrumentation, 10: 576-578.

Kolmogorov, A.N., 1933. "Grundbegriffe der Wahrscheinlichkeitsrechnung". Springer. Berlin. Translated by Morrison, N., 1956 as "Foundations of the theory of Probability". Chelsea, New York.

Leaper, D.J., Horrocks, J.C., Staniland, J.R., and De Dombal F.T., 1972. Computer assisted diagnosis of abdominal pain using "estimates" provided by clinicians. Br. Med. J., 4: 350-354.

Morrison, D.F., 1976. "Multivariate statistical methods". McGraw-Hill, Tokyo.

Turing, A.M., 1950. Computing machinery and intelligence, Mind LIX: 433-460.

Weizenbaum, J., 1967.   Contextual understanding by computers,
    Communications of the Association for Computing Machinery,
    10: 474-480.
Winston, P.H., 1977.   "Artificial Intelligence".   Addison Wesley,
    Reading.

A COMPUTER CONTROLLED BIOFEEDBACK SYSTEM: EFFECTS OF INVERSION OF

THE FEEDBACK SIGNAL ON HEART RATE

Harry McAllister

Department of Psychology
University of Aberdeen
Aberdeen

This experiment set out to investigate whether a purely operant account could be given of performance in a heart rate control experiment, based on the characteristics and performance of the feedback display, or whether the individual's own proprioceptive feedback plays some part in the process as suggested by McCanne and Sandman (1976).

EQUIPMENT, PROGRAMS, AND DATA-ACQUISITION

Over the past four years a computer controlled laboratory system has been developed by the author for the study of psycho-physiological responses and biofeedback effects. The physiological measurements are made using an 8-channel Grass Model 7D polygraph, and control of experiments is programmed using a DEC PDP 11/34 mini-computer. This both digitises and stores the physiological signals for future analysis, and produces all signals for control of experiments and for feedback to both subject and experimenter. The programs for this system are written in DEC FORTRAN IV (see McAllister, 1980). In this case the program PHYSIO was congifured for a heart-rate biofeedback experiment.

This program provides numerical feedback for the subject, in this case on a digital display, and an operant "shaping" of response schedule is followed, reward being illumination of a red light. Here increasing demands are made before success is signalled, as the subject's response proceeds in the desired direction. Likewise, decreasing demand follows persisting failure to reach the threshold of response required before being informed of success, or "rewarded".

147

The polygraph was used to record two physiological variables: heart-rate (HR) and respiratory rate (RR). Heart-rate was measured using a Grass 7P4 Cardio-tachometer set to output rates in the range 40-120 beats per minute (bpm) accurately on four centimetre per channel recording paper. Signals outside this range can still be acquired by the computer system, although precision of measurement may be reduced outside the stated values.

Respiratory activity was measured using a Grass nasal thermo-couple which yields an adequate signal for respiratory rate measurement when amplified through a Grass 7P1 Low Level D.C. pre-amplifier.

The computer input/output devices can scan up to 10 channels of physiological data on analog-to-digital convertors, and the program controls external apparatus through switch lines, and digital-to-analog outputs. Data acquired in this way can be used for computations immediately - "on-line" as in the feedback to the subject and shaping of response used in this experiment, and it is also stored for subsequent analysis. Analog-to-digital convertor samples of all physiological signals are stored, together with the time in milliseconds since start of the experiment, the current HR level for "reward", and the status of the reward light at that moment, ctc. The large files of data generated in this way are stored directly on RKO5 cartridge disks.

Programmed data manipulation

Calibration information supplied to the control program PHYSIO prior to commencement of each experiment proper, transforms all cardiac rate-meter signals numerically for storage as beats-per-minute (bpm) data, while respiratory activity is transformed simply as an amplitude measure corresponding to the graph paper millimetre measurements, identical to the polygraph written record.

For this experiment both physiological channels were sampled at quarter second intervals (4 Hz), thus ensuring that even the highest possible expected HR, from reclining and relatively relaxed subjects, would be detected. (A heart-beat lasting less than one quarter second occurs at 240 bpm plus, while we anticipated few hearts exceeding 120 bpm. The rough guideline of Shannon's information processing theorem suggests that sampling rate should be double that of the highest frequency of signal expected.)

Of course this implies that all heart beats at or below 240 bpm are represented on more than one occasion in the data, e.g. a beat occurring at less than 60 bpm will be represented four times, etc. Thus low rates are somewhat over-represented in the data and the results will as a result be somewhat biased towards "decrease" in

HR effects.   However, the overall effect is slight.

     With "inverted" HR feedback the digital display shows falls in
heart rate corresponding in magnitude to real rised, and vice versa.
Thus the subjects are presented with an apparent heart rate change
which is an inversion of the actual change.   The rationale behind
the use of this mode of feedback is very simple - if a subject has
no internal "perception" of his heart-rate and its changes, then
reward for appropriate shifts in HR in one direction, as shown by
the red light, will produce shaping of the response in that direction
regardless of <u>indicated</u> direction of these changes.   If, however, a
subject has "internal perception" of shifts in HR and their direction,
then inverting the <u>indicated</u> HR will disrupt the acquisition of the
shaped response because of conflict between the reinforced response
and the subject's perception of what might be appropriate.   Thus,
throughout all experiments the light gave consistent and valid
information - which would normally be expected to provide undisrupted
shaping of HR.   The light indicated that the subject was achieving
higher or lower HR, depending on which condition he was in.   No
indication was given to subjects that "inversion" existed prior to
the experiment, nor was any indication made that conditions might
change during the experiment.

     The polygraph record was marked in seconds by the Grass SMT7
event/time marker, but start and end of each trial was automatically
marked on the chart paper by computer signal to the event marker.
Multiple marks succeeding the start of a trial indicated the trial
number on the chart record.

The Subjects' Feedback display

     Feedback to subjects was provided directly from the computer
program, using a specially constructed subject display panel.   This
panel was placed on a trolley to one side of the subjects' recliner
and at a comfortable angle for viewing.   The display presented three
coordinated items of information:

1.   A four-digit, half-inch high red digital display showing heart
     rate in numbers, e.g. 75 or 123 bpm, only required digits being
     illuminated.

2.   A single red light beside the digital display, providing feed-
     back to the subjects, and illuminated when they were "doing
     well", i.e. achieving elevated or lowered HR's, according to
     the experimental group to which they were assigned.

3.   A quarter-inch green four-digit display showing, in tenths of
     seconds, how long the red light was on during that trial.   This
     time information persisted throughout the subsequent inter-trial

interval (ITI) and subjects were asked to maximise the time
registered.

SUBJECTS AND INSTRUCTIONS

The experiment reported here involved 18 male and 18 female
adults, aged 18 to 35 years, who were drawn from the departmental
subject panel. Three males and three females were randomly allocated
to each of six conditions. Three groups were "rewarded" for increasing their heart-rates (HR), three for decreasing them.

All groups of subjects were given identical instructions, both
in writing and in the style of answers to questions. They were told
basically that some people seem to be able to control their heart
rate when given information about it and that the display would show
their HR, while the red light would indicate when they were "doing
well". The information conveyed by the red light was the only
"reinforcement" delivered in this experimental context. The direction
of required HR change was not mentioned, although no endeavour was
made to conceal from subjects who asked that direction of change in
HR might be a critical variable in the experiment. Specific direction
of change in HR expected and other experimental conditions were not
discussed in any form until after the experiment.

PROCEDURE

All subjects were given the instructions to read and then
electrodes were attached while any questions were answered by the
experimenter. A push-button signal from the experimenter then
initiated calibration of the physiological amplifier signals for
computer analysis and storage. A one-minute computer controlled
demonstration showed what the subject display would look like both
during experimental periods and when the subject was to rest (during
inter-trial-intervals - ITI's). The subjects were then told that
they were to relax for ten minutes and that they would be warned
about half a minute before the experiment was to begin. The experimenter then initiated the automatic execution under program control
of the experiment itself. After eight minutes resting, acquisition
of the physiological signals was commenced without indication to
the subjects, providing a two-minute resting base-line record. Then
recording ceased for 30 seconds during which time the subjects were
alerted that the experiment would start soon, and to attend to the
display. After that half minute, recording of the physiological
signals started up for the duration of the experiment and trial one
commenced. All subjects were given 8 trials of two minutes duration,
each followed by an ITI of 30 seconds. After 30 minutes in total,
at the end of trial eight, the program closed down recording, stored
its data files, and the experiment ended.

The subjects' electrodes were removed and they were debriefed about their experimental conditions, and any questions were answered before departure. All subjects were paid £1.00 plus any travel expenses, for their participation.

Four of the six groups of subjects, two "increase" and two "decrease" groups, were given what the author has called "inverted" HR feedback for half the experiment, i.e. the first or the second set of 4 trials.

Groups of six subjects were allocated to experimental conditions as follows:

Group 1: Increasing HR feedback
Direct feedback, trials 1-4; inverted feedback trials 5-8.

Group 2: Decreasing HR feedback
Direct feedback, trials 1-4; inverted feedback, trials 5-8.

Group 3: Increasing HR feedback
Inverted feedback, trials 1-4; direct feedback, trials 5-8.

Group 4: Decreasing HR feedback
Inverted feedback, trials 1-4; direct feedback, trials 5-8.

Group 5: Increasing HR feedback
Increasing HR feedback only, on all trials.

Group 6: Decreasing HR feedback
Decreasing HR feedback only, on all trials.

Thus, the total experimental design was as shown in Table 1.

OFF-LINE DATA EDITING

All results were computed from data files derived directly from those generated on-line during the experiment. Physiological data always contains erroneous data, produced by large subject movements and amplifier malfuncitons, etc. HR data generated by an analog cardio-tachometer, as in this case, is particularly susceptible to these problems, due to the nature of the conversion from raw ECG to HR. These misrepresentations, if left in continuous numerical data could grossly distort any statistical analysis, and so they must be removed before such processing. This task was accomplished in this laboratory using a specially designed program, EDITOR.

Table 1: Experimental Design

	Inverted Trials 1-4	Inverted Trials 5-8	Direct Feedback
Feedback for Incr. HR	3m. 3f	3m. 3f	3m. 3f
Feedback for Decr. HR	3m. 3f	3m. 3f	3m. 3f

Because a subjective element enters into the identification of
spurious data, editing was carried out by an experienced research
assistant, who was not aware of any desired data outcomes. The
editing was done by both visual and numerical identification of invalid records on the computer's visual display unit. This program
facilitates inspection of the computer record by visually matching
numerically stored data with the polygraph trace, when the program
enables detailed inspection of potential artifacts using simultaneous
numerical and "magnified" visual presentation. All resulting spurious
HR data values are removed and replaced with the current running
mean HR for that subject, the running mean being computed over
"valid" data only.

Only small amounts of data are thus altered and automatic
insertion of the running mean can only militate against most hypotheses concerning change due to experimental conditions.

RESULTS

Data points represented in the accompanying Figures 1-3 are
means of difference between each trial HR and the pre-experimental
base-line HR for the six subjects in that group.

The results are expressed as differences from baseline, as this
is the most exacting way of examining whether an individual is
exerting HR control to an extent which produces a persisting shift
in HR.

Biofeedback derives from an operant philosophy and this experiment is based on a program designed to "shape" heart-rate in an
upward or downward direction as required. It should be noted that
no control is made in this experiment for breathing or muscular
changes which affect HR performance. Such control is critically

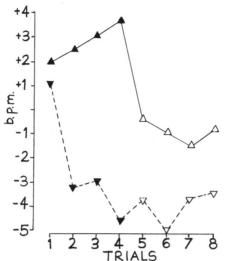

Figure 1: Groups 1 and 2. Direct feedback, trials 1-4; Inverted
           feedback trials 5-8. Group 1: increasing HR feedback.
           Group 2: decreasing HR feedback.

Key to Figures 1 to 3

Open triangles indicate inverted feedback

Solid triangles indicate direct feedback

Upward pointing vertex indicates increasing feedback

Downward pointing verted indicates decreasing feedback

Solid lines indicate reward for increase in HR

Broken lines indicate reward for decrease in HR

important where one is investigating the role of the autonomic
nervous system alone in exerting HR control. These variables, of
course, affect performance here, but voluntary changes are available
to all subjects involved and our concern is to see whether different
forms of feedback affect HR control given this freedom. All interacting systems, respiration, skeletal musculature, and heart innervation will be involved in the outcome. (See Brener, 1974).

     Each figure represents two groups of subjects in similar experi-
mental conditions, except that one is receiving "reward" for consistent HR increase, and the other for HR decrease. The figures
will be discussed as operant "cumulative records" of the HR control
learning which resulted.

     Dealing with each figure in turn, Figure 1 shows the clear

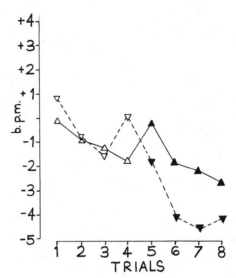

Figure 2:   Groups 3 and 4.   Inverted feedback, trials 1-4;   Direct
            feedback, trials 5-8.   Group 3: increasing HR feedback.
            Group 4: decreasing HR feedback.

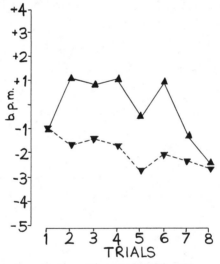

Figure 3.   Groups 5 and 6.   Direct feedback on all trials.
            Group 5: increasing feedback. Group 6: decreasing HR
            feedback.

divergence during trials 1-4 of two groups being shaped in opposite directions for increasing or decreasing HR, and the differences are in the expected directions. However, inversion of HR direction of change produced immediate loss of control on the part of the heart rate elevation group, whereas the HR reduction group showed no un-equivocal loss of control, merely no further decrease beyond the point already reached.

Turning to Figure 2, where conditions were reversed in their order of presentation, and inverted HR feedback was given for the first four trials, we see that neither group appeared to dramatically gain control. Both showed a very small fall in rates, which can only be interpreted as habituation to the experimental situation, and return to veridical feedback for both groups only produced some apparent effect on the HR reduction group. The HR elevation group continued in what could be a sort of learned helplessness condition, and the slight downward trend in their HR continued.

Work with groups 1-4 terminated the first phase of the experi-ment, but the interesting and equivocal outcomes prompted inclusion of the final two groups (5 and 6) who got veridical non-inverted feedback for the entire experiment.

At face value the results for groups 5 and 6 (Fig. 3) are quite equivocal. The HR elevation group shows small HR rises for the first four trials, but habituation after that despite the fact that the experimental conditions remained unchanged. Their elevation of rates does not compare with the group given HR speeding feedback in identical circumstances prior to inversion, shown in Figure 1. Likewise the HR decrease group show only what looks like half-hearted habituation throughout the experiment, and although always having lower HR's than the elevation group, habituation over the second half of the experiment is similar.

One explanation for these confusing findings may be one of those, frequently unmentioned and sometimes unmentionable, variations in experimental conditions which are not intended and certainly not controlled for. Between groups 1-4 and groups 5 and 6 undergoing the experiment at least three important extraneous variables altered.

1. A new laboratory became available, in which the subject is placed in a sound reduced room separate from the Grass polygraph.

2. The experimenter remained in the room with the subject and the Grass polygraph for Groups 1-4. The subjects in the last two groups were in the new room alone.

3. Groups 1-4 (Figures 1 and 2) were put through their experiment by a female research assistant. Groups 5 and 6 were run by the author (male) who supervised the apparatus, and in the new setting was therefore isolated from the subject.

These two groups (5 and 6) were added to the experiment with the empiricist's optimism that they would tighten up the design and clarify the earlier results! A quick scrutiny shows that this could hardly be further from the truth. So science progresses. These confounded and confounding variables could easily account for the failure of the last two groups to emulate the first two (Fig. 1) on trials one to four.

The large individual differences in HR control performance noted by all workers in the area (e.g. Levenson and Ditto, 1981) were observed in this experiment. However, all conclusions are based on mean data for each group. This is a weaker method of presenting the data than an intra-individual analysis, but despite this it does suggest the profound effect of some peripheral variables on biofeedback performance. The type of laboratory setting, the sex and proximity of the experimenter, may all be involved in prod- ucing the differences already mentioned. These possibilities are strongly supported when we consider the differences in pre- experimental basal level attained by the six groups. Basal HR for groups 1-4 were 74.6, 72.9, 75.1 and 78.2 respectively. Those for groups 5 and 6 were 69.7 and 59.9. There seems little doubt that the changes in conditions influenced the latter two groups. This could have considerable impact on HR performance in the experimental trials, especially in terms of the "law of initial values". (Lacey and Lacey, 1962).

Inspection of the figures as an operant cumulative record, and without reference to statistical significance, shows that straight- forward feedback at the start of the experiment does produce the expected differences between those signalled that they "are doing well" for increasing HR and those signalled for decreasing HR. After four two minute trials, however, these differences seem to have diminished through habituation, boredom, or fatigue, these being the only processes affecting groups 5 and 6. Disruption of HR control following introduction of inverted feedback, is shown by the HR increase group in Figure 1. The nature of the effect on HR decreasing group 2 is unclear.

Inversion of the heart rate signal early in the experiment with groups 3 and 4 (Fig. 2), certainly disrupted both increase and decrease HR learning, which is seen in varying amounts in the other four groups. This disruption continued when the true HR signal was restored in the second half of the experiment. Whether this failure to establish operant control is due to a learned helplessness effect, or simply due to habituation, etc. was not resolved by this experi- ment.

CONCLUSIONS

Learning of heart rate increase responses was demonstrated by both groups 1 and 5. Heart rate decrease responses were possibly shown by groups 2 and 6, but these were not clearly enough distinguished from passage of time (e.g. habituation) effects. Therefore it could not be unequivocally stated that operant control of decreasing HR had been demonstrated. This accorded with the findings of much of the literature, that HR slowing is less easily demonstrated than HR speeding, which may be due to the differences in innervation of the heart which are responsible for the two functions. (Lang, 1975).

The inversion of the change in HR shown to subjects, even in the presence of correct feedback about HR control, did disrupt learning. Therefore it was concluded that subjects do have internal proprioceptive cues about their HR, and that the contradiction resulting from the two feedback systems disrupts the operant learning process.

REFERENCES

Brener, J., 1974. A general model of voluntary control applied to the phenomena of learned cardiovascular change. In: Obrist, P.A., Black, A.H., Brener, J. and DiCara, L.V. (Eds.), "Cardiovascular Psychophysiology". Aldine, Chicago.

Lacey, J.I. and Lacey, B.C., 1962. The law of initial values in the longitudinal study of autonomic constitution: Reproducibility of autonomic responses and response patterns over a four year interval. Ann. NY. Acad. Sci., 98: 1257.

Lang, P.J., 1975. Acquisition of heart rate control: Method, theory, and clinical implications. In: Fowles, D.C. (Ed.), "Clinical Applications of Psychophysiology". Columbia University Press, New York.

Levenson, R.W., and Ditto, W.B., 1981. Individual differences in ability to control heart rate: Personality, strategy, physiological and other variables. Psychophysiol., 18: 91.

McAllister, H., 1980. Computer Program Abstracts: A flexible FORTRAN IV program for biofeedback experiments. Psychophysiol., 17: 511.

McCanne, T.R, and Sandman, C.A., 1976. Proprioceptive awareness, information about response-reinforcement contingencies and operant heart-rate control. Physiol. Psychol., 4: 369.

INTERNAL EVENTS AND PROCESSES

WITH PARTICULAR REFERENCE TO DEPRESSION

INTERNAL EVENTS AND PROCESSES WITH PARTICULAR REFERENCE TO

DEPRESSION - AN INTRODUCTION

B. Barnes
Liverpool Psychology
Service
Liverpool Health
Authority

D. Fielding
Sub-Department of Clinical
Psychology
University of Liverpool

This symposium, under the chairmanship of Professor John Copeland, addresses the relationship between internal events and psychopathology. Internal events, beliefs and cognitions have always had an uneasy status in psychology, being regarded by some as simply a 'by product' of events that result in overt behaviour and by others as the major force determining behaviour itself. The therapeutic endeavours of each clinician will reflect his or her interpretation of the nature and importance of these private phenomena. Accordingly, whilst the verbal psychotherapies have always made their prime concern the language and cognitions of patients, only latterly have behaviour therapists stressed the importance of internal processes. Indeed, some writers have suggested that it is unscientific to say, a priori, that covert events are by their nature unable to be studied. (Jacobs and Sachs, 1971).

Three of the papers in the symposium are concerned exclusively with the internal events and processes of the depressed person. The three perspectives from which depression is viewed are those of personal construct theory, dynamic psychotherapy and cognitive therapy. The fourth paper is written from the point of view of radical behaviourism. However, it differs from the other papers since it is not a consideration of depression alone. The authors take on a wider perspective and set out to critically evaluate a particular line of resistance (an 'ideological machismo') within the behaviour modification movement, that refuses to admit internal events into the behavioural analysis of any kind of human problem. Their reasoned argument provides a starting point for an examination of the phenomenon of depression from the standpoint of radical behaviourism. Their approach supports Forester's statement, (Forester, 1981) that depression is a verbal phenomenon in which the

main diagnostic characteristics are verbal behaviours that are facts
under the discriminative control of private events. Indeed in this
article Forester even goes so far as to include private reactions
to the depressed person in the functional analysis of the interaction
between the depressed patient and the therapist. The belief that
counter transference phenomena are both admissable and amenable to
behavioural analysis shows just how far the vanguard of this philosophy has progressed and how timely the fourth paper (by Higson and
Lowe) is in drawing our attention to the philosophical fitness of
such developments to the conceptual tradition of behaviour modification.

Over recent years there has been a considerable expansion in
psychological research on depression (Doefler, 1981). In particular,
attention has been drawn to the characteristic thinking style of
the depressed person. A major influence in this respect is the work
of Aaron Beck and his colleagues at the University of Pennsylvania
(see, for example, Beck, Rush, Shaw and Emery, 1979). These writers
believe that disordered thinking is not just a characteristic
feature of schizophrenia but that it is common to all types of
psychology, including depression. Cognitive distortions can be
identified in depression which, they argue, have aetiological
primacy in that they give rise to depressed affects in a continuous
cognition-affect cycle. The terms cognitive therapy and cognitive
behaviour modification have been used to describe treatments specifically aimed at identifying, reality-testing and correcting these
distortions and the assumptions or schemes upon which they are
based. A measure of the respect commanded by such approaches is
reflected in the investment of considerable sums of money by the
National Institute for Mental Health in a large scale outcome study
which compares the effectiveness of cognitive therapy with that of
psychopharmacological treatments in depression. (Kolata, 1981).

There is no doubt that the elasticity of the concept 'depression'
can lead to conceptual unevenness across theories with resulting
methodological problems in research. The concept has been used in
several contexts, for example, in terms of clinical depression and
its various subtypes, 'normal' depression, depression as an affect,
depression as a state and depression as a disposition or character-
ological trait. The word has different meanings to different
writers; moreover, it has different meanings to different patients
and it is in recognising this latter point that the four papers in
the symposium are truly psychological. That is, from each perspective presented, depression is not seen as an anonymous propulsive
entity that each patient 'has' but as an aspect of a unique person's
activity.

Dr. Rowe, like the cognitive therapists, is concerned with the
depressed patient's assumptions. However, using a personal construct
approach (see Rowe, 1978) she elicits assumptions at a different

level to those presented by Beck and his associates. In her paper
she describes the core constructs of the depressed person's world.
She points out that these constructs do not follow the pattern of
reason but are manifested in images and metaphor. In her view the
experience of depression eludes description in traditional psychiatric terms. Moreover the constructs used by the depressed individual
condemn that person to isolation behind a wall that Dr. Rowe believes
cannot be breached by an appeal to reason. So much is invested in
this self-imposed solitary confinement that the depressed person
will strongly defend this position in order to preserve his or her
sense of worth. As Dr. Rowe says, the depressed person's resistance
to change does not bring out the best in professional helpers when
faced with the tenacity with which this wall of constructs is
maintained. However, although the word resistance carries connotations of negativism, what Dr. Rowe's paper shows clearly are the
affirmations that are sustained in resisting any change in the
assumptive world upon which the experience of depression is founded.
That is, the risks attendant upon change seem too great to be taken
as they involve coming to face the mixture of good and bad in the
world, in one's parents and in oneself. In other words in defending
the core constructs of depression the depressed individual is at
least safe in, and sure of, a moral position that enhances his or
her significance by conferring momentousness upon the misery it
involves.

Mr. Symington's paper is an individual case study presented in
terms of psychodynamic theory and practice. However, many of the
features of the private world of depression described in his analysis
are strikingly similar to those presented by Dr. Rowe; his theoretical
description of depression as a result of love and hate towards the
parent which has led to being sealed off behind a presented self
finds support in Dr. Rowe's exposition of the depressed person's
own experience. Depression in its various forms, has always been
a subject extensively studied by psychodynamic writers (see Mendelson,
1974). Internal events are the main focus of such enquiry and
depression is usually seen as a response to a real or imagined loss
(or threat of loss) of a relationship or a possession or a physical
or psychological function that is important in terms of the person's
security or self-esteem. Depth psychologists generally believe that
certain people are primed to respond depressively to such losses on
the basis of early physical or emotional loss of contact with their
parents which has given rise to aggressive feelings that are in
conflict with their love for them. Mr. Symington takes this theoretical approach as read and deals instead with a particular kind of
depression that he has observed in his clinical practice. The
originality of his contribution lies in his careful investigation
of a particular aspect of a depressed girl's experience, the despair
arising from her having part of her personality permanently inoper-
ative, that part being her intelligence. Mr. Symington's formulation,
drawn from her presentation and history, clearly outlines the course

of events that led to her internal world being one of persecution of
her own capacities and shows how important it is to recognise this
kind of depression in order to help the intellectually able self
out of its shell of "psychic loneliness".

In the third presentation of the symposium Dr. Blackburn points
out that the study of internal events, although central to the verbal
psychotherapies, has given rise to some controversy amongst behavioural writers. However, she shows that the investigation of mediational
factors can be possible outside the frameworks provided by the
previous two speakers. In her view such an undertaking is in
accordance with the behavioural tradition and is of particular value
in the understanding and treatment of neurotically depressed patients.
The basic principles of the cognitive approach to depression having
been described (see Beck et al., op.cit.) the paper then addresses
a recently completed investigation which compares the effectiveness
of three treatment procedures with patients with unipolar depression.
Those treatments are cognitive therapy alone, pharmacotherapy alone,
and both treatments in combination. In her presentation, Dr. Blackburn states that in the research described, 'non-psychotic' does
not refer to 'not endogenous' but, rather, to the absence of delusions. About half her patients, in the treatment trial were diagnosed
as endogenously depressed. She also points out that in the pharmacotherapy and combined treatment groups, various drugs were used
depending on the opinion of the responsible clinician. The most
commonly used drug in these two groups was Amitriptyline. The
initial outcome data is presented, followed by an analysis of the
pattern of response through the course of treatment on a series of
cognitive, mood and behavioural measures. The pattern of change was
investigated in order to assess its relationship to outcome, to
examine the relative rates of improvement between treatments, to
measure the impact of the different treatments on the different
variables in the study and, finally, to see if it is possible using
the data to identify non-responders early in treatment. Dr. Blackburn gives a detailed presentation of her findings in relation to
these questions and summarises her findings in terms that have
implications for the clinical practice of cognitive therapy.

Dr. Higson, on behalf of Dr. Lowe and himself, presents a paper
they prepared together on the relationship between the cognitive
and radical positions within the behavioural corpus. The failure
of behaviour modification to live up to its early promise, almost a
repetition of the same mistake of promising too much committed by
early psychoanalysis, is laid at the door of those behaviourists
who have denied the importance of private events as a source of
control in human psychology. Like Dr. Blackburn, Dr. Higson reminds
us of Skinner's own advocacy of the critical significance of covert
behaviour to radical behaviourists seeking to comprehend the nature
of control in human behaviour. As humans differ from animals in
being able to respond verbally, and, therefore, potentially privately

to their own behaviour it is argued that the uncritical transposition of models of animal conditioning to human psychology misses that which is distinctively human about humans, and in so doing shapes a methodology that is quite insufficient for the task of analysing the behaviour of people. After reviewing the experimental evidence concerning schedules of reinforcement in human and animal behaviour and discussing the difference between the two (covert control) in terms of radical behaviourist philosophy and clinical behaviour modification the authors are able to conclude that all behaviour modification with humans is in a sense cognitive - or at least that it should be if the use of language (and, by extension, other covert behaviour) to describe contingencies of reinforcement is properly ascribed to human beings as the paper suggests. However, it is finally argued that although the emphasis that cognitive therapists place on covert behaviour is appropriate, their conceptual framework would benefit from theoretical insights proceeding from the radical behaviourist tradition.

Professor Copeland then opened the symposium to accomodate questions from the floor. As the ensuing discussion developed, its content came to focus more on the different theoretical positions of the speakers towards human psychology in general. Initially, however, it was their respective views of depression that were of immediate interest to the audience. Some members of the audience felt that depression is manifested in so many individual ways and in response to so many varied life events that the infinite variety of depressive phenomena was, in a sense, being forced to fit the theories of the speakers,and, particularly in the cases of Dr. Rowe and Mr. Symington, with their respective religious and cultural assumptions. Furthermore it was argued that their theories revealed more about the theorists than they did about the phenomena under observation. With regard to the problem of relating a consistent view of depression to its manifest complexity and its multifarious antecedents in terms of unique and individual life events, Dr. Rowe replied that she acknowledged fully the difference between depressed people and their circumstances but argued that the actual experience of depression as isolation is universal. Mr. Symington concurred with the view that life events are never identical for any two depressed individuals but was of the opinion that it is not the events in themselves that generate the experience of depression but the internal phantasies and feelings that come into private contact with these varied events. Dr. Blackburn stated that her position was rather different. She made it clear that, working as she does in a biological research unit, her definition of depression referred of necessity to a very specific pattern of symptoms for research purposes. Dr. Rowe, in response to the suggestion that she might be imposing religious and metaphysical assumptions of her own upon the experience of depression replied that this was not the case and that the core constructs of depression, like the core constructs of any world view including that of science, are metaphysical and overlap with the domain of theology. Mr. Symington, who was also implicated in the charge of theoretical bias, repeated that the specific concern of his paper being that of intellectual capacity was simply the result of his having observed a special category of depressed persons who had hitherto gone unnoticed in psychological theory and practice, a sub-set as it were of the depressed population whose understanding in dynamic forms he was taking as read. However, in terms of the general issue concerning the personal and the purely theoretical, Mr. Symington stated that he found it difficult to separate the two in dynamic practice. Interpretations, for example, if they are to be mutative must come from the psychotherapist's ego, or person, rather than from received wisdom.

The speakers were then asked whether or not they felt that depression might ever serve a useful function. Mr. Symington answered with an imaginary conversation between two psychoanalysts, one of whom remarks that his patient is becoming depressed, a statement to which his colleague responds with obvious approval. Mr. Symington's point about this seemingly sadistic dialogue is that depression is often a sign of progress from paranoid thinking to acknowledging one's own responsibility for the imagined damage being privately perpetrated in one's inner world. Dr. Rowe also believed that depression could be seen as a turning point. She argued that all widespread phenomena must have a function and, as it is an extremely common experience, that this must include depression. She believes that the biographies of several outstanding individuals have demonstrated that a period of depression can be the first time in a person's life when his or her own actions and their implications are accepted and thought through. Dr. Higson agreed that all behaviour must have a functional significance, including those behaviours which we label as depressive. However, as a member of the audience stated in relation to these views, to say that a behaviour may have a function is not to preclude the possibility that some other behaviour might well be capable of serving the same purpose less painfully.

It was suggested that the speakers were emphasising different facets of depression - getting depressed, being depressed and treating depression - and that the similarities and differences between approaches might be more intelligible when viewed in this light than in relation to a broader conception of the subject. For example, in terms of construing the experience of depression, Dr. Blackburn and Dr. Rowe found that they had a great deal in common in that they both look at the same sort of people in very similar ways, although using different terminology. The difference between them, however, emerges in therapy, for in the cognitive approach patients are dissuaded from discussing metaphysical questions and yet in the personal construct approach these very questions are the questions concerning core constructs. Therefore, as core

constructs are manifested in imagery and phantasy, Dr. Rowe's
approach is in this sense closer to that of Mr. Symington especially
in so far as the practical implications of selecting this level of
significance are that therapy becomes a long-term venture rather
than the short-term approach articulated by Dr. Blackburn. It was
further suggested from the floor that Dr. Blackburn and Dr. Higson
were prescriptive in their treatment of depression whereas Dr. Rowe
and Mr. Symington were more concerned with the patient's own agency
in handling his or her depression. Dr. Blackburn replied that her
cognitive therapy is indeed directive and that she regretted that
the behavioural measures used in her investigation had been too
weak to assess the efficacy of her approach in ways other than those
measured in terms of the self-reported statements about which the
therapy had been directive. However, Dr. Higson commented that the
trend in his own field, of behaviour modification, was now markedly
in the direction of enhancing the individual's self-control rather
than arrogating the locus of control to the therapist.

One member of the audience questioned the value of theory at
all, believing theoretical disputes to be of secondary importance.
to the pragmatic business of identifying and changing what is really
there. Dr. Higson replied that, in his opinion, all the speakers
were talking about what was really there but in different and useful
ways and that different theories are essential as one cannot simply
develop pragmatic procedures in the hope that one day they will
throw up a theory. Mr. Symington supported this view in saying
that one must have a theory to make sense of what is happening.
In illustration, he related an incident from his work with a
psychiatric patient who entered his room only to remain silent for
ten minutes before saying 'crocodiles', after a further ten minutes
of silence the patient said 'blue circles'. He believed that this
was to be made sense of in some way, that some theory or model was
required in order to make discrete elements of apparent nonsense
into an intelligible coherence. There was general agreement with
this view of the need for theory although there was some diversity
of opinion concerning the aims of theory building. For example, it
was felt that the vignette described above could simply have been
construed as a sample of contingency-shaped behaviour without
recourse to rendering it intelligible in terms of meaning. That
is, another difference between the speakers was implicit in the
ensuing discussion, the difference being between theories seeking
the determinants of behaviour and theories seeking the meanings of
actions (see Smail, 1978). This distinction appears to underlie
many of the other differences of emphasis between the four speakers
referred to above in terms of directive versus non-directive
treatment, short versus long-term therapy, concern with rational
thought and language versus concern with non-rational phantasy and
metaphor.

Although each paper is addressed to events 'inside the skin' and whilst there are many many interesting parallels and points of convergence, two mutually exclusive ranges of convenience for theory building remain nonetheless. Working within one, Dr. Blackburn and Dr. Higson are looking for causes and working within the other Dr. Rowe and Mr. Symington are seeking meanings; the treatment approach of each speaker derives its origin from his or her committment to one or the other of these two world views and, as Dr. Rowe has argued above, the core constructs of any world view are metaphysical, including those of science. Since that which is selected and referred to as fact and evidence in any theory is a reflection of the world view (or what Schafer (1976) calls the vision of reality) from which the theory has evolved, then theoretical disputes can often be conflicts between discordant visions of reality which cannot, therefore, be settled by resorting to fact and evidence alone. However, the four speakers avoided this error and demonstrated clearly that they respected theoretical positions other than their own, each being committed to the development of his or her approach without feeling it necessary to defensively attack everyone else's. They also avoided the opposite mistake of proposing a process of psychological syncretism whereby we all work towards merging our different approaches into one common theory. Mr. Symington argued that we would be mistaken to look for a single all-embracing theory. He believed that if one is to facilitate change in a patient then one's theory must make sense to oneself and to one's patient – an unlikely eventuality were theory ever to become uniformly codified. Dr. Higson was also strongly in favour of a diversity of theoretical approaches and this point was taken up by Professor Copeland in his closing remarks. He commented that the only thing we could be sure of with a comprehensive omnibus theory is that it would be wrong. Professor Copeland concurred with Dr. Higson and said that we need a number of different theories which we should try to develop as best we can, certainly trying to integrate them whenever possible but, as life is so complicated, he doubted that any real rapprochment would ever be likely. However, the symposium showed that this need not necessarily be a bad thing and that there can be harmony in discord between people viewing the indescribable complexity of the individual from different theoretical and metaphysical perspectives without closing their eyes to the possible virtues of other ways of looking at human beings.

REFERENCES

Beck, A.T., Rush, A.J., Shaw, B.F. and Emery, G., 1979. "Cognitive
     Theory of Depression". Guilford Press, New York.
Doerfler, L.A., 1981. Psychological research on depression: a
     methodological review. Clin. Psychol. Rev., 1: 119-137.
Forster, C.B., 1981. A functional analysis of behaviour therapy.
     In: Rehm, L.P. (Ed.), "Behaviour Therapy for Depression".

Academic Press, London.

Jacobs, A. and Sachs, L.B., 1971. "The Psychology of Private Events".
Academic Press, London.

Kolata, G.B., 1981. Clinical trial of psychotherapies is under way.
Science, 212: 432-433.

Mendelson, M., 1974. "Psychoanalytic Concepts of Depression".
Spectrum, New York.

Rowe, D., 1978. "The Experience of Depression". John Wiley, New
York and Chichester.

Schafer, R., 1976. "A New Language for Psychoanalysis". Yale,
New Haven.

Smail, D.J., 1978. "Psychotherapy: A Personal Approach". Dent,
London.

RESISTANCE TO CHANGE

Dorothy Rowe

Lincolnshire Area Department of Clinical Psychology

What is the difference between being unhappy and being depressed? Psychiatric textbooks list a number of symptoms, but do not describe the difference which, viewed from the inside of a depressed state, is startlingly clear. When we are unhappy, even if we have suffered the most terrible blow, we can seek and find some comfort. We can reach out for a comforting hand and find one; we can comfort ourselves. But when we are depressed a wall has come down between us and the rest of the world. There may be hands and voices offering comfort, but their message is lost on the other side of the wall and, if the message threatens to pierce the wall, we turn away in disgust. We do not deserve comfort, and so we give ourselves none.

Being depressed means being isolated, like a prisoner serving an indeterminate sentence in solitary confinement. Each person has his own image of the prison. It may be a pit, or an endlessly dark tunnel. The person may be alone in a vast desert, or wrapped in a shroud, or encased in an opaque sphere, or weighed down by an immovable load, or trapped on a ferris wheel turning endlessly in a deserted fairground. It would seem that no one would ever choose to undergo such an experience, but yet many of us do. We each construct our own world, and we are free to create for ourselves a spacious world, or we can build ourselves a prison.

Just as there are many different images of being depressed, but all with the basic sense of a person alone in a prison, there is a wide variety of constructs which can be used as bricks in the wall, but these constructs can be grouped into six main categories. So, if you want to build yourself a depression this is how you must construe yourself and your world.

171

First, be sure that no matter how nice you appear on the
surface, underneath, at your central core, you are bad, evil, unacceptable to God or man. The second construction follows naturally
from this. If other people are like you, basically bad, then you
must fear them, or, if they are basically good, you must also fear
them, because they will reject you if they find you out. Because
you see other people as either good (not like you) or bad (like
you, but not worrying about it the way you do) you envy and hate
them.

Feeling like this about yourself and others, it follows that
you find the world a frightening place from which death offers no
happy escape. When we each consider our death we see it in one of
two ways. Either we see it as the end of our existence, in which
case we have the problem of making our present life satisfactory,
or else we see it as a doorway to another life, in which case we
must live this life in terms of the next. So, if you want to be
depressed and if you see death as the end of your identity, then
you can never look at your life and see it as satisfactory. If you
want to be depressed and if you see death as a doorway to another
life, then you fear that you will fail whatever the test is which
allows entrance to a happy life. Since it is our construction of
death which determines our construction of life, to be depressed
you must base your life on a philosophy which is pessimistic and
fearful.

Having such a philosophy robs you of all hope for the future
and prevents you from becoming reconciled to the past which you can
never construe in any favourable or pleasant terms. Living in such
a dangerous and unrewarding world, surrounded by people who inspire
fear, hate and envy, and hating yourself, it is not surprising that
you are constantly angry. But anger is evidence of the badness
within you, and you must fear it, just as you must fear the anger
of other people. And because anger is bad you must never forgive
it. You live by the rule of never forgiving yourself nor other
people. Since Jesus has told us that God will forgive our tres-
passes as we forgive those who trespass against us, we know that if
we do not forgive others God will not forgive us.

Using this interlocking set of constructions you build yourself
a prison and put yourself in solitary confinement. Solitary confinement, as we know, is the worst torture that we can encounter.

Some people find themselves in the solitary confinement of
depression only once in their lives. Afterwards if asked about
their experience they will say, "It was terrible, but I learnt a
lot from it - I see things differently now." But some people get
depressed more than once. They seek treatment, and it works, but
not for long, and then they are depressed again, and again they
look for treatment. Whenever I ask therapists - be they psycho-

therapists, psychologists, doctors or nurses - to give their images
of what it is like to try to help a depressed person two kinds of
images are described. One is of being outside an impenetrable wall;
the other of wandering in a fog. The emotions aroused are of anger,
frustration, helpless confusion and guilt. Trying to help a
depressed person does not always bring out the best in us. The
depressed client challenges our picture of ourselves as competent
therapists. He fends off our skilful approaches, and we get angry.
If we then feel guilty about being angry with someone needing our
help, we shall then feel the stirring of our own latent depression,
and become frightened. It is no wonder that many doctors respond
to depressed patients by giving them a prescription and bundling
them out the door or by removing the sight and sound of them with
electroconvulsive therapy. Similarly many psychologists deal with
depressed clients by refusing to take them on, or by giving them
short-term contracts for therapy, or by setting them tasks which,
it is hoped, will quickly change them. However, we soon find that
anyone who has spent the best years of his life in constructing his
depression is not going to let it be quickly knocked down by any
therapeutic endeavour.

When a client first comes to see us his immediate demand is
"Take the pain away but don't change me." He wants to continue in
his selfish, egotistical way, but without any suffering. Don't we
all! But life, unfortunately, is not like that. We may not always
be punished for our sins, but we are always punished by them. We
cannot escape the consequences of our acts, and so the therapist
has to explain that he has no magic wand. If the client wants to
reduce his suffering then he must change. So some clients leave in
disgust when they discover that the therapist claims not to be a
magician, but others stay and promise that they will make all
efforts to change, provided the therapist will promise that when
the course of therapy is finished the client will live happily
ever after. To the unwary therapist this may appear to be no more
than a naive request, but it is, in fact, a ploy used by the
depressed client to put the therapist in the wrong.

Now where the future is concerned, the depressed person has
always operated on two linked rules. One is "Always expect the
worst" and the other is "Make sure you know exactly what is going
to happen". When each of us looks forward to some event we decide
whether to anticipate it optimistically or pessimistically. If we
are optimistic, we can enjoy a pleasurable anticipation, but we run
the risk of painful disappointment. If we are pessimistic, we
experience a continuing low-level misery, but we may suddenly be
surprised by joy. People who get depressed regard optimism as the
height of foolishness. "Expect the worst and you are never dis-
appointed" is the rule they live by. So, if the therapist promises
his client that the course of therapy will result in happiness, the
client immediately knows that the therapist is either stupid or
lying.

Suppose, then, the therapist, being wise to the ways of the world, answers truthfully and says that no one ever lives happily ever after and that change, any change, brings effects that cannot be predicted. This response reveals the therapist as a very dangerous person. He is threatening to destroy the cocoon of security which the depressed person has built up. As any depressed person will tell you if he trusts you enough, being depressed is horrible, but at least you are safe. Inside the prison of depression you can make sure that everything remains the same and that nothing from the outside can get in to disturb you and make you behave in a way in which you do not wish to behave. Such security the depressed person may be prepared to defend to his last breath. Every time someone on the outside of the wall suggests something which might make a hole in the wall, the depressed person counters with a "Yes, but... ."

The depressed person defends his position not simply as the one to which he has retreated in fright. He also holds his position, this particular position, for very positive reasons. He is defending a moral position from which he does not wish to budge. The particular moral position he is defending can be described in many ways, but the basic proposition is simply "I'd rather be good than happy".

Now all of us follow this rule. We all want to think well of ourselves and to have other people think well of us. The difference between those people who cope with life and those who don't is that the people who cope define their "good" in ways which are not too difficult to live by. They set themselves standards which they have a chance of reaching, and, whenever they fail, they reproach themselves only in the mildest of terms and they give themselves encouragement to do better next time. But the people who do not cope have set themselves standards which are impossible to reach, and when they fail, as they must, they berate and punish themselves. People who cope see happiness as something they have the right to enjoy and suffering as something which must be abolished, ameliorated, or, if all else fails, simply endured. People who do not cope feel that they have no natural right to be happy. Either they have espoused the Calvinist work ethic, where every pleasure must be first earned by effort, or the Catholic ethic where every pleasure must be paid for by acts of penance and reparation. As the old Spanish proverb states, "Take what you like, says God, and pay for it." People who do not cope have elevated suffering from simply being the outcome of certain events to being good in its own right - a state of being which expiates past sins, or propitiates the Gods, or redeems one's soul, or reveals one's goodness to the world. Martyrdom is probably the most popular career that has yet been devised. Whether one martyrs oneself to the applause of thousands by acts of extreme heroism, or whether one martyrs oneself in

obscurity, slaving over a hot stove to serve food to an ungrateful
family, the reward is plain. By my martyrdom I overcome my inherent
badness and make myself into a good person. The degree of suffering
must be commensurate with the degree of badness perceived within,
and the greater the martyrdom the more distinct, unique, superior
to the conglomerate mass of humanity the person can see himself as
being. When a person believes "I suffer; therefore I am" he is
not prepared to be relieved of his suffering. An expert in suffering comes to a therpist not to have his suffering taken away from
him but to prove that it cannot be taken away from him. He is
himself the cross he has to bear.

The first act of self-sacrifice usually takes place when the
child discovers that the people on whom he depends for his security
are capable of causing him much pain. He then has to decide what
is the source of the evil, the badness that causes his parents to
act in this way. If he decides that the badness resides in his
parents he then puts his security at risk. The only way he can
preserve his parents as good is to locate the badness within himself.
Once having done that, he has to devote the rest of his life to
keeping his badness a secret by striving to be good. The first
act of self-sacrifice begets a million others. These acts may
range from a life devoted to good works, to the ritualisation of
the act in an obsessional phobia, to the relinquishing of one's
belief in the right of one to exist and thus falling prey to the
terrors of a psychosis.

To live freely - free from psychosis or obsessions, or the
need to be for ever doing something for other people - we have to
be able to accept that everybody is a mixture of good and bad, and
that the bad is just as much a part of life as the good. Now this
is just what the depressed person cannot do. He has high standards.
He expects that he should be perfect, that everyone else should be
perfect, that the world should be perfect, that the universe should
be perfect, that God should be perfect. Unfortunately events in
the world do seem to suggest that God is at best inefficient and
at worst malicious. This makes the depressed person very angry.
He gets angry with everyone (including himself) who is not perfect.
Thus his high standards keep him in a constant rage. If the unwary
therapist suggests that perhaps the depressed person's standards
are too high - that it is not necessary to take work home with him
every night, or to scrub the kitchen floor every day - then the
therapist has simply revealed himself as an imperfect, unacceptable,
untrustworthy person.

To be able to accept the bad with the good, we have to be able
to forgive. But not everyone regards forgiveness as a virtue. If
you forgive someone, then you lay yourself open to be hurt again,
and if you regard yourself as a sensitive person, as so many

depressed people do, you strive to avoid situations where you may
be hurt. By not forgiving we can exert a control over the behaviour
of others. How often we say to ourselves, "If I did that, my
mother would never forgive me," and, fearing our mother's lack of
forgiveness, we refrain. Not forgiving can become an integral part
of maintaining one's self-respect, while a vow of revenge can become
the whole framework and purpose of a person's life. Such a life
may be lived to avenge the crimes of Cromwell or the neglect of an
unloving mother, and such a life may not be experienced as happy
but it is experienced as significant.

Even those of us who want to lead a quiet, peaceful, pleasant
life still want to feel that their life has some significance, that
they are not merged into the great mass of humanity, that their
existence is noted and remarked upon by others. We want more than
just to be born, live and die. We want to make our mark upon the
world, to leave, as Samuel Beckett said, "a stain upon the silence."
We would all like to fill that silence with applause, to be
revealed and recognised as the most amazing, wonderful, intelligent
person the world has ever seen. Unfortunately, the world is very
stingy with its applause. Many people may find themselves loved
but few are famous. Many people find themselves without love or
fame or recognition. The world passes them by. How are they to
give their lives some significance?

Now suppose you had to choose between living in one of two
communities, the only communities which were available to you. If
you lived in one community you would find that everyone there
ignored you. If you lived in the other community you would find
that everyone there noticed you but only to be hostile to you.
Which would you prefer - to be noticed with hostility or to be
ignored? I find that quite a few people, not just clients, prefer
a hostile world to one that ignores them. Those people who know
their own existence only through the eyes of others and who dread
hostility regard the alternatives as equally impossible and state
that in such a situation they would prefer to die. To live in a
world which is indifferent to our existence we need to feel secure
in our own self-worth, and to be able to look to ourselves for
love, reassurance and entertainment. This requires a great deal
of self-confidence, and so for some people lacking in self-
confidence paranoia can supply the missing security and comfort.
When paranoia is too great a threat, the only alternative is death.

Yet, in truth, we all live in a world which largely ignores
us. Most of the world's population is ignorant of my existence,
and of those who are aware of me most are so wrapped up in their
own concerns that they become aware of me only when I cross their
minds as someone who might meet one of their needs. Unconditional
positive regard is a rare commodity. And though a small part of
the human race may occasionally pay attention to me, nature is

indifferent to human existence. We are, so physicists tell us, part of the changing cosmic pattern, but not an important part. If we want to feel that we are an important part of the cosmos then we have to create and believe in a religion. Every religion is in essence a drama where the believer holds the centre of the stage, as the protagonist in the battle between good and evil. Good and evil can be dressed in many guises - as the God of Love who is also the God of Wrath, or as God and the Devil, or as a multitude of benign and dangerous gods, or as the Force of Good and the Force of Evil, or as the abstract ideals of Humanity, Wisdom, Science, Progress, Nature, Ignorance, Oppression and so on. When life goes well for us we can believe that, in the drama, we are participating in the victory of the good. When life goes badly for us we can believe that we are the victim of the bad - that someone Up There does not like us, that we have incurred the wrath of the gods, that a malign fate has stricken us, that the forces of Ignorance and Oppression have marked us for destruction. In the philosophy of the depressed person, the forces of evil, however conceived, always have the edge over the forces of good. If the depressed person is told that he is mistaken, that God is good, that life on earth is getting better, he knows that he is talking to a fool or a liar. To be told that he is not a protagonist in a cosmic drama of good and evil is no comfort either. It takes enormous strength of character to face with equanimity the evidence that I am one of countless millions on an insignificant planet headed for destruction if not by our own stupidity then by the collapse of our solar system. Our vanity requires us to play a much bigger role in the cosmos.

So it is that when the depressed person builds his prison, the bricks are made of fear - fear of himself, fear of other people, fear of life and death, fear of the past, fear of the future, fear of anger, fear of change. But the cement that he uses to bind the bricks together with is vanity, and this is where the therapist meets resistance. You may take my pain away, but not my pride.

BIBLIOGRAPHY

Rowe, D., 1978. "The Experience of Depression". Wiley, New York and Chichester.
Rowe, D., 1982. "The Construction of Life and Death". Wiley, New York and Chichester.
Rowe, D., 1982. "Depression: The Way Out of the Prison". In preparation.

DEPRESSION CAUSED BY ARRESTED INTELLECTUAL DEVELOPMENT

Neville Symington

The Adult Department
The Tavistock Clinic
London

    Some years ago a psychiatrist rang me and asked if I would see
a girl who had been under his care in hospital for the previous six
weeks. She had been admitted as an in-patient following a massive
overdose. I arranged to see her and a few days later a very sullen
girl clumped into my consulting room. She came from the north of
England and was working in a residential home for children in care
as a sort of social work assistant. She spoke in a toneless voice,
was dressed smartly but in a rather old fashioned manner. I had the
impression of someone who had been dressed up by mother to visit an
elderly relative. She might have had with her a box of chocolates
to give or a bunch of flowers. She would speak politely to the
relative for a dull half hour and then depart. She was a solid
girl, walked heavily and when she sat down she looked like an over-
grown schoolgirl. She did not have the appearance of somebody who
had had sexual relations. She was aged about twenty-five and I
would have guessed that she probably left school at sixteen. My
immediate impression was that she was rather dim and poorly educated.

    Now, all these impressions of mine were based on non-verbal
cues but they created a powerful stereotyped attitude of mind in me.
My way of being towards her was determined by this fixed mental
image. I decided, slightly reluctantly, to take this girl on for
weekly psychotherapy. I felt I had been landed with a dull, boring
patient who would not prove to be very rewarding. However quite soon
in the sessions two themes began to emerge. She kept complaining
about all the people who did not take much notice of her. She
described to me an occasion when she was one of twelve people going
out on a picnic for the day and when the travel arrangements had
been made the organisers had forgotten about her. I began to
realise that she was complaining bitterly about my own stereotyped

179

reaction to her and that I was not noticing another part of her
personality although it was there to see. So the other theme was
the passing comments - that I was supposed not to notice - that
indicated education and intelligence. Slowly I discovered that she
spent most of her spare time going to the theatre, visiting art
galleries and reading. She was extremely well read and she soon
discovered that I was a Freudian and not a Jungian. She had read
Freud and Jung and had her own intelligent opinions about the merits
and demerits of both. She had tackled quite a bit of philosophy
and had read most of the classics of English literature. Yet, this
only emerged slowly, bit by bit, and when I began to articulate this
side of her which was so hidden it caused considerable anxiety. It
became clear that the non-verbal presented self was a precipitate
of an identification with her mother. She had introjected a mother
who was bitterly envious of her intelligence and capacity, a mother
who did not want her to marry, a mother who wanted her to be a
plain domestic girl, a mother who wanted her as a devoted daughter
who would be a good virgin all her life. This internal object
strangled the intelligent, adventurous and sexual self. Now all
this is fairly familiar; in jargon language that destroys all
subtlety we could say that the patient's depression was caused by a
persecuting superego. But this misses out something. Why did this
patient take a massive overdose? Why did another part of her revolt
so savagely against this maternal superego? If she had been un-
intelligent I do not think she would have arrived in my consulting
room, I doubt whether she would have taken an overdose. I think
the despair resulted from a vision of her intelligent self having
the last drop of blood strangled out of her. Of course depression
resulted largely from guilt arising from her attacks upon her mother
whom she loved as well as hated. But there is a difference between
depression and despair. Despair is always that some part of the
personality is doomed to paralysis for ever.

Therefore I do not want to discount those psychodynamic factors
in the personality which lead to depression. Clearly this patient's
condition was determined by guilt and bad internal objects to a
large degree but it is not the whole story. It is also important
to look at those parts of the personality which these introjects
strangle. This girl's sexual side was also strangled but I do not
think that awareness of her state, leading therefore to despair,
would have emerged had her intelligence not also been a victim of
her internal persecutor.

I want at this point to interpose for a moment to reflect on
the case history I have given and wonder how common a situation
it is. I suppose that many will say that such a condition is quite
rare. I should like to think that this is the case but my experience
tells me that it is a good deal more common than may be supposed.
I have not of course done any research to determine, for instance,
how many cases of suicide or attempted suicide could come into the

category I am describing but I would be very surprised if it were
below 10%. I have come across this category of patient also among
alcoholics and delinquents. I am struck by the fact that not much
account of it is taken in case histories. I came across a man who
was working as a warehouse porter and who was referred to me for
depression. I estimated his IQ and he came out at 128. Can you
imagine a man heaving sacks all day in a warehouse with an IQ of
128? An alcoholic was referred to me who was working as a clerk in
a department of local government and he had an IQ of 154. Can you
imagine him adding up invoices all day when he had an IQ of 154?
That particular patient was one of the best read people I have ever
come across. I asked him once if he had read 'The Brothers Karamazov'
and he replied curtly: "Four times". In a psychiatric prison I
came across an inmate whose welfare officer was trying to find him
a job as a painter and decorator on his release. I estimated his IQ
and it was 146; we changed his release plan. He got into university
and ended by getting a good degree in Economics. Now in all these
cases there was a side of the personality which was strangling the
intelligent self and it was the dull pedestrian side which established itself as the presented self. It was this side which determined
the person's role in the public sector.

Now, it has seemed to me to be extremely important in all these
cases first to recognise the fact that a patient belongs to this
special category. Secondly it is important to foster and encourage
the victim self. The therapist needs to give it support against
this envious strangling introject. This is often more difficult
than it first appears because there is often an overlay of omnipotent assertive behaviour that tempts the therapist to try and
bring the patient down a peg or two. The therapist may concentrate
on attacking this omnipotent and assertive side. There is no doubt
that it needs to be dealt with but if the intelligent self is not
nourished and supported then the patient will not regain psychic
health. In all these cases the patient has ended by changing his
or her external role and replaced it with an occupation more in
accord with his or her intelligence and capacity. The patient
remains ill until this has happened.

But why is it that when the intelligent self is strangled that
it clamours so that the patient has a breakdown? Of course intelligence is so closely linked with a person's autonomy and capacity
to forge his or her own individual existence. Intelligence level
determines to a very large extent in our society a person's role
and social position, the sort of friends he will have and the type
of exchange that he or she can have with those friends. If there
is no access or communication within the framework of that guiding
intelligence then the frustration is enormous. The person finds
him or herself surrounded by people who do not satisfy his or her
needs.

In the formulation of Winnicott (1958) it is the intelligent self which is the True Self and the dull or uneducated side is the False Self. Winnicott used this formulation to describe the patients whose real self was hidden by another side and it was the latter which the world saw. The True Self remained hidden and often it took a lot of therapeutic work to reach this centre. The True Self was the vulnerable loving part of the personality usually hidden under a hard brittle exterior. What I am describing is something similar but what I want to assert is this: that the True Self in these cases is always located around the nucleus of the intelligence. The True Self is determined by the intelligence level and that the intelligence and the capacity to think is what forges the person's place in the world. A person's happiness is determined to a large degree by the extent to which his or her inner self permeates the rest of the personality and makes contact with the external world. The presented self is that part of the personality which the social world encounters and through which the core self makes contact with the social environment. If that contact hardly occurs at all then the patient is sealed off in psychic loneliness.

Looked at from an evolutionary point of view, what I am saying is rather obvious. Man's capacity to think gives him an autonomy and an ability to adapt his environment to his needs. When his intelligence does not function he goes under and becomes victim to the forces around him. Similarly in relation to others the person whose intelligence does not function successfully is not able to adapt the situations around him so as to give satisfaction. He is dependent upon others to provide it. Now, this is alright if the level of intelligence is itself low, but when it is unusually high as in the cases I have quoted then the awareness that potential for forging an individual existence, for taking a certain place in society and contributing to it is there but cannot be mobilised has all the ingredients of tragedy and leads to suicide or what Herman Hesse referred to as suicides in his novel 'Steppenwolf': in other words to a self-destructive existence. I will just quote Hesse's words:

> "And here it must be said that to call suicides only
> those who actually destroy themselves is false. Among
> these, indeed, there are many who in a sense are suicides
> only by accident and in whose being suicide has no
> necessary place. Among the common run of men there are
> many of little personality and stamped with no deep
> impress of fate, who find their end in suicide without
> belonging on that account to the type of the suicide
> by inclination; while, on the other hand, of those who
> are to be counted as suicides by the very nature of
> their beings are many, perhaps a majority, who never
> in fact lay hands on themselves." (Hesse, 1965, p 58).

And it is in this group that intelligence is often high but the capacity remains hidden and unmobilised. The person feels inwardly cheated of what is his or her birthright. They envy those who have achieved their rightful place in society so in despair they turn to a suicide-existence in Hesse's sense. They turn to drink, to drugs, to a criminal way of life or just surrender to an unfulfilling way of life.

Now this means of course that a very powerful force in the personality sets itself up against the development of intelligence. What is this and how does it arise? I will return to the patient with whom I started this talk. She began to report statements about her mother that made it look as if the latter was very puritanical and controlling. She was evidently a very efficient mother who managed the household and looked after her father's affairs. Father had a public role of some importance in the local community. As a child the patient was always given secondary roles compared with other children. When there was a party in the village the patient was expected to help mother and was stopped from playing with the other children. "You must always put others first, dear", she told her daughter on various occasions. The father, it appeared was a very intelligent man who was gifted naturally and carried out his profession with an ease which was quite enviable. It appeared further that mother had trained as a doctor in her youth but, on marrying, had forsaken her career and it seemed that she was deeply resentful towards her husband. During the period of engagement she had been at some distance from him most of the time. It seemed that she had built up a romantic picture of the future marriage and was prepared to sacrifice her own chosen career for a vision of a happy, loving marriage. She had a son and a daughter and it seems that mother fastened onto the daughter as the object of her resentment. When the daughter did well at school and showed promise of future educational achievement mother began to put obstacles in the way. The daughter was very attached to mother but in her description of her she always painted her as someone who had a child out of duty. There was no sense of maternal feelings or maternal warmth. One got a picture of a mother who lived a very puritanical life, guided by duty and principles and very little place for pleasure and natural satisfactions. Such a situation created a clinging reaction in the patient towards her mother but also a combination of love and hatred. What emerged most strongly was mother's intense envy of her daughter's developing capacities and in particular her intellectual ability. The patient had internalised this envious mother as a defence against her hatred of her. It was for this reason that she felt so threatened when I began to point out her unnurtured intellectual capacity. It began to put her in touch with her hatred and enormous guilt. Her attempt at suicide, which I feel certain was designed to succeed, was principally a savage attack on her internal mother. The therapy of this patient centred around nurturing this intellectual self and at the

same time combatting a fateful sense that the dice were loaded
against her and that whatever she did she was destined to be a
suicide.

Therapy was stopped at the end of two years by mutual consent.
She knew and I knew that this deep sense of an unconquerable fate
was still in her though it did not hold sway over her personality in
the way it had. She knew and I knew that she was in danger of being
overwhelmed by a sudden moment of despair in which she might kill
herself. She knew and I knew that to tackle this would involve
psycho-analysis which she did not want to undertake. However at
the end of two years she had changed her job, moved from a dank and
miserable hostel into a house where she shared with two other people
of her own age, she had had a moderately satisfactory sexual relationship with a boyfriend and was reading for a degree in Literature and
Philosophy at University. Friends were taking notice of her in a
new way; people perceived her intelligence and education. Her
intellectual self was making contact with her social environment.

REFERENCES

Hesse, H., 1965. "Steppenwolf". Penguin Books.
Winnicott, D.W., 1958. "Collected Papers: Through Paediatrics to
      Psychoanalysis". Tavistock, London.

PATTERN OF CHANGE IN MOOD AND COGNITION WITH COGNITIVE THERAPY

AND PHARMACOTHERAPY

Ivy M. Blackburn   Steven Bishop

MRC Brain Metabolism Unit   Brown University
Thomas Clouston Clinic   Rhode Island
Edinburgh

INTRODUCTION

The emergence of interest in mediational cognitive factors in clinical psychology in the last 10 years or so - after a long period of strictly behavioural paradigms - has been called the "cognitive revolution" after Thomas Kuhn's (1970) expose of scientific revolutions. As all revolutions, this one has been welcomed by many (e.g. Mahoney, 1974; Meichenbaum, 1977; Ellis, 1962) and reviled by others (Ledwidge, 1978; Rachlin, 1974; Wolpe, 1978; Greenspoon and Lamal, 1978) and some may have taken it too far. However, taking into consideration what the patient thinks and treating thoughts as important mediational factors between stimulus and response, which are amenable to change techniques, were advocated by Skinner himself (1963). "It is particularly important that a science of behaviour faces the problem of privacy ... An adequate science of behaviour must consider events taking place within the skin of the organism ... as part of behaviour itself."

Cognitive factors have played a particularly important role recently in the understanding and treatment of depressive disorders. Inspired by clinical theoreticians like Beck (1967, 1976), Ellis (1962), Goldfried et al. (1974) and Rehm (1977), and experimentalists like Seligman (1975), Meichenbaum (1977) and Mahoney (1974), clinical psychologists have now begun to involve themselves with the patients who, in fact, make up the bulk of psychiatric referrals and community cases, namely neurotically depressed patients. The literature reveals an increasing number of experimental and treatment papers (Hollon and Beck, 1979). In Edinburgh, in addition to descriptive and experimental studies (Blackburn, 1974, 1975; Blackburn et al., 1979; Lyketsos et al., 1979; Blackburn and Bonham, 1980; Wilkinson

185

and Blackburn, 1981), we have recently completed a treatment study
comparing cognitive therapy with pharmacotherapy, each alone and in
combination, in the treatment of non-psychotic, unipolar depressed
outpatients (Blackburn and Bishop, 1981; Blackburn et al., 1981).

The basic tenet of the cognitive approach can be seen as an
extension of the Cartesian dictum:
    I think, therefore I am.
    I think with a negative bias, therefore I am depressed.
    I think and feel depressed, therefore I act depressed.
As can be seen in the schematic representation:

$$S \longrightarrow \text{cognitive} \rightleftharpoons \text{feeling} \longrightarrow \text{behaviour}$$

the emphasis is on thinking as the primary link in the chain, though
there is a feed-back mechanism and also, very likely, a reciprocal
interaction between feeling and cognition. Cognitive therapy is
therefore directed at improving mood and behaviour by modifying the
mediating "dysfunctional" thoughts, through cognitive and behavioural
techniques. Beck et al. (1979) have provided a detailed account of
therapy techniques which need not be elaborated here. The cognitive
deficits or dysfunctions which the therapist aims to alter are seen
at different levels:
    (1) in the cognitive content (negative views of self, the world
    and the future);
    (2) in cognitive processing (i.e. appraisal, attention, reten-
    tion, abstraction, etc.); and
    (3) in cognitive structures (basic assumptions, beliefs,
    attitudes).

REVIEW OF THE EDINBURGH OUTCOME STUDY

In the treatment trial, patients from two sources of referral,
psychiatric outpatient clinics and a general practice, were assessed
for inclusion in the study. All patients had to satisfy Spitzer's
criteria for primary major depressive disorder (Spitzer et al.,
1978) and to have a score of at least 14 on the Beck Depression
Inventory (Metcalfe and Goldman, 1965). Table 1 indicates the
number of patients assessed, those rejected because of inclusion
and exclusion criteria, and those finally accepted (for more details,
see Blackburn et al., 1981).

The results shown in Table 2 indicate that at outcome of
treatment (about 12 weeks), all but three treatments were effective
in the hospital patients, but in the general practice patients, the
drug group responded poorly (response was assessed as scores of ≤ 8
on the Beck Depression Inventory and/or ≤ 9 on the Hamilton Rating
Scale for Depression).

Table 1.   Populations studied

	Hospital O.P.	General Practice
Numbers assessed	71	69
Numbers rejected	22 (31%)	30 (43%)
Drop-outs	9 (18%)	15 (32%)
Completers	40	24

When more detailed analyses of outcome were done on 18 dependent variables measuring mood, cognitive and behavioural variables, using a two-way analysis of covariance (treatment x location) for change scores (i.e. baseline scores minus end-of-treatment scores), the relative efficacy of the three treatment modes from the two sources of referral became more obvious. Four variables which differentiated the two groups at baseline were used as co-variates: duration of illness episode, total score on the Present State Examination, education level and socio-economic level. Figures Ia and 1b show in histograms those variables which differentiated treatments significantly, i.e. Beck Depression Inventory (BDI), Hamilton Rating Scale for Depression (HRS-D), Anxiety (Anx.), Inward Irritability, Total Irritability (Total Irrit.) - these three variables were measured by the Irritability, Depression and Anxiety Scale (IDA) by Snaith et al (1978), view of self, view of the world and view of the future, as measured by semantic differential scales (Osgood et al., 1957). It can be seen that for the hospital out-patient group (HOP), the usual pattern of response is that the combination treatment group did better than the cognitive therapy alone or drug alone groups, with little difference between the latter. In the general practice group (GPP), the combination treatment group and cognitive therapy group performed similarly and better than the drug group. These results have been partly reported, in the form of percentage change scores, by Blackburn et al. (1981).

THIS STUDY

Aim

In addition to outcome at the end of treatment, the design of the study allowed us to investigate pattern of response over the course of treatment, as all patients were regularly re-assessed every two to three weeks. The questions addressed in the analysis reported here were:
   1. Is final outcome mirrored by pattern of response through

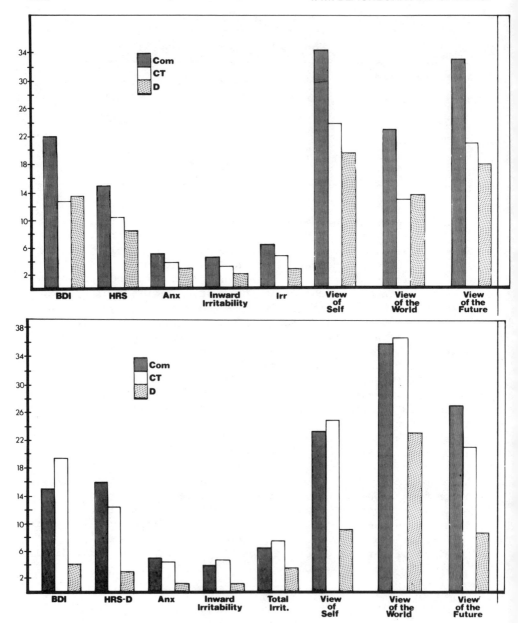

Figure 1: Significant change scores in analysis of covariance in
           (a) hospital outpatients (above) and (b) General Practice
           patients (below). COM = Combination treatment; CT =
           Cognitive therapy; D= Drugs; BDI = Beck Depression
           Inventory; HRS-D = Hamilton Rating Scale for Depression;
           Anx = Anxiety; Total irrit or irr = Inward and outward
           irritability.

Table 2. Number of responders and non-responders in each treatment for each source of referral

	Hospital Outpatients		General Practice Patients	
	Responders	Non-Responders	Responders	Non-Responders
	(1)	(2)	(3)	(4)
Drugs	11	2	1	6
		13		7
Cognitive Therapy	9	5	8	0
		14		8
Combination Treatment	11	2	8	1
		13		9
	31	9	17	7
		40		24

treatment?

2. Does one treatment work faster than another?
3. Do responses on different types of variables, mood and cognition, vary among treatments: for example, mood may change more quickly on drug treatment and cognitions on cognitive therapy.
4. How early can non-responders be identified?

Method

Subjects   All 64 patients who completed treatment were divided into responders and non-responders, as described above, i.e. responders scored $\leq$ 8 on the BDI and/or $\leq$ 9 on the HRS-D. There were 48 responders: 19 on combination treatment (Com), 17 on cognitive therapy (CT), 12 on drug (D) and 16 non-responders: 3 Com, 5 CT, 8 D. Hospital and general practice patients were combined for this analysis.

Measures   Pattern of response was analysed on a series of mood and cognitive measures: BDI (Beck et al., 1961); HRS-D (Hamilton, 1960); Anxiety (IDA, Snaith et al., 1978); Irritability (IDA, Snaith et al., 1978); Hopelessness (Beck et al., 1974), view of self, the world and the future (semantic differential scales with 12 bipolar adjectives for each concept representing evaluation, activity and potency, Osgood et al., 1957). Writing speed, as a behavioural measure, was also included to measure the vegetative symptom of retardation.

Procedure   All patients were retested every 2 - 3 weeks to the end of treatment by the authors and a psychiatrist not involved in therapy did the ratings on the HRS-D.

Statistical analysis   The analysis uses the usual end-point procedure, i.e. to keep the N constant at each point of testing, the last score of an individual who completed treatment early is repeated (Friedman, 1975). A multiple analysis of variance (MANOVA) was used to analyse differences among treatments at each point of re-testing. Significant F's were followed by Scheffe's a-posteriori tests to locate differences. The scores analysed were cumulative percentage change scores to take into consideration basal level, i.e.

$$\frac{(\text{occasion}) \ 1 - (\text{occasion}) \ 2}{(\text{occasion}) \ 1} \times 100, \quad \frac{1 - 3}{1} \times 100, \quad \frac{1 - 4}{1} \times 100, \text{ etc.}$$

Results

Correlations   Table 3 indicates that all the measures were on the whole highly correlated at baseline (N = 64), except for the behavioural measure (writing speed). Self-rated depression (BDI)

Table 3. Correlations of variables at baseline (N = 64)

	HRS-D	ANXIETY	IRRIT-ABILITY	HOPE-LESSNESS	VIEW OF SELF	VIEW OF ENVIRON-MENT	VIEW OF FUTURE	WRITING SPEED
BDI	.51***	.37**	.26*	.51***	-.57***	-.50***	-.45***	-.21
HRS-D		.26*	.24	.10	-.25*	-.22	-.08	-.18
ANXIETY			.42***	.25**	-.31*	-.34*	-.17	-.31*
IRRITABILITY				.32*	-.36**	-.27*	-.19	-.26
HOPELESSNESS					-.57***	-.55***	-.74***	.14
VIEW OF SELF						.64***	.60**	.28
VIEW OF ENVIRONMENT							.53***	.26
VIEW OF FUTURE								-.04

* p < .05   ** p < .01   *** p < .001

covaried significantly with other self-rated measures (anxiety,
irritability, hopelessness, view of self, the world and the future)
and with observer-rated depression (HRS-D). The HRS-D appeared a
more independent measure as it correlated significantly, at a modest
level, only with anxiety and view of self, apart from its highly
significant correlation with BDI. The highest correlation was
between hopelessness and view of the future ($r = -.74$) giving
concurrent validity to this semantic differential measure. The
behavioural measure did not correlate with any other measure
(except anxiety) and therefore appears to lack validity as a measure
of depression in this group of patients.

   Patterns of response   Figures 2 - 10 show the pattern of
response over the course of treatment for responders (solid lines)
and non-responders (broken lines) for the three modes of treatment
and in respect of the nine dependent variables. The notations at
the bottom of the figures indicate points of comparison, for example
1/2 = occasion 1 with occasion 2, and the ordinate represents percentage change scores.

   The pattern of response on the Hamilton Rating Scale for
Depression (HRS-D) is shown in Figure 2. It can be seen that
responders on combination treatment (RCOM) have the highest rate
of response at the beginning of treatment, though from the fifth
occasion of testing onwards their response was very similar to that
of responders on cognitive therapy alone (RCT). Responders on drugs
(RD) had a lower rate of response throughout. The differences in
rate of response were significantly different on the third occasion
of testing ($F = 3.3$, $p < .05$), but a-posteriori tests (Scheffe's)
failed to locate the significant differences. The significant
differences at fourth ($F = 5.92$, $p < .01$), 5th ($F = 4.62$, $p < .05$)
and 7th occasions ($F = 4.63$, $p < .01$) were located, as indicated by
the ticks on the figure. At fourth testing, the responders on combination treatment had improved significantly more than drug
responders ($p < .01$) and cognitive therapy responders had improved
more than drug responders ($p < .05$), while at 5th and 7th testing,
cognitive therapy responders had improved more than drug responders
($p < .05$).

   Among non-responders, the drug group (NRD) and the combination
treatment group (NRCOM) were similar in their pattern of response,
obtaining a mild response which decreased over time. The non-
responders on cognitive therapy (NRCT) actually got worse from the
start of treatment. The differences among non-responders did not
reach significance.

   Figure 3 shows the pattern of response on the Beck Depression
Inventory (BDI). Again, it can be seen that responders on combination treatment (RCOM) had the edge over the other two groups of
responders at the start of treatment and the drug group responded

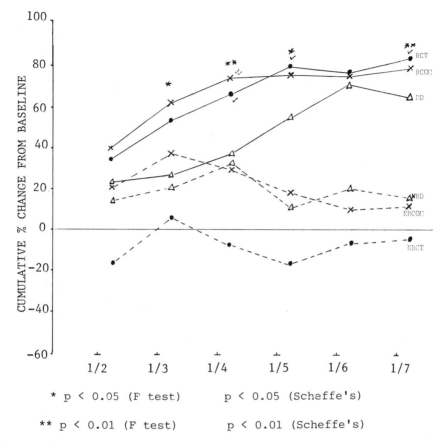

* p < 0.05 (F test)   p < 0.05 (Scheffe's)

** p < 0.01 (F test)   p < 0.01 (Scheffe's)

Figure 2: Hamilton Rating Scale for Depression. Legend also
           applies to Figures 3 to 10.

—x——x——x— Recovered on combination treatment (RCOM, N=19)

—•——•——•— Recovered on cognitive therapy (RCT, N=17)

—△——△——△— Recovered on drugs (RD, N=12)

—x— —x— —x— Not recovered on combination treatment (NRCOM, N=3)

—•— —•— —•— Not recovered on cognitive therapy (NRCT, N=5)

—△— —△— —△— Not recovered on drugs (NRD, N=8)

1/2   1/3   Change from occasion 1 to occasion 2, change from
                 occasion 1 to occasion 3, etc.

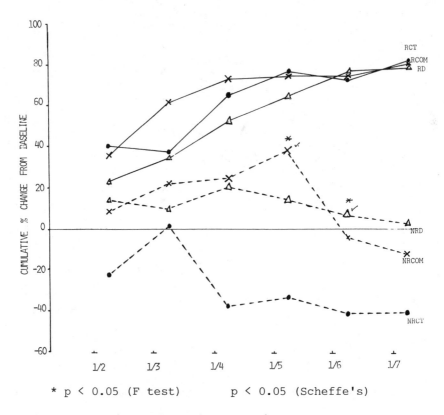

* p < 0.05 (F test)   p < 0.05 (Scheffe's)

Figure 3: Beck Depression Inventory

at a slower rate, but at the end of treatment, there was no difference among groups. There was no significant difference in response
among the groups of responders at any point of testing.

The non-responders on cognitive therapy (NRCT) again deteriorated with treatment, while the non-responders on drugs (NRD) and on
combination treatment (NRCOM) had a mild response which decreased·
over time. Significant differences were obtained at the 5th occasion
of testing (F = 4.81, p < 0.05), where NRCOM differed significantly
from NRCT at the 0.05 level and 6th occasion of testing (F = 4.72,
p < 0.05) where NRD differed from NRCT at the 0.05 level.

Figure 4 shows the same pattern of response on self-rated
anxiety (IDA sub-scale). Combination treatment and cognitive therapy
gave a similar response rate with combination treatment being slightly superior at the start. The drug responders (RD) did significantly
worse right from the start, with significant differences at all

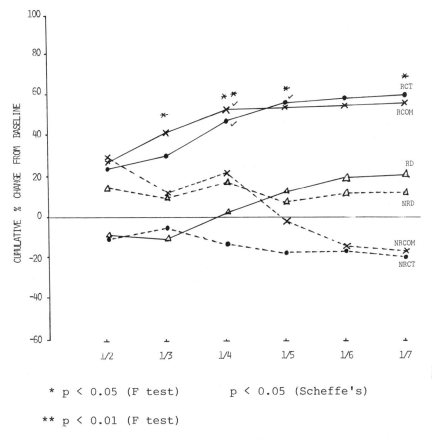

* p < 0.05 (F test)   p < 0.05 (Scheffe's)

** p < 0.01 (F test)

Figure 4: Anxiety

points, except the second and sixth occasions. It is surprising
that drug responders felt worse at the beginning of treatment in
spite of the sedative effect of antidepressant medication. Significant differences at third (F = 3.32, p < 0.05) and seventh occasion
(F = 3.29. p < 0.05) were not located, but on the fourth occasion
(F = 5.61, p < 0.01) both combination treatment and cognitive
therapy were superior to drugs at the 0.05 level, and on the fifth
occasion (F = 4.03, p < 0.05), cognitive therapy was superior to
drugs at the 0.05 level.

The non-responders followed the same pattern as on previous
variables, i.e. the non-responders to cognitive therapy (NRCT) did
worst of all, having deteriorated from the start of treatment. The
non-responders on drugs (NRD) maintained a slight improvement through
treatment and the non-responders on combination treatment (NRCOM),

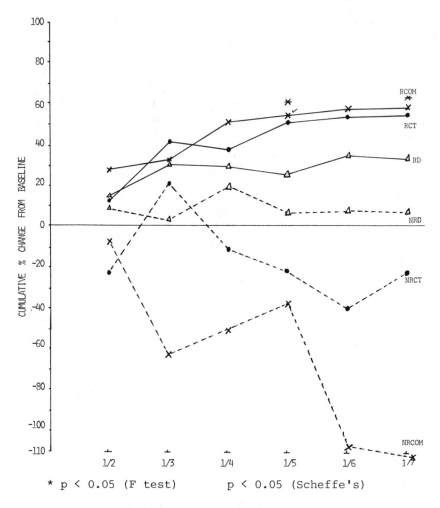

* p < 0.05 (F test)   p < 0.05 (Scheffe's)

Figure 5: Irritability

having started with a moderate response (30%), had increased anxiety
at the end of treatment. There were no significant differences
among non-responders.

Percentage change on the last mood variable, irritability (IDA
sub-scale) is shown in Figure 5. The responders on drugs (RD) did
worse than the other two groups of responders from the 4th occasion
of testing. Significant differences occurred on the 5th occasion
of testing (F = 4.05, p < 0.05) where the combination group did
significantly better than the drug group at the 0.05 level and on
the 7th occasion of testing (F = 3.44, p < 0.05) where significant

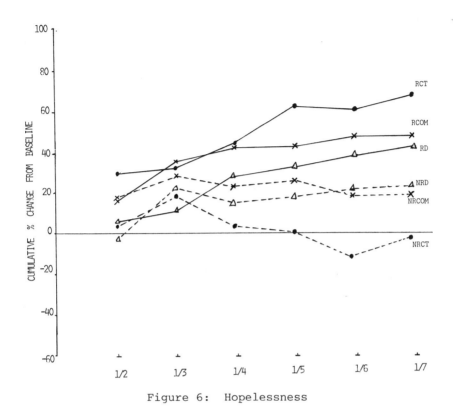

Figure 6: Hopelessness

differences were not located. The non-responders on combination treatment (NRCOM) and on cognitive therapy (NCT) deteriorated over time, i.e. got more irritable, while the non-responders to drugs (NRD) maintained a slight improvement. No significant differences were located among the non-responders.

The next four figures show the pattern of change on cognitive variables. In Figure 6, change in <u>hopelessness</u> follows the same pattern as in mood variables. The drug responders, at the end of treatment, remained more hopeless (42% improvement) than the responders on combination treatment (44% improvement) and the responders on cognitive therapy (69%). The drug responders had a lower level of response throughout treatment, which was not signif-icantly different from that of the other two groups of responders at any point.

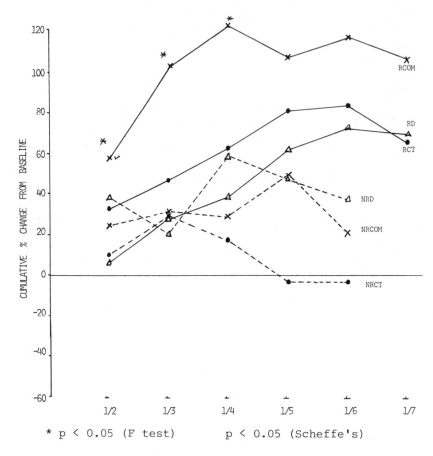

* p < 0.05 (F test)   p < 0.05 (Scheffe's)

Figure 7: View of self

No significant differences were located among non-responders, though again the non-responders to cognitive therapy did worst of all.

Changes in the three concepts of the cognitive triad, view of self, the world and the future, as measured by the semantic differential, are shown on Figures 7, 8 and 9. In Figure 7 showing the percentage change in <u>view of self</u>, it can be seen that responders to combination treatment had a higher level of response throughout treatment than the other two groups and that responders to cognitive therapy improved their view of self quicker than responders to drugs, with no difference at the end of treatment. Significant differences were seen at 2nd occasion of testing (F = 3.89, p < 0.05) where the

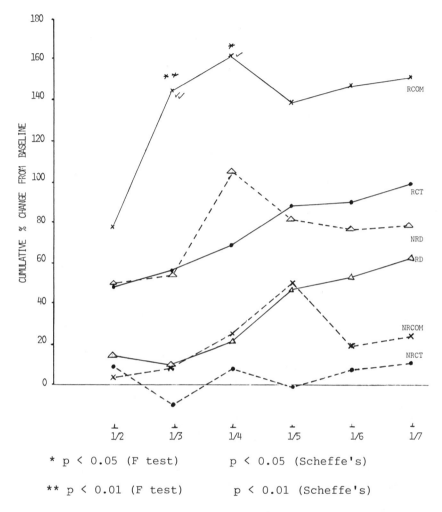

* p < 0.05 (F test)   p < 0.05 (Scheffe's)

** p < 0.01 (F test)   p < 0.01 (Scheffe's)

Figure 8: View of the environment

combination group was significantly different from the drug group
(p < 0.05) at 3rd (F = 3.43, p < 0.05) and 4th (F = 3.24, p < 0.05)
occasions of testing where differences were not located.

No significant differences were found among non-responders,
though non-responders to cognitive therapy did worse than the other
two groups, having deteriorated by the end of treatment.

Figure 8 shows the same patters of response for view of the

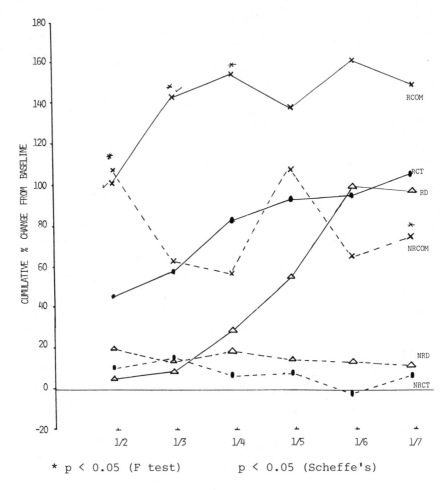

* p < 0.05 (F test)   p < 0.05 (Scheffe's)

Figure 9:   View of the future

environment, responders to combination treatment improved to a
higher level and more rapidly (over 100%), followed by responders
to cognitive therapy, while responders to drugs changed the way
they view their environment only minimally and very slowly (60% at
the end of treatment). Significant differences were obtained at
3rd occasion of testing (F = 5.98, p < 0.005) with the combination
group differing from the drug group at the 0.01 level, and at the
4th occasion (F = 4.91, p < 0.05) where the combination group
differed from the drug group at the 0.05 level.

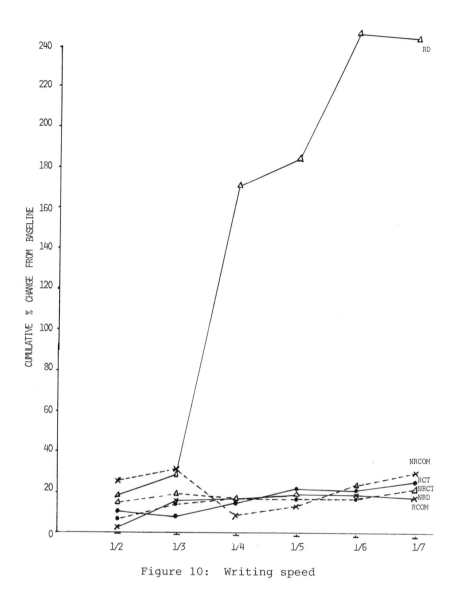

Figure 10:   Writing speed

There were no significant differences among the non-responders, where the non-responders to drugs did best (better than the respond- ers to drugs) and the non-responders to cognitive therapy did worst, remaining near baseline throughout treatment.

Figure 9 shows again the same pattern for change, in view of the future.   Responders to combination treatment had a better and

quicker response than the other two groups (over 100%) and though
response on cognitive therapy and on drugs was similar at the end
of treatment, response on cognitive therapy was more rapid at the
beginning of treatment than on drugs. Significant differences were
obtained at 2nd occasion of testing ($F = 3.94$, $p < 0.05$) where
combination treatment was significantly better than drug treatment
($p < 0.05$), on 3rd occasion ($F = 4.4$, $p < 0.05$) where combination
treatment differed from drug treatment ($p < 0.05$) and on 4th
occasion ($F = 3.19$, $p < 0.05$).

Among non-responders, those on combination treatment were
clearly separated from the other two groups, throughout treatment,
with a significant difference ($F = 4.21$, $p < 0.05$) at the last
occasion of testing; while non-responders to drug and to cognitive
therapy showed minimal improvement (less than 20%) throughout
treatment, non-responders to combination treatment responded at a
high level, sometimes undiscriminated from responders, showing a
relatively high increase in optimism.

The last figure, Figure 10, shows the pattern on a behavioural
measure of speed, namely writing speed. Here, the drug responders
showed a high level of improvement from the 4th occasion of testing,
with little difference between responders on combination treatment
and on cognitive therapy and non-responders to all three treatments.
The large variation in response, however, prevented these differences from reaching significance. There was little difference
among non-responders, all groups showing minimal improvement.

Discussion

1. Looking at the pattern of response over course of treatment,
as reflected in cumulative percentage change scores, indicated that
the results obtained at outcome were mirrored by progress throughout
treatment. The combination of cognitive therapy and antidepressant
drugs gave on the whole a quicker and greater rate of improvement
than either treatment on its own and cognitive therapy was superior
to drugs alone. The pattern applied both to mood and cognitive
measures, so that it cannot be said that there is a specific effect
of pharmacotherapy or of cognitive therapy on different aspects of
depression.

2. If rapid improvement is desirable, it is clear that combination treatment should be the treatment of choice according to these
results in depressed outpatients. In depression in particular, a
significant change early in treatment in hopelessness and negative
view of the future is often a question of life and death as hopelessness has been found to predict suicide better than level of
depression (Minkoff et al., 1973).

3. The results on a behavioural speed measure were at variance with other results, in that the response of the drug group was of a greater magnitude. This could be interpreted as indicating that retardation, a vegetative symptom of depression, responds best to pharmacotherapy. However, if that were so, it would be difficult to explain why the same response was not shown by patients receiving pharmacotherapy and cognitive therapy in combination. A better explanation may be the lack of validity of writing speed as a measure of retardation. It was pointed out in the table of intercorrelation that writing speed did not correlate significantly with any other baseline measure, except weakly ($r = -0.31$) with the level of anxiety (i.e. the higher the level of anxiety, the slower was writing speed).

4. A question which is often put to the clinician is how soon will you know whether your treatment is working? The data from the non-responders in this study indicated that, on the whole, from 2nd and 3rd assessments, that is by 2 - 4 weeks, it is possible to predict response. This applied in particular to the general depression measures and to irritability, the cognitive measures appear to differentiate responders and non-responders later, that is by 4th and 5th assessments, i.e. at about 6 - 8 weeks. Decrease in anxiety also occurred early in responders to cognitive therapy and combination treatment, but much later in responders to drugs, in spite of the sedative effect of antidepressant medication. The separation of responders on general depression scales at about 4 weeks agrees with biological clinical practice and experience, a change of treatment often being considered after about 3 - 4 weeks if no response is seen on current medication. It must be remembered, however, that the non-responders on each treatment were very small, so that caution must be exercised in interpreting the results.

5. Bearing in mind this caveat, the consistently poorer response of the non-responders to cognitive therapy is intriguing. Practically, the conclusion to be drawn seems to be that if a patient does not respond to cognitive therapy by 2 - 4 weeks, it is better to offer him an alternative treatment or to prescribe antidepressants, even if his psychotherapy is continued. Theoretically, it may be that CT responders are a specific type of depressed patients, differing from non-responders in specific ways. In a study of predictive factors of response (Blackburn et al., 1981) we found that long duration of index episode of illness was a negative predictor of response to CT, as was a positive view of the environment. However, more detailed studies are necessary to differentiate between potential responders and non-responders to cognitive therapy.

In conclusion, cognitive therapy alone or in combination with drugs was superior to drugs alone in the treatment of depressed outpatients. This superiority was shown not only at final outcome, but in the rate and extent of progress through treatment on both

mood and cognitive parameters. Pharmacotherapy is well known to
be efficacious in the treatment of depressive disorders. This study
supports this general view but shows that the combination of cognitive therapy with drugs has an additive effect. The theoretical
explanation of these empirical findings are far from clear at the
moment, though, in my view, they open up possibilities for constructive speculations and hypotheses which could be put to the test.

REFERENCES

Beck, A.T., 1967. "Depression: Clinical, Experimental and Theoret-
    ical Aspects". Staples Press, London.
Beck, A.T., 1976. "Cognitive Therapy and the Emotional Disorders".
    International University Press, New York.
Beck, A.T., Ward, C.H., Mendelson, M., Mock, J. and Erbaugh, J.,
    1961. An inventory for measuring depression. Arch. Gen.
    Psychiat., 4: 53.
Beck, A.T., Weissman, A., Lester, D. and Trexler, L., 1974. The
    measurement of pessimism: the hopelessness scale. J. Consult.
    Clin. Psychol., 42: 861.
Beck, A.T., Rush, A.J., Shaw, B.F. and Emery, G., 1979. "Cognitive
    Therapy of Depression". Guilford Press, New York.
Blackburn, I.M., 1974. The pattern of hostility in affective
    illness. Brit. J. Psychiat., 125: 141.
Blackburn, I.M., 1975. Mental and Psychomotor speed in depression
    and mania. Brit. J. Psychiat., 126: 329.
Blackburn, I.M., Lyketsos, G.C. and Tsiantis, J., 1979. The temp-
    oral relationship between hostility and depressed mood. Brit.
    J. Soc. Clin. Psychol., 18: 227.
Blackburn, I.M. and Bonham, K.G., 1980. Experimental effects of a
    cognitive therapy technique in depressed patients. Brit. J.
    Soc. Clin. Psychol., 19: 353.
Blackburn, I.M. and Bishop, S., 1981. Is there an alternative to
    drugs in the treatment of depressed ambulatory patients?
    Behav. Psychother., 9: 96.
Blackburn, I.M., Bishop, S., Glen, A.I.M., Whalley, L. and Christie,
    J.C., 1981. The efficacy of cognitive therapy in depression:
    a treatment trial using cognitive therapy and pharmacotherapy,
    each alone and in combination. Brit. J. Psychiat., 139: 181.
Blackburn, I.M. Bishop, S. and McGuire, R.J., 1981. Prediction of
    response to cognitive therapy. Paper presented at 1st European
    meeting on cognitive behavioural therapy, Lisbon, 10th Septem-
    ber, 1981.
Ellis, A., 1962. "Reason and Emotion in Psychotherapy". Lyle
    Stuart, New York.
Friedman, A., 1975. Interaction of drug therapy with marital therapy
    in depressed patients. Arch. Gen. Psychiat., 32: 619.
Goldfried, M.R., Decenteceo, E.T. and Weinberg, L., 1974. System-
    atic rational restructuring as a self-control technique.

Behav. Ther., 5: 247.

Greenspoon, J. and Lamal, P.A., 1978. Cognitive behaviour modification, who needs it? Psychol. Rec., 28: 354.

Hamilton, M., 1960. A rating scale for depression. J. Neurol. Psychiat., 23: 56.

Hollon, S.D. and Beck, A.T., 1979. Cognitive therapy of depression. In: Kendall, P.C. and Hollon, S.D. (Eds.), "Cognitive Behavioural Interventions". Academic Press, New York.

Kuhn, T., 1970. "The Structure of Scientific Revolutions". University of Chicago Press.

Ledwidge, B., 1978. Cognitive behaviour modification: a step in the wrong direction? Psychol. Bull., 85: 353.

Lyketsos, G.C., Blackburn, I.M. and Tsiantis, J., 1978. The movement of hostility during recovery from depression. Psychol. Med., 8: 145.

Mahoney, M., 1974. "Cognition and Behaviour Modification". Ballinger, Cambridge, Mass.

Meichenbaum, D., 1977. "Cognitive Behaviour Modification". Plenum, New York.

Metcalfe, M. and Goldman, E., 1965. Validation of an inventory for measuring depression. Brit. J. Psychiat., 111: 240.

Minkoff, K., Bergman, E., Beck, A.T. and Beck, R., 1973. Hopelessness, depression and attempted suicide. Am. J. Psychiat., 130: 455.

Osgood, C.E., Suci, G.J. and Tannenbaum, P.H., 1957. "The Measurement of Meaning". University of Illinois Press, Chicago.

Rachlin, H., 1974. Self-control. Behaviourism, 2: 94.

Rehm, L.P., 1977. A self-control model of depression. Behav. Ther., 8: 787.

Seligman, M.E.P., 1975 "Helplessness". Freeman, San Francisco.

Skinner, B.F., 1963. Behaviourism at fifty. Science, 140: 951.

Snaith, B.P., Constantopoulos, A.A., Jardine, M.Y. and McGuffin, P., 1978. A clinical scale for the self-assessment of irritability. Brit. J. Psychiat., 132: 164.

Spitzer, R.L., Endicott, J. and Robins, E., 1978. Research diagnostic criteria (RDC) for a selected group of functional disorders. Biometrics Research, New York.

Wilkinson, I.M. and Blackburn, I.M., 1981. Cognitive style in depressed and recovered depressed patients. Brit. J. Clin. Psychol., 20: 283.

Wolpe, J., 1978. Cognition and causation in human behaviour and its therapy. Am. Psychol., 33: 437.

IS ALL BEHAVIOUR MODIFICATION 'COGNITIVE'?

C.F. Lowe
Department of Psychology
University College of
      North Wales
Bangor
Gwynedd

P.J. Higson
Department of Psychology
North Wales Hospital
Denbigh
Clwyd

> The technical trick of conducting our
> thinking in auditory word-images, instead of
> in spoken words, does indeed secure secrecy
> for our thinking, since the auditory imaginings
> of one person are not seen or heard by another...
> But this secrecy is not the secrecy ascribed to
> the postulated episodes of the ghostly shadow-
> world (of mind). It is merely the convenient
> privacy which characterises the tunes that run
> in my head and the things that I see in my mind's
> eye.
>
>   - Gilbert Ryle (1949)

INTRODUCTION

Behaviour modification arose out of the study of animal behaviour in controlled experimental settings. Skinner and others had shown that the behaviour of animals could be considered to be an orderly function of contingencies of reinforcement. As Morse (1966) put it 'Even people with a minimum of training can follow simple specified procedures for producing stable, standard behaviour patterns of various types in any individual of a variety of different species ... Furthermore, any member of most species will give a similar performance on the same schedules.' Apart from the power to change behaviour imparted by this approach an explanatory system was also offered according to which any particular performance, for example on a schedule of reinforcement, could be analysed in terms of the operation of discriminative and reinforcing stimuli. The response was usually the operation of some mechanical device like a lever; the reinforcer was typically food and discriminative stimuli were environmental events such as the illumination of coloured lights All of these variables were publicly observable events. The creation of explanatory fictions, 'events taking place somewhere else, at some other level of observation' (Skinner, 1950), was eschewed.

This was the model adopted by the behaviour modification movement. It focussed upon observable behaviour and environmental stimuli and was taken by many to exclude consideration of covert events. The basic conditioning principles having been established, all that was required it was thought was the development of an appropriate technology to deal with clinical problems. The principal difficulty envisaged at the time appeared to be, not the question of whether the model was efficacious, but the ethical problems which would arise as a consequence of behaviour modifiers being in possession of such a powerful technology! (cf. Ulrich, Stachnik and Mabry, 1970).

Some years on, the ethical dilemmas have lessened as it has become apparent that the power to predict and control complex human behaviour remains elusive. Instead, behaviour modification's lack of success in many areas has led to a great deal of soul-searching within the field (cf. Brigham, 1980; Michael, 1980; Branch and Malagodi, 1980; Reppucci and Saunders, 1974). Indeed, it has led some to abandon the traditional behaviour modification approach altogether, rejecting the radical behaviourist philosophy upon which behaviour modification is based in favour of the "new" cognitivism.

The new approach, known as cognitive behaviour modification (CBM) or cognitive behaviour therapy (CBT), covers a variety of research and clinical activities. It is difficult to establish precisely what are the 'cognitive', as opposed to the mere behavioural, elements in much of this work. However, most of the therapies have in common a concern with psychological events which are not publicly observable. Such covert or 'private' events include, for example, imagining and covert speech, activities which are frequently labelled 'cognitive' (Catania, 1979). It is this issue of private events which is the focal point in the continuing controversy surrounding CBM. Advocates of the cognitive approach argue that (i) understanding and control of private events is of great importance for clinical psychology; and (ii) behaviourism rejects the study of private events. They have concluded, therefore, either that behaviourism should be abandoned or that it should be fundamentally revised to take into account the cognitive aspects of human functioning (Bandura, 1977; Kendall and Hollon, 1979; Locke, 1979; Mahoney, 1974; 1980; Meichenbaum, 1977; Wilson, 1978).

Much of the exchange between the two camps has taken the form of a trial of strength to establish which approach can produce the

most effective therapy. One feature to emerge from the debate so
far has been the extraordinary confusion of participants on both
sides with respect to the theoretical foundations of behaviour modification. Little consideration has been given to the possibility
that both sets of practitioners are engaged in qualitatively similar
activities.

THE EXPERIMENTAL EVIDENCE

A central theoretical assumption underlying a great deal of the
behaviour modification enterprise is that the principles of behaviour
established in animal studies have a general applicability and
govern not only the behaviour of animals but also that of humans.
However, relatively few experimental studies have systematically
investigated the effects of reinforcement contingencies with humans
and such studies as do exist raise serious questions about the notion
of generality. Schedules of reinforcement is the context in which
animal operant behaviour has been most intensively studied and a
great many studies have shown that, over a wide range of species,
the effects of each particular schedule are similar both within and
across animal species (but see also Lowe and Harzem, 1977). The
schedule performance of humans, on the other hand, frequently bears
little resemblance to that of animals (cf. Lowe, 1979). A series of
studies by one of the present authors and colleagues (Bentall and
Lowe, 1982; Lowe, 1979; Lowe, Beasty and Bentall, 1983; Lowe, Harzem
and Bagshaw, 1978; Lowe, Harzem and Hughes, 1978) has shown that in
situations where schedules of reinforcement are arranged for human
responding, the effects of the reinforcer are greatly affected by
subjects' covert verbal behaviour and their formulation of the
contingencies. Indeed, effects of changes in the reinforcing
contingencies can be completely overridden by the subject's own
"self-instructions". The only studies where human performance
consistently resembles that of animals are those which (a) employ
devices such as response-produced clock stimuli to attenuate inter-
ference from subjects' verbal behaviour, or (b) have as subjects
young infants who have not yet developed language (cf. Lowe, 1983).

Unlike humans, animals are not able to use language to describe
their own behaviour and its environmental consequences; lacking this
ability their behaviour is affected in very different ways by reinforcing contingencies. The experimental evidence suggests that
animal conditioning models which do not provide for the controlling
role of verbal behaviour are inadequate for a human psychology.
This research also provides good empirical support for those approaches to therapy, such as CBM, which emphasise the importance of
private events.

RADICAL BEHAVIOURISM

The recognition of the effectiveness of private speech in controlling behaviour may pose problems for some traditional accounts of behaviour modification but does it also mark the demise of radical behaviourism? Clearly, if private events are important determinants of overt behaviour but are ignored in behavioural analyses then this would be a serious, if not fatal, deficiency in behaviourism. The standard critique is well expressed by Mahoney as follows:

> 'Watson and Skinner have been among the more outspoken proponents of a non-mediational approach to human behaviour. In brief, their arguments have included assertions that (a) science can only deal with publicly observable events and (b) inferential accounts of behaviour are to be avoided because they are unparsimonious'.

(Mahoney, 1977, p.9)

Certainly as far as Skinner's philosophy of science is concerned, it is difficult to believe that there could be a greater travesty of his position than this statement. And yet it is a view which is widely held by participants on both sides of the CBM debate (see, for example, Kendall and Hollon, 1979; Ledwidge, 1978; Locke, 1979; Strupp, 1979; Wilson, 1978; Wolpe, 1978).

Theoretical objections to the study of covert events, largely on the grounds that there can be no public agreement about their validity, has come from methodological behaviourism, a theoretical position which has been adopted by many behaviour therapists. But Skinner has consistently argued against this view claiming that it is misguidedly adhering to the outmoded tenets of logical positivism and operationism. Indeed the principal distinguishing feature of his radical behaviourism is that it considers that a science of behaviour, like other sciences, must deal with events which are not directly observable; inference, therefore, is held to be essential in the study of behaviour, regardless of parsimony.

Our characterisation of the Skinnerian positon is very much at odds with that of Mahoney and other commentators but it is very easily substantiated as Skinner's writings on these issues since 1945 consistently make the same points. Some examples may serve to convey the degree to which the radical behaviourist position has been misconstrued:

> 'When someone solves a problem in mental arithmetic the initial statement of the problem

, and the final overt answer can often be related
only by inferring covert events'

(Skinner, 1957, p.434)|

'A science of behaviour must consider the
place of private stimuli ... The question then
is this: What is inside the skin, and how do
we know about it? The answer is, I believe
the heart of radical behaviourism.'

(Skinner, 1974, p. 211-212)

Clearly, covert behaviour is a critical feature of radical
behaviourist theory. But even when it is accepted that this is a
legitimate subject matter for study many experimentalists and
clinicians, who are avowed radical behaviourists, cannot bring
themselves to grant private events the same causal status as is
accorded to stimuli that occur 'outside the skin' in the environment.
For example, in a recent attempt to combat the growing threat of
cognitivism, Branch and Malagodi (1980) have written "Radical
behaviourism eschews bestowal of causal status to private events...
(they) can be thought of as coincidental, collateral products of
events that result in overt behaviour". They go on to justify this
with the following argument: 'The real problem then, is one of
accessibility. Private events are not accessible and therefore not
directly manipulable. They provide prescriptions for actions based
on indirect manipulations of things unseen' (p.33). It is possible
that someone may once have argued in a similar vein for the futility
of studying electrons but the accessibility argument seems to have
as little to recommend it for psychology as it did for physics.
the key to some of psychology's central problems is hidden in a
troublesome location, surely, this is not a reason for giving up the
search or for looking elsewhere in convenient but empty places.

An even more remarkable defence of the epiphenomenalist view
of covert behaviour, again directed at cognitive critics, comes
from Rachlin (1977, and see also Brigham, 1980). This at least has
the merit that is does not discriminate between overt and covert
verbal behaviour but assigns them both to a condition of causal
impotence. For example, Rachlin (1977, p. 662) writes: 'It makes
little sense that verbal behaviour should cause other behaviour'.
Of course, to give causal status to overt verbal behaviour would be
to open the door to granting similar status to covert verbal behaviour; something said quietly to oneself should be no less effective
than that which is said aloud. But there seems little reason to
single out verbal behaviour from other events in the universe of
stimuli as having no determining role in human action. To do so is
to ignore the findings of many experimental studies which have demonstrated that what a subject says to himself can influence the rest
of his behaviour (e.g. Bem, 1967; Kendler, 1964; Lowe, 1979; Lowe,
1983; Luria, 1961; Sokolov, 1972).

The epiphenomenalist argument appears to be an unfortunate last ditch stand against what is seen to be the invasion of cognitivism. But it has little in common with the radical behaviourism of Skinner which unashamedly recognises the causal role of verbal behaviour, both covert and overt. This is, perhaps, most evident in Skinner's account of rule-governed behaviour. According to Skinner (1969) a rule is a description of a reinforcement contingency which specifies the occasions when a behaviour occurs, the behaviour itself, and its consequences. Rule following is contrasted with contingency-shaped behaviour where an individual's behaviour is shaped through repeated exposure to a particular reinforcement contingency. It is not, of course, necessary for an individual to be able to describe a particular contingency to be affected by it. For example, a skill acquired through long exposure to reinforcing conditions, such as the one quoted by Skinner (1969) of a blacksmith operating a bellows, may not be dependent upon the individual being able to describe the contingencies; passing on the skill to another individual, however, is greatly facilitated if the blacksmith can formulate a rule accurately describing his own behaviour and its consequences. Individuals may learn rules from others or construct their own, given that they have been taught to do so by a verbal community. It is this capacity to describe our own behaviour and its effects on the environment which is a critical factor in the creation of a 'consciousness' which is unique to humans (Skinner, 1974):

> 'The verbal community generates "awareness" when
> it teaches an individual to describe his past and
> present behaviour and behaviour he is likely to
> exhibit in the future and to identify the variables
> of which all three are presumably functions. The
> description which is thus generated is not yet a
> rule, but the person may use the same terms to
> mould his own behaviour (as a form of self-control),
> to make resolutions, to formulate plans to state
> purposes, and then to construct rules'

> (Skinner, 1969, p.159)

Although it has to date received little attention from clinical psychologists, Skinner's analysis, particularly that of rule following, appears to have much to recommend it as a framework for understanding the processes involved in the acquisition and maintenance of complex human behaviour.

Thus both radical behaviourist theory and research might be said to be 'cognitive' in that they point to the importance of verbal behaviour, overt and covert, in controlling human behaviour. Indeed, understanding the nature of control by covert stimuli is at the 'heart of radical behaviourism' Skinner (1974). Why then should the behaviour modification movement have proceeded without drawing upon this theoretical background? One possible explanation is that the aversion to considering private events and verbal behaviour as controlling stimuli may be a hangover from earlier forms of behaviourism of the methodological variety, under the influence of which many behaviourists strive to deny either the existence or efficacy of any event which cannot be publicly and directly observed and measured. There is also the point that because the animal conditioning model is the one which is adopted by behaviour modifiers then no allowance is made within their theoretical system for the controlling function of human verbal behaviour.

What we have been considering up to now has been the theoretical basis of behaviour modification but can it be the case that behaviour analysts in practice really do eschew control by covert events and verbal behaviour? Presumably, from the moment a client enters the clinician's office and is told by the behaviour modifier to 'sit down' we can begin to collect evidence to the contrary.

VERBAL CONTROL IN BEHAVIOUR MODIFICATION

Token Economies

One form of behaviour modification that has become very widespread is that of token economy programmes. Since the early work of Ayllon and Azrin (1968) with chronic psychiatric patients, token economy programmes have been conducted with a variety of clinical and non-clinical subject populations in a variety of different settings (cf. Kazdin, 1977). This work is frequently cited as evidence for the effectiveness of operant contingencies with humans.

A standard description of token economies would be that they (i) specify a series of target behaviours for the particular client group, (ii) present tokens contingent upon the subjects' performance of the target behaviour, and (iii) allow subjects access to items from a variety of back-up reinforcers through the exchange of tokens (cf. Ayllon and Azrin, 1968). Such a description might apply equally well to a study of animal operant behaviour; there is no reference to the role of verbal behaviour and covert events. But does the description, in fact, accurately characterise what happens in token economies?

For the past five years, one of the present authors (Higson) has conducted a token economy programme with long stay patients in a psychiatric hospital. Detailed analysis shows that verbal control is an integral part of this programme, for example, staff provide (i) verbal prompts to initiate target behaviour, (ii) verbal accounts,

accompanying token presentation, of whether the subject's performance
of the target behaviour matched the specified criteria, (iii) verbal
instructions about the contingencies in operation to subjects at
group meetings, especially when a subject is new to the programme,
(iv) brief written verbal descriptions of the contingencies, which
are posted throughout the ward (e.g. 'make your bed and earn six
tokens'), and (v) a full written description of the contingencies
for each new subject upon arrival on the ward. Most token economies
with psychiatric patients that we know of make extensive use of
verbal behaviour in both initiating and maintaining behaviour.

     Now it might be argued that this is not the way for a good
behaviourist to conduct a token economy programme, that it results
in the reinforcing contingencies being contaminated by verbal complexities (cf. Michael, 1980) and that instead, one should minimise
instructions and concentrate on getting the response-reinforcer
relationships correct as is customary in animal experimentation.
The evidence suggests that this would be a recipe for failure. In
reviews of the token economy literature, Franks and Wilson (1974)
and Kazdin (1977) have argued that one of the reasons why some
clients' behaviour is insensitive to the reinforcing contingencies
is that the therapist's verbal descriptions of the contingencies
have not been sufficiently detailed or explicit. For example,
Franks and Wilson (1974) write: 'Instructions combined with reinforcement seem to facilitate performance ... The staff concerned
have to be well-trained - they must know how best to reinforce
behaviour, and how to accompany reinforcement with an explicit
statement of the contingencies which are operating (e.g. "I gave
you four tokens because of the good cleaning job you did this morn-
ing")'. A number of studies confirm this view. For example, Ayllon
and Azrin (1964) found that providing a tangible reinforcer to modify
the meal-time behaviour of psychiatric patients had no effect on
performance unless it was accompanied by instructions that specified
the reinforcing contingency; it should also be noted, however, that
instructions alone had no enduring effect unless accompanied by
reinforcement. Herman and Tramontana (1971) reported that presenting
tokens to children as reinforcers for appropriate classroom behaviour
did not markedly alter behaviour until the contingencies were described to the children. Similarly, studies by Suchotliff, Greaves,
Stecker and Berke (1970), Hall, Baker and Hutchinson (1977) and Baker,
Hall, Hutchinson and Bridge (1977) testify to the central role of
instructions in token economy programmes.

     This evidence raises the critical question of what it is that
controls the behaviour of clients in these situations: is behaviour
under instructional control or under the control of the putative
reinforcing contingencies, or some combination of both. As Kazdin
(1977) has pointed out, in most programmes little attempt has been
made to assess the extent to which reinforcement contributes to
changes in behaviour over and above instructions and yet, in general,

little credit has been given to instructions as a factor involved in behaviour change. This is exemplified by a report of a token economy programme conducted by Nelson and Cone (1979). Token contingencies were introduced to increase the appropriate behaviour of psychiatric patients in four different areas: personal hygiene, personal management, ward work and social skills. Nelson and Cone attribute the observed increase in subjects' performance of the target behaviours entirely to the introduction of the token economy contingencies.
In their description of the programme, on the other hand, they devote a section to what they term 'prompts'. Here the authors state that:

> 'After token reinforcement was initiated
> for a category of behaviours, verbal instructions,
> reminders and modelled demonstrations were freq-
> uently provided. In addition, posters were
> placed on the ward walls indicating target
> behaviours, token values, ward rules, and the
> ward schedule ... Observation of 130 instances
> of subjects' performing the target behaviours
> during the implementation and probe phases
> indicated that subjects received some type of
> individual prompt ... during 24% of constructive
> activity, 71% for inappropriate behaviour, and
> 100% for inactivity'.

(Nelson and Cone, 1979, pp. 260-261)

Given that the controlling role of verbal instructions is recognised as it now is in the experimental literature (cf. Catania, 1981; Lowe, 1979) the plea to get back to instruction-free contingencies for 'pure' contingency control (Matthews, Shimoff, Catania Sagvolden, 1977; Michael, 1980) might seem appealing. But this aspiration is founded upon a basic misunderstanding of the nature of human behaviour as opposed to that of animals. Because humans, when they have acquired language, do not just simply respond to contingencies of reinforcement as animals do. Humans respond verbally to their responding; they comment upon the contingencies to themselves; they reflect; they consider possibilities; they imagine alternatives; they formulate rules. This ongoing commentary on their own behaviour and its likely environmental consequences will not normally go away regardless of how much the therapist's instructions have been mini- mised. Indeed, the fewer instructions provided by the therapist the greater is the scope for the influence of the client's own 'self- instructions', which may provide a completely erroneous account of the contingencies. It is the influence of such misleading self- instructions which often leads to the contingency insensitivity reported in token economy programmes (Franks and Wilson, 1974; Kazdin, 1977) and in the experimental literature on human operant

behaviour (cf. Lowe, 1979). Thus we would contend, not just
Meichenbaum (1977), but all behaviour modifiers are involved in
dealing with clients' self-instructions.

Contingency Management

The effects of verbal behaviour can also be seen in various
contingency management procedures which involve the systematic
scheduling of both positive and negative consequences for behaviour.
One form of contingency management is achieved through the use of
contingency contracting. This procedure involves the negotiation
of a written contract between two or more individuals which clearly
specifies the 'target behaviours' that each have agreed upon and the
consequences arranged for successful performance of these behaviours.
The contract may also specify setting conditions for the target
behaviour and the consequences of non-compliance with the terms of
the contract. Contingency contracting has been successfully employed
in a variety of clinical settings and with a variety of problems,
for example, marital problems (Crowe, 1978; Stuart, 1969), child
delinquency (Stuart, 1971; Tharp and Wetzel, 1969), classroom
management (Homme, Csanzi, Gonzales and Rechs, 1970), alcohol abuse
(Miller, 1972), and obesity (Foreyt, 1977; Mann, 1972; 1977). The
following examples may serve to illustrate the processes involved in
standard contingency management and contracting procedures.

The typical contingency management approach employed with problem
drinkers has involved providing either positive consequences for a
reduction in the rate of drinking or amount of alcohol drunk, or
negative consequences for the occurrence of alcohol drinking, or
some combination of both. Cohen, Liebson and Faillace (1971), for
example, describe a series of studies conducted with a 39 year-old,
hospitalised chronic alcoholic with a 10-year history of alcohol
abuse. The target behaviour for this individual was a reduction in
the overall amount of alcohol drunk each day, for which a positive
or negative consequence was presented according to whether the
subject drank more or less than the specified limit. In one study
a free-operant drinking phase was employed in which the subject had
access to 24 ounces of 95 proof ethanol each day. During a contingent
reinforcement phase, if the subject drank 5 ounces of alcohol or less
on a particular day, he was placed in an enriched ward environment
which provided the opportunity to work for money, private telephone,
recreation room, and television. If, on the other hand, the subject
drank over 5 ounces he was placed in an impoverished environment
(loss of all privileges) for the rest of the day. During control
conditions no contingencies were in operation. The results of this
single-case study indicated that controlled drinking (under 5 ounces
per day) was maintained for as long as 5 weeks during contingent
phases, with a return to excessive drinking during non-contingent
phases.

A study by Mann (1977) concerned with weight-reduction in male and female subjects provides an example of contingency contracting. The contract (i) required each subject to surrender a large number of items considered to be valuable to him/her self, (ii) required the subject to be weighed regularly, (iii) prescribed the manner in which the subject could earn back or permanently lose his valuables (i.e. statement of the contingencies), and (iv) stipulated that the researcher, at his discretion, would change the procedures from baseline, to treatment, back to baseline, and back to treatment conditions (a single-subject design was used). Three forms of re-inforcement contingency were specified in the contract: (a) as soon as each 2 lb weight reduction was achieved the subject received one valuable; (b) the subject was presented with a 'bonus' valuable for losing a minimum number of pounds by the end of each successive two-week period during the treatment condition; (c) some of the valuables were delivered to the subject only if and when the target weight requirement (specified at the outset) was met. In addition, if the subject decided at any time to opt out of the programme the researcher kept possession of all the remaining valuables. Mann reported that the contract procedure was successful in producing significant red-uctions in weight for all subjects.

Although these examples, together with many other studies show that contingency management procedures can be successful, they also show, contrary to what is often believed, that the changes brought about cannot be attributed to the direct effects of reinforcement. For, as Michael (1980) has previously observed, in cases such as these the behaviour being affected is so distanced from its prog-rammed consequences, that it cannot be directly influenced by them. In animal operant research even very short delays between the operant response and the presentation of the reinforcer (i.e., ranging from a few seconds to a few minutes) can seriously retard or eliminate the acquisition of behaviour (Davey, 1981; Skinner,1938). In many contingency management studies, however, including the two examples presented above, the delay between the occurrence of the behaviour to be 'reinforced' and the putative reinforcer may be several hours, or even days, long. We would agree with Michael (1980) when he suggests that 'Such effects are probably always mediated through some form of rule statement or rule control, which is typically not mentioned or analysed'. These rule statements will incorporate the instructions given to the subject or, as in the case of contingency contracting, the written descriptions of the contingencies. But where our account differs radically from that of Michael's is that he cites such cases as being exceptional to the general behaviour modification situation where contingencies operate directly; he assumes that when human behaviour is followed closely in time by a particular consequence that it will be free of 'rule statements' and 'rule control'. There can be no good grounds, theoretical or empirical, for this assumption. On the contrary, it seems that, having acquired language, humans will persist in using it to construe

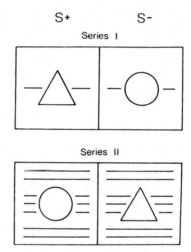

Figure 1: Two simple discriminations, labelled 'Series I' and
           'Series II'. The task requires the subject to discriminate
           between the correct (S⁺) and incorrect (S⁻) form-background
           configuration. Each series is learned independently and
           then performance is assessed on a conditional discrimin-
           ation test consisting of trials that intermix Series I
           and Series II. (After Schilmoeller et al., 1979).

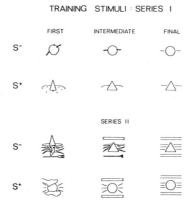

Figure 2:   Some of the shaping steps for Series I and Series II,
            showing the initial stimuli presented to subjects (FIRST),
            stimuli from the middle range of steps (INTERMEDIATE),
            and the final stimulus configurations (FINAL) (After
            Schilmoeller et al., 1979).

their environment, regardless of the temporal relationship between
their behaviour and its consequences.

Discrimination Training

    One final example of behaviour analysts ignoring the role of
verbal behaviour comes from the literature on errorless discrimination
learning. Terrace (1963), employing animal subjects, showed that fine
discriminations between colours could be established by reinforcing
responses in the presence of one stimulus (S$^+$), and witholding reinforcement in the presence of the second stimulus (S$^-$) which was
gradually introduced (faded in) along the dimensions of duration and
intensity. This technique has subsequently been used with normal
human subjects and with clinical populations (cf. Sidman and Stoddard,
1967; Schilmoeller and Etzel, 1977; Cullen, 1981). Recently, an
additional procedure has been developed called 'stimulus shaping'
(cf. Schilmoeller, Schilmoeller, Etzel and Le Blanc, 1979); this
involves manipulating the topographical configuration, rather than
the intensity, of visual stimuli.

    The effectiveness of both procedures and a trial-and-error
procedure was compared in a study by Schilmoeller et al. (1979); the
subjects were 4-5 year-old children. Figure 1 shows two simple
discriminations. The task was to learn each of the series independently and then performance was assessed on a conditional discrimination test consisting of trials that intermixed Series I and Series
II as shown in Figure 1. Some of the stimulus-shaping steps for
Series I and II are illustrated in Figure 2 which shows, for example,
how an S$^-$ stimulus which looks like an apple with a worm is transformed into a circle with a single line background, and how an S$^+$
stimulus which resembles a tree on a hill is changed in successive
steps into a triangle with a single line. The authors reported that
training by stimulus shaping was more effective than either stimulus
fading or trial-and-error for facilitating transfer of correct responding from the two simple discriminations to the conditional discrimination. Their explanation of these results is particularly
interesting. They write:

> The success of stimulus shaping was
> most likely due to (a) the selection for
> initial trials of stimuli that were clearly
> different from one another and whose shape
> resembled the stimuli involved in the
> ultimate discrimination, i.e., criterion-
> related stimuli (Schilmoeller and Etzel,
> 1977); and (b) the progressive topograph-
> ical transformation of these criterion-

related stimuli into the actual criterion
stimuli involved in the ultimate discrimination.

(Schilmoeller et al., 1979, p. 418)

Thus the principal reasons cited for success do not include any
mention of verbal behaviour but instead they are couched in the
stimulus discrimination terms familiar from animal experimentation
(although the possibility is conceded that labelling the initial cues
correctly may have 'contributed' to the success of shaping).   An
alternative explanation of the results is that they are due almost
entirely to verbal control.   The initial stimuli chosen for the
shaping procedure were such as to virtually ensure that the subjects
would label them as 'worm with an apple' and 'tree on a hill' (S^-
and S^+, Series I), and 'witch over broom' and 'sun breaking through
clouds' (S^- and S^+ , Series II).   Moreover, both of the labelled S^-
scenes are probably aversive to young children while the S^+ stimuli
are clearly benign.   Luria (1961) and others have shown that difficult
discriminations are more easily learned when labels are provided and
in this study it may well be the case that it is this labelling
aspect which is critical; topographic transformations may not be
necessary and, indeed, if the original stimuli could not be labelled,
might not be of any benefit.   Preliminary findings from a follow-up
study with mentally handicapped patients, conducted by the first
author of the present paper (in conjunction with S. Hobbs and L.
Tennant; see Hobbs, 1982), support this analysis and show that
explicitly providing subjects with labels for S^+ and S^- results in
even better discrimination learning than is achieved by stimulus
shaping alone.

But our argument extends beyond saying that subjects label
stimuli in stimulus shaping procedures.   Human subjects will normally
engage in this activity when any discrimination procedure is employed,
including fading and trial-and-error, and this will affect performance
for better or worse.   Thus, for example, in the study by Schilmoeller
et al., the fading procedure may have resulted in the children labelling differences between the stimuli in terms of intensity characteristics or some other idiosyncratic formulation; these may have
actively interfered with discrimination of the form-background
relationship which was necessary for the conditional discrimination.
Unfortunately, we have no information about the labels and other
formulations of the contingencies which the subjects used in any of
the discrimination conditions because the authors did not ask the
subjects about this aspect of their behaviour.   In this, as in many
other behavioural studies, it appears that the 'introspection' taboo
inherited from earlier forms of behaviourism continues to be responsible for the loss of valuable data which could help to reveal some
of the hidden, but important, determinants of behaviour.

BEHAVIOURISM OR COGNITIVISM?

The evidence from both the theory and practice of behaviour modification clearly indicates that private events play a central role in the determination of human behaviour. If to acknowledge the importance of private events is to be 'cognitive' then all behaviour modification with humans who have developed language is, or should be, cognitive. But what is to be gained or lost by adopting the conceptual apparatus of cognitivism?

It seems that the first, and perhaps most fundamental problem encountered by the aspiring cognitivist is to establish what the core concept of 'cognition' refers to. It might, for example, refer simply to covert behaviour. But in this case 'cognition' would be a subset of behaviours distinguished only by the criterion of observability; there is little reason, for example, to believe that going through the steps of solving an arithmetical problem aloud obeys different scientific laws from doing so in subaudible speech. (The point is made very well by the quotation from Ryle which occurs at the beginning of this chapter.) According to this account of the term 'cognition', however, all cognitive therapy would be behavioural!

An alternative position, necessary perhaps to justify the introduction of the term 'cognitive', would be that cognitive refers to events which are non-behavioural. The problem then is to specify what kinds of things these events are, whence they originate, and how they come into contact with behaviour. At this point, the mists of Cartesian dualism begin to gather once again, and the good work done by behaviourism in dispelling dualistic confusion appears to have been to no avail. Faced with this prospect, there is much to be said for Ryle's (1949) dismissive suggestion that '(The term) "Cognitive" belongs to the vocabulary of examination papers'.

There is too the neo-Kantian aspect of CBM whereby it adopts as its guiding dictum Epictetus' contention that 'Men are disturbed not by things but by the views they take of them' (cf. Ellis, 1970) and Castenada's (1972) declaration that 'The world is such-and-such or so-and-so only because we tell ourselves that it is the way it is' (cf. Mahoney, 1974; Meichenbaum, 1977). According to this view the way to change the world and ourselves it to recite daily the kind of self-statement commended by Emil Coue (1922) 'Day by day, in every way I am getting better and better'. The problem comes when day by day in every way I get worse and worse, and I and my world around me collapse. In this event my verbal behaviour, and perhaps anything else the cognitive therapist has told me to say, will rapidly lose credibility. As any good behaviourist would point out, the efficacy of stimulus events, such as self-statements, originates from, and is sustained by, the consequences of behaviour (cf. Ayllon and Azrin, 1964). The real world has multitudinous ways of maintaining its effectiveness despite our views or wishful thinking.

It is in relation to these basic theoretical issues, which ultimately inform practice (cf. Lowe and Higson, 1981), that the radical behaviourist approach has most to offer. It avoids the serious problems involved in a bifurcation of human activity into 'cognition' and 'behaviour', where cognition is seen as something non-behavioural and subject to different scientific principles (cf. Ullman, 1970). Rather than the world being determined by our view of it, the environment is considered to be the <u>primary</u> determinant of all behaviour, non-verbal and verbal, overt and covert. But there is room within this account for a dialectical view of the relationship between verbal and non-verbal behaviour. This may be summarised as follows: In the lifetime of the 'normal' individual, (i) the world exists prior to his being able to talk, (ii) the world, that is his particular social environment, establishes in him many skills, including the skill of being able to talk about the world and himself, and (iii) being able to speak about his interactions with the environment has a profound effect on the way he behaves; his actions and the consequences of these actions determine what he says to himself. At least in principle and to some extent in practice, radical behaviourism can account for the acquisition and maintenance of operant behaviour in animals, in humans who have not yet developed speech (e.g. Lowe, 1983; Lowe, Beasty and Bentall, 1983), and in verbal humans unable to describe to themselves particular contingencies, i.e., who are not aware (Hefferline, Keenan and Harford, 1959). It provides a framework for understanding the development and maintenance of verbal behaviour in both overt and covert forms (Skinner, 1957) and, perhaps most critically with regard to future prospects, the relationship between verbal and non-verbal behaviour. In short, it is a coherent and integrated conceptual system for clinical psychology which compares very well with its cognitive rivals.

Our wish would be for those who are working within the CBM tradition to consider seeking a philosophical and conceptual home under the radical behaviourist roof. The practical benefits, in relation to therapy, that might accrue from such a move should be considerable (cf. Lowe and Higson, 1981; Zettle and Hayes, 1982). We would also ask behaviour analysts to look objectively at the achievements of cognitive behaviour therapy, which have come about largely as a result of recognising the importance of covert behaviour. To ignore the causal role of verbal behaviour, much of which is covert, is to deny what is essentially human about our clients. It is also passing over one of the most potent means for bringing about behaviour change.

Hall, J.N., Baker, R.D. and Hutchinson, K., 1977. A controlled evaluation of token economy procedures with chronic schizophrenic patients. Behav. Res. and Ther., 15: 261-283.

Hefferline, R.F., Keenan, B. and Harford, R.A., 1959. Escape and avoidance conditioning in human subjects without their observation of the response. Science, 130: 1338-1339.

Herman, S. and Tramontana, J., 1971. Instructions and group versus individual reinforcement in modifying disruptive group behaviour. J. App. Behav. Anal., 4: 113-119.

Hobbs, S.D.W., 1982. "An investigation of the Role of Verbal Labelling in Errorless Discrimination Learning with Mentally Handicapped Adults". Research dissertation submitted to the British Psychological Society.

Homme, L., Csanzi, A., Gonzales, M. and Rechs, J., 1970. "How to use Contingency Contracting in the Classroom". Research Press, Champaign, Ill.

Horne, P.J. and Lowe, C.F., 1982. Determinants of human performance on multiple concurrent variable-interval schedules. Behav. Anal. Letters, 2: 186-187.

Kazdin, A.E., 1977. "The Token Economy: A Review and Evaluation". Plenum Press, New York.

Kelleher, R.T., 1966. Chaining and conditioned reinforcement. In: Honig, W.K. (Ed.), "Operant Behaviour: Areas of Research and Application". Appleton-Century-Crofts, New York. 160-212.

Kendalll, P.C. and Hollon, S.D., 1979. Cognitive-behavioural interventions: overview and current status. In: Kendall, P.C. and Hollon, S.D. (Eds.), "Cognitive-Behavioural Intervention: theory research and procedures". Academic Press, New York.

Kendler, H.H., 1964. The concept of the concept. In: Melton, A.W. (Ed.), "Categories of Human Learning". Academic Press, New York. 212-236.

Ledwidge, B., 1978. Cognitive-behaviour modification: a step in the wrong direction? Psychol. Bull., 85: 353-75.

Locke, E.A., 1979. Behaviour modification is not cognitive - and other myths: a reply to Ledwidge. Cog. Ther. and Res., 3: 119-125.

Lowe, C.F., 1979. Determinants of human operant behaviour: temporal control. In: Zeiler, M.D. and Harzem, P. (Eds.), "Reinforcement and the Organisaiton of Behaviour". Vol. 1: Wiley, Chichester UK.

Lowe, C.F., 1983. Radical behaviourism and human psychology. In: Davey, G.C.L. (Ed.), "Animal Models and Human Behaviour". Wiley, Chichester, UK.

Lowe, C.F., Beasty, A. and Bentall, R.P., 1983. The role of verbal behaviour in human learning: infant performance on fixed-interval schedules. J. Exper. Anal. Behav.,

Lowe, C.F. and Harzem, P., 1977. Species differences in temporal control of behaviour. J. Exper. Anal. Behav., 28: 189-201.

Lowe, C.F., Harzem, P. and Bagshaw, M., 1978. Species differences in temporal control of behaviour II: human performance.

REFERENCES

Ayllon, T. and Azrin, N.T., 1964. Reinforcement and instructions
    with mental patients. J. Exper. Anal. Behav., 7: 327-331.
Ayllon, T. and Azrin, N.H., 1968. "The Token Economy: A Motivational
    System for Therapy and Rehabilitation". Appleton-Century-Crofts,
    New York.
Baker, R., Hall, J.N., Hutchinson, K. and Bridge, G., 1977. Symptom
    changes in chronic schizophrenic patients on a token economy:
    A controlled experiment. Brit. J. Psychiat., 131: 381-393.
Bandura, A., 1977. "Social Learning Theory". Prentice Hall,
    Englewood Cliffs, N.J.
Bem, S.L., 1967. Verbal self-control: The establishment of effect-
    ive self-instruction. J. Exper. Psychol., 74: 485-491.
Bentall, R.P. and Lowe, C.F., 1982. Developmental aspects of human
    operant behaviour: the role of instructions and self-
    instructions. Behav. Anal. Letters, 2: 186.
Branch, M.N. and Malagodi, E.F., 1980. Where have all the behaviour-
    ists gone? The Behaviour Analyst, 3: 31-38.
Brigham, T.A., 1980. Self-control revisited: or why doesn't anyone
    actually read Skinner anymore? The Behaviour Analyst, 3:
    25-33.
Castaneda, C., 1972. "A Separate Reality: Further Conversations
    with Don Juan". Pocket Books, New York.
Catania, A.C., 1979. "Learning". Prentice Hall, Englewood Cliffs,
    N.J.
Catania, A.C., 1981. The flight from experimental analysis. In:
    Bradshaw, C.M., Szabadi, E. and Lowe, C.F. (Eds.) "Quantifica-
    tion of Steady-State Operant Behaviour". Elsevier/North Holland
    Biomedical Press, Amsterdam. pp. 49-64.
Cohen, M., Liebson, I. and Faillace, L.A., 1971. The role of rein-
    forcement contingencies in chronic alcoholism: an experimental
    analysis of one case. Behav. Res. and Ther., 9: 375-379.
Coue, E., 1922. "The Practice of Autosuggestion". Doubleday, New
    York.
Crowe, M.J., 1978. Behavioural approaches to marital and family
    problems. In: Gaince, R.N. and Hudson, B.L. (Eds.) "Current
    Themes in Psychiatry 1". Macmillan, London.
Cullen, C., 1981. The flight to the laboratory. The Behaviour
    Analyst, 4: 81-83.
Davey, G., 1981. "Animal Learning and Conditioning". Macmillan,
    London.
Ellis, A., 1970. "The Essence of Rational Psychotherapy: A Comp-
    rehensive Approach to Treatment". Institute of Rational
    Living, New York.
Foreyt, J.P., 1977. "Behavioural Treatments of Obesity". Pergamon
    Press, New York.
Franks, C.M. and Wilson, G.T., 1974. "Annual Review of Behaviour
    Therapy and Practice". Brunner/Mazel Publishers, New York.

J. Exper. Anal. Behav., 29: 351-361.

Lowe, C.F., Harzem, P. and Hughes, S., 1978. Determinants of operant
     behaviour in humans: some differences from animals. Quart. J.
     Exper. Psychol., 30: 373-386.

Lowe, C.F. and Higson, P.J., 1981. Self-Instructional Training and
     Cognitive Behaviour Modification: A behavioural analysis.
     In: Davey, G.C.L. (Ed.), "Applications of Conditioning Theory".
     Methuen, London.

Luria, A., 1961. "The Role of Speech in the Regulation of Normal
     and Abnormal Behaviour". Liveright, New York.

Mahoney, M.J., 1974. "Cognition and Behaviour Modification".
     Ballinger Publishing Co., Cambridge, Mass.

Mann, R.A., 1972. The behaviour-therapeutic use of contingency
     contracting to control an adult behaviour problem: weight
     control. J. App. Behav. Anal., 5: 99-109.

Mann, R.A., 1977. The behaviour-therapeutic use of contingency
     contracting to control an adult behaviour problem: weight
     control. In: Foreyt, J.P. (Ed.), "Behavioural Treatments of
     Obesity". Pergamon Press, New York.

Matthews, B.A., Shimoff, E., Catania, C. and Sagvolden, T., 1977.
     Uninstructed human responding: Sensitivity to ratio and
     interval contingencies. J. Exper. Anal. Behav., 27: 453-467.

Meichenbaum, D., 1977. "Cognitive-Behaviour Modification: An
     Integrative Approach". Plenum Press, New York.

Michael, J., 1980. Flight from behaviour analysis. The Behaviour
     Analyst, 3: 1-21.

Miller, P.M., 1972. The use of behavioural contracting in the
     treatment of alcoholism: A case report. Behav. Ther., 3:
     593-596.

Morse, W.H., 1966. Intermittent reinforcement. In: Honig, W.K.
     (Ed.), "Operant Behaviour: Areas of Research and Application".
     Appleton-Century-Crofts, New York. 52-108.

Nelson, G.L. and Cone, J.D., 1979. Multiple-baseline analysis of a
     token economy for psychiatric patients. J. App. Behav. Anal.,
     12: 255-271.

Rachlin, H., 1977. A review of M. Mahoney's Cognition and Behaviour
     Modification. J. App. Behav. Anal., 10: 369-374.

Reppucci, N. and Saunders, J., 1974. Social psychology of behaviour
     modification: problems of implementation in natural settings.
     Amer. Psychol., 29: 649-660.

Ryle, G., 1949. "The Concept of Mind". Penguin, Middlesex, England.

Schilmoeller, K.J. and Etzel, B.C., 1977. An experimental analysis
     of criterion-related and noncriterion-related cues in 'errorless'
     stimulus control procedures. In: Etzel, B.C. Le Blanc, J.M.
     and Baer, D.M. (Eds.), "New Developments in Behavioural
     Research: Theory, Method and Application". Lawrence Erlbaum
     Associates, Hillsdale, NJ.

Schilmoeller, G.L., Schilmoeller, K.J., Etzel, B.C. and LeBlanc, J.M.
     1979. Conditional discrimination after errorless and trial-
     and-error training. J. Exper. Anal. Behav., 31: 405-420.

Sidman, M. and Stoddard, L.T., 1967. The effectiveness of fading in programming a simultaneous form discrimination for retarded children. J. Exper. Anal. Behav., 12: 3-15.

Skinner, B.F., 1938. "The Behaviour of Organisms". Appleton-Century-Crofts, New York.

Skinner, B.F., 1950. Are theories of learning necessary? Psychol. Review, 57: 193-216.

Skinner, B.F., 1957. "Verbal Behaviour". Appleton-Century-Crofts, New York.

Skinner, B.F., 1969. "Contingencies of Reinforcement: A Theoretical Analysis". Appleton-Century-Crofts, New York.

Skinner, B.F., 1974. "About Behaviourism". Knopf, New York.

Sokolov, A.N., 1972. "Inner Speech and Thought". Plenum Press, New York.

Strupp, H.H., 1979. Psychotherapy research and practice: an overview. In: Garfield, S.L. and Bergin, A.E. (Eds.), "Handbook of Psychotherapy and Behaviour Change: An Empirical Analysis". (2nd edition). Wiley, New York.

Stuart, R.B., 1969. Operant interpersonal treatment for marital discord. J. Cons. and Clin. Psychol., 33: 675-682.

Stuart, R.B., 1971. Behavioural contracting within the families of delinquents. J. Behav. Ther. and Exper. Psychiat., 2: 1-11.

Suchotliff, L., Greaves, S., Stecker, H. and Berke, R., 1970. Critical variables in the token economy system. Proceedings of the 78th Annual Convention of the American Psychological Association, 5: 517-518.

Terrace, H.S., 1963. Errorless transfer of a discrimination across two continua. J. Exper. Anal. Behav., 6: 223-232.

Tharp, R.G. and Wetzel, R.T., 1969. "Behaviour Modification in the Natural Environment". Academic Press, New York.

Ullman, L.P., 1970. On cognitions and behaviour therapy. Behav. Ther., 1: 201-204.

Ulrich, R., Stachnik, T. and Mabry, J., 1966, 1970. "Control of Human Behaviour,Volumes 1,2". Scott Foresman, Glenview, Ill.

Wilson, T., 1978. Cognitive behaviour therapy: Paradigm shift or passing phase. In: Foreyt, J. and Rathjen, D. (Eds.), "Cognitive Behaviour Therapy: Research and Application". Plenum Press, New York.

Wolpe, J., 1978. Cognition and causation in human behaviour and its therapy. Amer. Psychol., 33: 437-446.

Zettle, R.D. and Hayes, S.C., 1982. Rule-governed behaviour: A potential theoretical framework for cognitive behaviour therapy. In: Kendall, P.C. (Ed.), "Advances in Cognitive Behavioural Research and Therapy (Vol. 1)". Academic Press, New York. 76-118.

LONG TERM CARE

LONG-TERM CARE - AN INTRODUCTION

F.M. McPherson

Tayside Area Clinical Psychology Department
Royal Dundee Liff Hospital
Dundee

This symposium is about long-stay psychiatric patients. The Introduction will remind you of the features of this group, will outline public policy since 1962 and will suggest the place of psychological methods in treatment and management.

THE LONG-STAY PATIENT

Size of the Problem

The usual practice now is to describe as 'long-stay' any patient who has been resident in hospital for one or more years. The Mental Health Enquiry showed that in 1974 there were about 60,000 men and women who had been resident in English mental illness hospitals for one year or more, of whom 47,000 had been there for five years or longer. When estimating the future service needs of this population, statisticians distinguish between the 'old' and 'new' long stay. The former are those patients who were admitted several years ago when treatment and management were less advanced than now. Had they fallen ill recently rather than, say, thirty years ago, they might not have been admitted to hospital at all, or might have been discharged after only a brief stay. Their numbers are, of course, declining although they will remain substantial for many years. Thus, Easson and Grimes (1976) estimated that of 72,000 'old' long stay patients in England in 1971, 28,000 would still be in hospital in 1981, 11,000 in 1991 and 4,000 at the end of the century. The 1981 figures are the equivalent of 55 beds per 100,000 population. The 'new' long stay are those patients who are currently accumulating in hospital, despite modern methods of treatment and management.

Their numbers are increasing, and Easson and Grimes (1976) estimated
that in 1981 they would require 51 in-patient beds per 100,000
population, of which 18 would be for the elderly severely mentally
infirm, and 19 for patients under 65 years of age.

Clinical Features

No systematic study has been carried out of the diagnoses of
'old' long stay patients; in any case, little weight can be placed
on the original diagnosis, made often decades ago, and most of
these patients are now too deteriorated for a standard diagnostic
interview to be useful. However, it is usually assumed that the
majority are schizophrenic. 'New' long stay patients were studied
by the MRC (Mann and Cree, 1976). Four hundred patients who had
been resident in 15 mental illness hospitals for between one and
three years were sampled. 44% were found to have a diagnosis of
'schizophrenia', 16% one of 'affective psychoses and neuroses', 14%
'senile and presenile dementia' and 7% 'personality disorder'.

Chronic schizophrenic patients are thus by far the largest of
the diagnostic groups represented among 'new' long stay patients,
and probably among the 'old' long stay also. Certainly rehabilitation practice in this country has been influenced to a significant
extent by assumptions made about chronic schizophrenia and its
management, and most writing and research has concentrated on these
patients.

Wing (1978) describes the two main features of chronic schizophrenia as being 'the clinical poverty syndrome', which is made up
of a cluster of behaviours including flattening of affect, poverty
of speech, social withdrawal, psychomotor slowness and apathy, and
'schizophrenic thought disorder' - sometimes called 'thought-process
disorder' - which can include 'knights-move' thinking, the use of
neologisms and 'word salads', and talking 'past the point'. In
addition, some chronic schizophrenic patients, either regularly or
during infrequent episodes, show the florid features typical of the
acute phase of the illness - delusions, hallucinations, bizarre and
disturbed behaviour etc.

Institutionalism

Superimposed upon these symptoms are the features of 'institutionalism'. This term refers to the gradual deterioration in
personal and social behaviour shown by many long term residents in
mental hospitals. They often develop a shambling gait, become
careless in dress, appearance, and personal hygiene, may engage in
socially embarrassing behaviour, and appear to have lost a wide

range of personal, social and vocational skills. Allied to this,
is an increasing contentment with - or more accurately, unwillingness
to leave - the institution. It is a feature of the 'new' as well as
of the 'old', long stay: thus, only 30% of the Mann and Cree (1976)
sample said that they definitely wanted to leave hospital, whereas
30% said that they definitely wished to stay. Also, as we will
discuss later, it is found not only in mental hospitals, but is a
feature of chronic schizophrenic patients in many different environments. 'Institutionalism' was first brought to general notice by
the descriptive writing of Barton (1959), Goffman (1961) and
Gruenberg (1967) and by the research of Wing and Brown (1970), who
studied female chronic schizophrenic patients in three hospitals.
Both institutionalism, and the clinical poverty syndrome, were
found to be associated with the extent of social deprivation in
each hospital, as measured by the number of possessions owned by
patients, the restrictiveness of the ward regime, amount of contact
with the outside world, and the amount of time which the patients
spent doing absolutely nothing.

Social deprivation, and hence the clinical poverty syndrome
and institutionalism, was particularly apparent in the large, old-
fashioned mental hospitals and findings such as those of Wing and
Brown (ibid.) gave rise to the hope that these chronic handicaps
could be overcome if these hospitals were improved or were replaced
by other forms of care.

PUBLIC POLICY SINCE 1962

It would be useful now to consider the policies for the long-
stay mental patient which have been promulgated - although often
not implemented - by successive British Governments over the past
20 years.

The Hospital Plan

The Report of the Royal Commission on Mental Illness and Mental
Deficiency in 1957 drew attention to the appalling conditions in
many mental hospitals of the time, and to the stigma which attached
to inpatient treatment, which often prevented successful rehabilitation. Possibly influenced by this Report, and by the statistical
research of Tooth and Brooke (1961), the Minister of Health, Mr.
Enoch Powell, announced in 1961 that a number of mental hospitals
in England and Wales would be closed, and the number of beds reduced
by about half by 1975. Although Mr. Powell referred to "setting
the torch to the funeral pyre" the actual methods by which this was
to be achieved were somewhat less inflamatory and were detailed in
'A Hospital Plan' for England and Wales published by the Ministry
of Health in 1962. Acutely-ill psychiatric patients were to be

treated in the District General Hospitals which would be built in
large numbers, each to serve a population of 100,000 - 150,000.
For those patients who did not require hospital treatment, e.g.
those with chronic mental and physical handicaps, 'the aim will be
to provide care at home and in the community'. There was to be no
place for the traditional mental hospital. The assumptions being
made were: i) that treatment in DGH's would prevent all but a
handful of acutely-ill psychiatric patients from becoming chronic,
ii) that those who did require long-term care could receive it
adequately in the community, and iii) that the great majority of
patients then in mental hospitals could be discharged.

It is important to note that at the time when 'A Hospital Plan'
became policy, there was little evidence for any of those assumptions.
The decision to replace residential care by community care was
justified by moral imperatives (Hawks, 1975) - 'community is good,
institution is bad' - although the late Richard Titmuss and more
recently Scull (1975) suspected economic motives: community care
was probably cheaper, and in any case involved the transfer of the
financial burden from central Government to the local authorities.
Tooth and Brooke (1961) had provided evidence for the third assumption, but some of the conclusions drawn from their data were soon
shown to have been invalid. They had noted the sharp decline in
long-stay patients from 1954 to 1959, had extrapolated the trend,
and had concluded that by 1975 the mental hospitals would be almost
empty. But these years were atypical, for they were marked by a
gust of therapeutic optimism, coincident with but not wholly explained by the introduction of the phenothiazenes, which has never
subsequently been repeated; the annual rate of discharge since then
has always been slower. Further, Tooth and Brooke (1961) failed to
predict the growth of the 'new' long-stay population.

Failure to Implement 'A Hospital Plan'

Although the run down of the mental hospitals has not been as
dramatic as was hoped in the early 1960's, and no large mental
illness hospital has yet been closed down, the shift in patient
population has been impressive, and the number of mental hospital
inpatients has fallen from 150,000 in 1955 to 80,000 in 1977.
Unfortunately, although 'A Hospital Plan' has been quite successful
when judged by statistical criteria, on clinical grounds it can be
said to have been something of a disaster. Clinically, the Hospital
Plan policy depended upon the District General Hospital psychiatric
units coping with almost all acute psychiatric illness, and upon
adequate community care being available to the chronic population.
However, despite occasional, local successes, the DGH units have
not over the country as a whole, resulted in a major change in the
way in which patients are managed. The Report of the Royal Commission on the NHS (1979) commented that: 'The relatively small size

of the DGH units, the lack of money to create many more of them, and the nature and extent of the patient populations which the psychiatric services have had to continue to look after, have frustrated (the policy). Some DGH units have been selective either in their admission policies or about those for whom they would continue to care, and the mental hospitals have had to receive those patients whom the DGH units have thought were unsuitable in the first place or whom they had failed to cure' (para. 10.57).

Secondly, and more crucially, the great increase in local authority provision on which the whole community care policy depends has simply not happened. Despite clear evidence of this, the DHSS appeared to continue with its plan to run-down the mental hospitals. Thus, Better Services for the Mentally Ill (DHSS, 1975) reaffirmed the policy of community orientated care: 'We believe that the failures and problems are at the margins and that the basic concept remains valid' (para. 2.17). They were wide margins. 'Better Services' estimated (conservatively in the opinion of many) that the number of local authority day care places required for the mentally ill was 30,000 whereas the number in existence in 1974 was only 5,000 - a short fall of 83%. The short fall in residential places was 67% (4,000 in existence, 12,000 required). In 'Priorities for Health and Personal Social Services in England', the policy was again reaffirmed, and it was also vigorously promoted by bodies such as MIND. However, apart from exhortation, no practical steps were taken to ensure that resources, and not merely patients, were transferred from the NHS to local authorities, or to increase by some other means the overall level of spending by social services departments on the mentally ill.

Consequences of this failure

As a consequence of this miss-match between policy and provision, tens of thousands of patients have been discharged into communities whose resources are grossly inadequate to provide acceptable levels of care. Creer and Wing (1974) found that few of their samples of discharged schizophrenic patients had any contact with social workers or other professional staff. Instead, the objective and subjective burdens were borne by their relatives, of whom 24% considered that their health and well-being had been 'very severely' impaired by the experience. Another 14% considered themselves to have suffered 'severe' impairment and only 15% reported no adverse consequences. Other studies have reported the deteriorating psychiatric, social and physical condition of those many discharged patients who have become institutionalised in seaside boarding houses, lodgings or poorly-staffed and equipped local authority homes - whose dormitories are sometimes as large and stark as any back ward.

A further consequence has been that, because the long-term

goal was to close the mental hospitals, Health Authorities have been
reluctant to spend any money on them. There have been long periods
during the last 20 years when NHS Revenue and Capital Expenditure
on the mentally ill, as a percentage of total NHS expenditure, has
actually been falling. The cost per patient week of patients in
mental illness hospitals remains well below that of general hospitals
- in my own District, in 1979/80 it was £151 in the teaching psychiatric hospital and £426 in the teaching general hospital. The
Royal Commission Report observed that: 'New hospitals have not been
built and old ones have been inadequately maintained and upgraded
.... the morale of staff in these hospitals has been damaged, and
recruitment to what have seemed to be condemned relics of the past
has been affected' (para. 10.59). A succession of mental hospital
scandals, covering the country from Whittingham to St. Augustines,
has been one consequence.

Future Plans

     Possibly in response to the Royal Commission's criticisms,
there appears recently to be evidence of a more purposeful approach
by the DHSS. It is regularly being emphasised that the mental
illness hospitals will continue for many years to have an important
role in the provision of services for the long-stay patient. And
in the consultative document 'Care in the Community' (DHSS, 1981)
the DHSS outlined some practical plans for the reallocation of
resources from the NHS to the community. Any systematic planning
would be welcome, for the past 20 years have indeed been a sorry
tale of ineptitude and lack of resolution both nationally and,
almost everywhere, locally by those in charge of health and personal
social services, and by their political masters.

SOME RESEARCH EVIDENCE

     It is obvious from even a cursory examination that policies
for the mentally ill in recent years have been influenced more by
moral attitudes and economic and administrative considerations
than by scientifically-based evidence concerning the efficacy of
different types of programme, or the types of patient for whom, e.g.,
community as opposed to hospital care would be appropriate. However,
some evidence does exist, and although it is not my purpose to
review the literature comprehensively, it might serve as a useful
introduction to the symposium to remind you of several conclusions
which the literature does permit to be drawn with some confidence.

Possibility of Discharge

     Inpatient hospital provision is required for a proportion even of the 'new' long-stay population, who have handicaps which prevent them from being discharged. For example, Mann and Cree (1976) estimated that while 70% of their sample could have been discharged if appropriate community facilities existed, the remainder required the intensive care which only hospital can provide; of these, about half would need long-term care; Todd et al. (1976) found that of 261 schizophrenic patients admitted in 1967-70, 33 were still in hospital, of whom only three were well enough to be discharged.

Reduction of institutionalism

Merely transferring patients from the back wards to the community does not necessarily produce dramatic improvement, even in the features of institutionalism; indeed, there may even be harmful effects. Although much of the success of the early rehabilitation programmes was due to the changes which they brought about in the patients' social environment (Wing, 1978), more recent research has led to the early optimism being tempered. Institutionalism seems to depend in part upon factors 'within' the individual, and can thus develop and be maintained in almost any social environment. For example, Creer and Wing (1974) reported that of two samples of chronic schizophrenic patients living in the community, 74% showed social withdrawal of 'very' or 'rather' marked severity, 56% and 54% respectively showed similar degrees of underactivity, and low conversation. In addition, it has been known for some time that social stimulation can have harmful effects on chronic schizophrenic patients. Wing et al. (1964) noted that during rehabilitation some patients suffered a return of the delusions and hallucinations which had not been present for some time. Brown, Leff and their colleagues (e.g. Brown et al., 1972) have isolated one apparently important variable by showing that the amount of 'expressed emotion' in the families of long-stay schizophrenic patients had a crucial effect on their clinical condition.

Psychological methods employed with long-stay patients

Within conventional treatment settings, i.e. the psychiatric hospital and its aftercare facilities, behavioural methods are more effective than alternatives both in effecting successful discharge to the community, and in improving the status of long-stay hospital residents. The classic study of Paul and Lentz (1977) showed the superiority of 'social learning' methods over milieu therapy and the normal hospital environment, especially when followed by after-care consultation. Token economies have been shown to be highly effective in promoting positive behaviour and in reducing bizarre and disruptive behaviour among institutionalised patients (Azrin, 1977) although as Douglas Fraser will tell us, the 'crucial ingred-ients' of token economies have not yet been identified. Social

skills training programmes have also been shown to be valuable (e.g.
Goldstein et al., 1975).

To sum up, therefore, it appears that national policies for
long-stay psychiatric patients have been based on the fallacies
that all of them can be discharged from hospital, and that merely
to discharge them is sufficient to produce major improvement in their
functioning. However, significant numbers will remain in hospital,
many of them 'new' long-stay patients with severe handicaps which
will respond only to specialist intervention. Many of the others
will survive in the community only if greater resources than at
present are expended, and only if they receive adequate rehabilitation
and after-care. With the long-stay residents, the rehabilitation
patients, and the discharged group, psychological approaches such
as behavioural methods and social skills training are of crucial
value.

REFERENCES

Barton, R., 1959. "Institutional Neurosis". Wright Bros., Bristol.
Brown, G.W., Birley, J.L.T. and Wing, J.K., 1972. Influence of
     family life on the cause of schizophrenic disorders: a
     replication. Brit. J. Psychiat., 121: 241.
Creer, C. and Wing, J.K., 1974. "Schizophrenia at Home". National
     Schizophrenic Fellowship, Surbiton.
Department of Health, 1962. "A Hospital Plan for England and Wales",
     Cmnd 1604. HMSO, London.
Department of Health and Social Security, 1975. "Better Services for
     the Mentally Ill", Cmnd 6233. HMSO, London.
Department of Health and Social Security, 1976. "Priorities for
     Health and Social Services in England: a consultative document".
     HMSO, London.
Department of Health and Social Security, 1981. "Care in the Comm-
     unity - A Consultative Document on Moving Resources for Care in
     England", HC(81)9, HMSO, London.
Easson, R.J. and Grimes, J.A., 1974. In-patient care for the mentally
     ill: a statistical study of future provision, Health Trends,
     8: 13.
Goffman, E., 1961. "Asylums". Penguin, Hamondsworth.
Goldstein, A.P., Gershaw, N.J. and Sprafkin, R.P., 1975. Structured
     learning therapy - skill training for schizophrenics. Schizo-
     phrenia Bull., 1: 83.
Gruenberg, E.M., 1967. The social breakdown syndrome - some origins.
     Amer. J. Psychiat., 123: 12.
Hawks, D.V., 1975. Community care: an analysis of assumptions.
     Brit. J. Psychiat., 127: 276.
Kazdin, A.E., 1977. "The Token Economy". Plenum Press, New York.
Mann, S.A. and Cree, W., 1976. 'New' long-stay patients: a
     national sample survey of fifteen mental hospitals in England

and Wales. <u>Psychol. Med.</u>, 6: 603.

Paul, G.L. and Lentz, R.J., 1977. "Psychosocial Treatment of Chronic
    Mental Patients: Milieu versus Social-Learning Programmes".
    Harvard University Press, Cambridge, Mass.

Scull, A.T., 1975. "Decarceration: Community Treatment and the
    Deviant. A Radical View". Prentice Hall, New York.

Todd, N.A., Bennie, E.H. and Carlisle, J.M., 1976. Some features of
    the 'new long-stay' male schizophrenics. <u>Brit. J. Psychiat.</u>,
    129: 424.

Tooth, G.C. and Brooke, E.M., 1961. Trends in the mental inpatient
    population and their effects on future planning. <u>The Lancet.</u>
    ii: 70.

Wing, J.K., 1978. "Schizophrenia". Academic Press, London.

Wing, J.K. and Brown, G., 1970. "Institutionalism and Schizophrenia".
    Cambridge University Press, Cambridge.

Wing, J.K.,Monck, E., Brown, G.W., and Carstairs, G.M., 1964.
    Morbidity in the community of schizophrenic patients discharged
    from London mental hospitals in 1959. <u>Brit. J. Psychiat.</u>,
    110: 10.

INITIATIVES IN LONG-TERM RESIDENTIAL CARE

John Hall

Department of Clinical Psychology
Warneford Hospital
Oxford

The nineteenth century saw an explosion in the growth of public
provision of residential facilities for the physically and mentally
sick. Earlier centuries had seen small-scale provision of private
infirmaries and asylums. Yet both types of institution grew in the
nineteenth century at a larger rate than the rate of population
growth, and the size of individual institutions grew during the
century, so that, for example, the average size of British public
lunatic asylums grew from 116 in 1827 to 1,072 in 1910. Arising
from this rich provision of buildings, care of the physically and
mentally ill has been dominated by hospital provision, so that
hospital medicine rather than community medicine, has been historically the high status branch of the profession.

While most people enter hospital, hostel or residential home
in any one admission for a relatively short period of time, a small
proportion of those admitted go on to stay for a considerable period
of time. The periods of time in hospital are longest for the
severely mentally handicapped, who may still enter hospital at a
very early age, and for the mentally ill, when a chronic psychiatric
condition does not necessarily imply any reduced expectation of life.
The physically handicapped are often at risk from medical complic-
ations of their handicap, and the "geriatric" patient enters
residential care at an already advanced age. Even so, members of
both these latter groups may still be receiving residential care
for several years.

People enter long-term residential care for a number of reasons,
apart from the requirement that the full panoply of hospital services
be readily available. They may come in because the family member
who has cared for them is ill, or has indeed died. Possibly the

241

day care facilities in the locality are very poor, and no suitable intermediate level of support, short of residential care, is available. Certainly it is difficult to set clear criteria which will differentiate, for any given clinical problem, between those people who are in hospital and those who are cared for at home.

In any one institution, and indeed in any one ward or unit within an institution, there will be a wide range of physical and psychological needs of the residents which should be met. The way in which these needs are met is determined in part by how those needs are conceptualised: can they be prevented, can they be cured, or can they be relieved.

Smith (1977) has suggested that there are other ways of approaching the medical task: prevention, cure and alleviation. Specialists in public health might claim that the achievement of preventative medicine, such as large-scale immunisation programmes or monitoring of the purity of public water supplies, has played a far larger part in reduction of morbidity and mortality than curative medicine. However, cure is still possible for a number of conditions. Alleviation is the remaining approach to those who cannot be cured, and accordingly alleviation is the approach most often taken in long-term care. Yet alleviation itself is confounded with the concept of care. To care for someone has the ring of passivity, and indeed much long-term care is passive, with little expectation of positive benefit to, or change in, the patient.

Does long-term care have to be passive? Historically long-term institutions have tended to attract less resources than the more glamorous acute treatment institutions. Most health-care professions are trained in acute settings, and come to expect relatively rapid response to treatment, so that the recruitment of good calibre professional staff to work in long-term cases is often extremely difficult: a tragically clear example of this problem is the difficulty in finding consultant medical staff to work whole-time in mental handicap. Yet despite these problems, there is now evidence of increasing interest in the nature of long-term care, and in its improvement. This evidence is to be found from several different sources: it is not exclusively psychological but it lends increasing support to the value of a psychological approach to the design and implementation of regimes of long-term care.

Identification of the specific needs of the handicapped

Psychologists have long been suggesting the relevance of behavioural, rather than diagnostic formulations of the needs of individual patients. Psychological approaches to improving long-term care thus encompasses the identification of the current behavioural assets, deficits, and deviations of patients, and the derived identification of clear goals of treatment and care (Hall, 1981). It is accordingly highly significant that the World Health Organisation have now developed an International Classification of Impairments, Disabilities and Handicaps (ICIDH) to complement the well established International Classification of Diseases (ICD). Wood (1980) has outlined the reasons for the development of ICIDH, and points out that "the burden of illness is coming to be dominated by chronic and disabling conditions". He discusses the restricting effects of the medical model of illness, which stops short of the consequences of illness, and the value of the new system for reflecting change in chronic or disabling conditions.

Apart from considering the presenting form of the patient's problems, it may also be useful to consider their etiology. Wing and Brown (1970) developed a three-fold categorisation of the causes of chronic psychiatric disability. One category they consider is the pre-morbid state of the patient: people who have a chronic course to their psychiatric illness are less intelligent and have poorer occupational records than those with a less chronic course. Thus there may be a "ceiling" to the effectiveness of any rehabilit- ation or alleviative procedures which could be recognised in advance rather than a failure to respond being attributed to the psychiatric condition itself. Apart from Wing and Brown's other two categories of primary and secondary handicaps, there may be handicaps caused specifically by living in an institution, or caused as side-effects of psychotropic medication. The more precisely the cause and nature of the handicap of those in long-term care can be specified, the more readily can change be detected, and useful intervention procedures recognised.

Statements of clear overall objectives

It is not uncommon to find staff who work in long-term care settings who have no overall policy or aims to guide them in their work. Apart from approaches based on identification of individual need, another way of approaching the alleviative task is to formulate some superordinate goal, from which subordinate targets may be derived. "Community care" is one such goal, implying that community care is good, and institutional care is bad. This assumption has much popular appeal, but itself rests upon a number of other un- tested assumptions, so it has been said that community care has been pursued more as a moral endeavour, than as a rationally analysed objective (Hawks, 1975).

A related overall goal is the choice of the "least restrictive environment", which has guided much of the deinstitutionalisation movement in the United States, especially since the classic legal judgement of Wyatt v. Stickney in Alabama in 1972. Bachrach (1980) similarly examines the semantic confusion surrounding the use of this concept, and the need for a more complex conceptual approach to this issue.

It is not then surprising to find that there are some overall goals widely supported and used, which have little empirical support. Russell Barton (1975) identifies seven main causes of the "institutional neurosis" syndrome, and suggests seven corresponding remedies. One of the causes he states to be lack of personal events and possessions and hence the corresponding remedy would be the provision of such events and possessions. Accordingly many institutions take trouble to individualise patients' counterpanes on their beds, and encourage patients to array pictures and ornaments near their bed. Yet little is known about the psychological value of such individualisation to long-term patients, or the benefits following the introduction of such personalisation of the patient's environment (Slater and Gill, 1981).

Superordinate goals can be helpful in providing an overall guiding philosophy to a ward or unit, and in preventing a mundane preoccupation with low-level short-term goals. The assumptions underlying such goals and the degree of empirical support for them, require examination. It needs to be recognised that the set of subordinate goals logically deduced from one superordinate goal may be incompatible with the set of subordinate goals derived from another equally defensible and humane superordinate goal. Whatever the merits of the goals, the more public they are made, the greater the chance that they will be adhered to.

Monitoring progress

Change, when it occurs, in long-term settings tends to happen slowly. This means that quite substantial change may occur in a given patient but may not be identified by the direct-care staff in day-to-day contact with the patient. This raises the need for some system of regular review or monitoring of progress of residents.

Monitoring is best conducted along some form of guidelines, which are common to both internal and external monitoring agencies. Internal agencies - the institutional staff of various grades and levels should be the best informed professionally and technically, but will also be the most involved personally. It is often useful to supplement such monitoring by involving an external agency such as the lay managers of the institution, or an inspectorial/advisory body, such as the Health Advisory Service in the British National Health Service.

The worry of many professional staff is that such monitoring may become in itself a time-consuming activity with little useful outcome. This risk can be minimised by paring down the main issues

kept under regular review so that they comprise the most important
aspects of the service, or those aspects suspectd to be most deficient in the individual ward or unit so monitored. There are
several outline checklists or guidelines to assist in this task.
The "Nodder" Report (Department of Health and Social Security, 1980)
gives as appendices a model standard document and the derived check-
list, and in chapter three of the main report, discusses how standards and monitoring systems can be set up and implemented. A further
implication of the Nodder Report is that preventing bad practice,
or reducing the risk of abuse to patients is one goal of such
monitoring, but is not the same goal as positively encouraging good
practice. Sadly it has to be acknowledged that preventing bad
practice, or at least careless or indifferent practice requires
constant vigilance in most longer-term care settings.

Examination of the caring environment

Behaviour can only occur to the extent that the physical
environment permits it to happen. Thus a whole range of rehabilita-
tive activities depend on the availability of appropriate rooms,
facilities, or items of equipment, such as quiet private rooms for
writing, money to relearn cash-economy skills, or cookers or washing
machines to relearn domestic skills. If the physical environment is
deficient, then an apparent deficit in the patient may be due to the
inadequacies or restrictions of the setting in which he lives.

This suggests that close examination, indeed assessment and
"treatment" of the environment may produce more gains than direct
treatment of the patient. Moos (1973) has suggested that there are
six major ways in which characteristics of environment are related
to indices of behaviour. These include, for example, the architect-
ural or physical design variables of the setting, and the organisational structure of the environment. Polsky and Chance (1980) looked
at the way in which chronic schizophrenic patients showed preference
for particular chairs or areas of a ward, and found that the patient
who interacted least on the ward showed no preference for any
particular area of the ward, a finding consistent with some previous
research in the same field. This suggests that simplistic analyses
of patient-environment interactions fail to do justice to the finer
detail of "ward ecology".

Another problem in the design of therapeutic environments is
that of the failure of patients who have convincingly displayed
skills in one setting to exhibit them in another setting to which
they are transferred or discharged. This generalisation problem is
common to many modes of treatment, but is illustrated most clearly
by the care needed to successively modify token economy programmes
so they gradually approximate more and more closely to the contingencies of the "real" world. Failure to modify the programmes in

this way can lead to catastrophic failure of transfer of learning
from even one ward to another. Shepherd (1980) discusses some of
the problems which this phenomena creates in the treatment setting.

Examination of the caring personnel

Even the most superficial analysis of long-term care shows that
the staff who are in greatest contact with patients tend to be the
least well-trained, at least in terms of formal job-relevant
qualifications and experience. Kushlick (1976) has proposed a
classification of Direct Care, or DC staff, ranging from DC 24 hours
(the natural family, if still in contact with the patient) to DC
10 minutes (the specialised professional staff, such as doctors).
On this analysis, it is likely that the staff who have the greatest
degree of impact on the patients will be the self-same least well-
trained staff.

It is accordingly alarming to find out how at least some such
staff feel about their work. Moores and Grant (1977) found that
many nursing staff in hospitals for the mentally handicapped are
not involved in their work. A factor analysis of their attitudes
suggested three main factors: the level of expectation of the
patients' accomplishments, intolerance and involvement.

A major task in long-term care is accordingly to produce at
least some degree of communication between the staff concerned and
hopefully active co-operation as well. Attempts to do this need to
take account of the differing concepts of different professions.
Alaszewski (1979) looked at the role concepts of occupational
therapists and physiotherapists who were working in rehabilitation.
While the occupational therapists tended to favour holistic -
considering the whole person - approaches and to see their interventions as alleviative, the physiotherapists were more technique
orientated, and emphasised the curative aspects of their job. Thus
two apparently similar professions and in this case professions
which are contemplating merging into one common profession, approach
the task of rehabilitation with different assumptions. Perhaps with
this in mind, the creation of a "multi-purpose rehabilitation
therapist" has been proposed (Helander, 1980). While a common
training may not be the solution, some degree of joint training
experience could reduce some of the suspicion and ignorance that
exists between professions, as noted by the Nodder Report.

Given the availability of staff with the appropriate skills,
they then need to be organised and allocated effectively. This
implies the existence of some sort of criterion of work load or
dependency, so that a given number of staff can be allocated as
equitably as possible over a given number of patients. This
exercise was attempted in the Jay Report (Department of Health and

Social Security, 1979), which proposed a totally new scheme of
training direct-care staff to work with the mentally handicapped.
One effect of this exercise was the recommendation, based on dependency studies, that the number of such direct-care staff should
be doubled from 30,000 to 60,000!

Given the right number of direct-care staff in the right place,
they still need to do the right things. Studies in staff-patient
interaction show that levels of interaction in long-term care
settings may be low and that simply increasing the numbers of staff
may improve staff-staff interaction more than staff-patient interaction. The concept of engagement has been developed to allow levels
of involvement between patients and activities, or other people, to
be evaluated. Porterfield and Blunden (1978) have introduced a
"Room Manager" procedure into activity sessions for the levels of
engagement.

Considerable ingenuity may be needed from staff in many long-
term care settings, since there may not be enough of them, and they
may lack necessary facilities. A fascinating feature of some long-
stay wards is the astounding degree of success or improvement in
staff functioning that can be produced by a single enthusiastic
sister or charge nurse. Perhaps more than in the acute setting, a
willingness to innovate or 'have a bash' is welcome. An important
factor may then be the extent to which such an enthusiast is per-
mitted to innovate in content alone, or to make innovation in their
role and function as well. Schein (1971) has distinguished between
content innovation and role innovation and has drawn attention to
the value of role innovation in settings such as long-term care,
when traditional role prescriptions may simply not fit the reality
of the skills and calibre of the people available.

Definition of the type of Intervention

It is common to describe therapeutic procedures as if they were
some sort of package that could be adequately defined by reference
only to the "package" term. Thus references are made to token
economy programmes and therapeutic community regimes, as if the use
of such terms is sufficient description of the practices that go on
within such regimes.

Yet consideration of different token economy programmes for
example, can show how different two such programmes can be. A
token programme for profoundly mentally handicapped patients will
probably concentrate on improving the deficits of a group of people
with very limited social functioning who appear to respond to a very
limited range of environmental events, and whose lives are led
largely within a very sheltered setting.

A token programme for disturbed adolescents, on the other hand, may have to focus on the control of the deviant or disruptive behaviour of a group of people highly sensitive to the opinion and influence of their peers, highly aware of what is going on in the world about them, and intervention must take account of the home environment to which they will ultimately return.

Thus, rather than use blanket terms on their own for such programmes, it may be helpful, firstly, to additionally describe the nature of the client or patient group being treated, the nature of the behaviour which is the target of the programme, and the nature of the setting in which the interaction occurs.

Secondly, it may be helpful to identify a programme by main ingredients of it, rather than the 'type' or 'category' of inter-vention which describes it. For example, the main components of an intervention may consist of an initial assessment of the patient, followed by detailed goal-planning which may be much more controlled and consistently controlled than the subsequent reinforcement regime, so that the assessment/goal planning phase of the programme is the major component of it. Similarly, an intervention may vary in the intensity with which it is applied, depending on both the availability of staff to conduct the programme, and on the relevance of an intensive approach to the patient problem being treated. Thus it may be more important for a physically handicapped patient to have sporadic episodes of high-intensity treatment, thus encouraging at least occasional requirement of maximum effort, while for a person suffering from schizophrenia it may be more important to provide a moderate level of intensity of stimulation for a longer period of the day specifically avoiding any intensive stimulation (Leff et al., 1982). Such factors as overall levels and scheduling of particip-ation in activities, variety of activity and material and social feedback and reinforcement from staff may need to be identified as key ingredients and definers of the type of intervention appropriate in particular settings.

Constraints upon the process of change

One of the major findings of the growing literature on institu-tional change is that introducing and maintaining change is costly. It is costly in staff time, because often new procedures have to be learned and tried, if only for an interim period. It is costly in intellectual effort, because problems have to be anticipated, acknowledged and resolved under circumstances when there is little clear guidance on what to do. It can be costly in social terms, as staff groups who have previously jogged along happily together now divide into the progressives and the diehards. While Georgiades and Phillimore (1975) draw attention to the myth of the "hero innovator", there may be an opposing figure of the "hero stabiliser", who is as

invested personally in maintaining the status quo as the innovator
is in creating change.

Since change is costly, more resources are demanded from both
staff and patients than in an unchanging setting. These resources
may be material, and in particular may involve the availability of
more staff. A careful appraisal of the manpower available to the
agent of change, and the possibility of more people becoming
available, is the main resource issue to be settled before change
is initiated. Simple staff numbers are not enough, however: people
must be free to do the right things, and be in the right places and
this often requires an examination of the relationship between all
the various people involved, and how some overall cohesion can be
achieved in their efforts. It then becomes helpful to analyse these
relationships: can a person prescribe the activities which another
does, can he manage the work of another, or can he only co-ordinate
it? In health care settings surprisingly complex variants of these
relationships may exist, and similarly there may be confusion about
the way in which these people meet together. Are they a true team,
meeting together in a way that permits face-to-face communication,
or are they only a network, never meeting all together but still
reliant on each other for effective functioning (Rowbottom and Hey,
1978)?

A number of writers have made detailed suggestions about how
to change institutions (Reppucci and Saunders, 1974; Towell, 1981).
Among these suggestions are several which essentially are consequences of the recognition that change is costly. Thus the proposal
that "change agents" should create a "critical mass" of associates
to give team support, is a recognition of the personal demands that
change places upon people. Other suggestions are more specific,
like the reference to the "port-of-entry" problem: this refers to
the initial "honeymoon" period, during which the newly-introduced
innovator-to-be is closely watched, and during which important
expectations and attitudes may be established. It may be important
to have documentary support for proposals being made. Carefully
worded and carefully distributed reports and proposals which are
prepared early on in a programme can be invaluable reference points
if the going becomes tough, and doubts set in.

What initiatives are possible

One of the strongest challenges to develop new patterns of
long-term residential care comes, paradoxically enough, from a group
of people who receive very little such care. This group is the
dossers and destitute, apparent in the centres of most major cities.
The work of the Cyrenians, the Salvation Army, and other similar
organisations shows how large is this problem and how little the
resources or imagination devoted to it. This group of (largely)

men is characterised by their active resistance to enquiry and offers
of help, although many of them are in poor health and with major
psychiatric disabilities. The age of onset among the destitute is
dropping, and the evidence is that their numbers are increasing
(Leach, 1979). Meeting the needs of this group would require a
considerable degree of co-operation between voluntary, health and
social agencies and would require a marked degree of imagination and
innovation to design and provide a pattern of care for them.

What initiatives, then, are possible in long-term residential care?

1. A reconsideration of the classification of the problems presented
   by patients and residents. A move away from a medical disease
   model to a disability/impairment model can give more direction
   to treatment of the chronically ill and handicapped patients.

2. An appropriate use of superordinate or high level goals of long-
   term care. While superordinate goals themselves need to be
   critically evaluated in terms of their relevance to a particular
   client group, they give cohesion and overall purpose to procedures
   which can otherwise appear fragmented and pointless.

3. A recognition of the value of some form of positive and open
   monitoring of the progress of patients and indeed the performance
   of staff. Positive, because otherwise we only notice the failures. Open, because otherwise day-to-day contact can blunt
   sensitivity to the individual needs of patients, so that an
   outside view preserves a sense of proportion and external reality
   in the appraisal of what is really going on.

4. A greater interest in the physical environment of the institution.
   How do residents use the spaces and facilities available to them,
   and what attributes of that environment contribute to a fuller
   and more varied use of it?

5. A recognition of the key role of staff, most of all the direct-
   care staff in greatest contact with the residents. Do they
   consider themselves involved in decisions which affect their
   and their patients' lives? Are they equipped with the skills
   to help their patients, and encouraged to employ those skills?
   Are any changes of role necessary to bring staff and patients
   together in the most appropriate way?

6. An analysis of the ingredients of therapeutic regimes to identify
   those which are active in bringing about therapeutic benefit in
   a particular setting. The emphasis of regime design and maintenance can then be modified to pay most attention to those
   ingredients which really work.

7. A greater amount of attention to the organisational systems and
    administrative networks which support good care and permit
    innovation.

    There are uncertainties about the future of long-term residential
care. Certainly, many of the older hospitals, some of them old poor-
law institutions, are too large and ill-adapted to provide the pattern
of care possible in smaller and modern purpose-built units. Yet
economic factors alone mean that alternative accomodation is unlikely
to be provided in the forseeable future, and the present facilities
are likely to remain the backbone of residential care services at
least until the end of this century. This does not mean that institutional care practices need go unchanged. Kathleen Jones has
pointed out that we are much clearer about what we are running away
from in this field, than where we are running to. David Towell (1978)
has commented that we are not exactly running anywhere! At least
there are some signposts available to guide a walk in some of the
directions outlined here.

REFERENCES

Alaszewski, A., 1979. Rehabilitation, the remedial therapy profess-
    ions and social policy. Social Science and Medicine, 13:
    431-443.
Bachrach, L.L., 1980. Is the least restrictive environment always
    the best? - sociological and semantic implications. Hospital
    and Community Psychiat., 31: No. 2, 97.
Barton, R., 1975. "Institutional Neurosis". John Wright, Bristol.
Department of Health and Social Security. 1979. Report of the
    Committee of Enquiry into mental handicap nursing and care.
    (Jay Report) Cmnd 7468. HMSO, London.
Department of Health and Social Security. 1980. Organisation and
    management problems of mental illness hospitals: report of a
    working group (Nodder Report). HMSO, London.
Georgiades, N.J. and Phillimore, L., 1975. The myth of the hero-
    innovator and alternative strategies for organisational change.
    In: Kierne, C.C. and Woodford, E.P. (Eds.), "Behaviour Modifi-
    cation with the Severely Retarded". Associated Scientific
    Publishers, Amsterdam.
Hall, J.N., 1981. Psychological assessment. In: Wing, J.K. and
    Morris, B., "Handbook of Psychiatric Rehabilitation Practice".
    Oxford University Press, Oxford.
Hawks, D.V., 1975. Community care: an analysis of assumptions.
    Brit. J. Psychiat., 127: 276-285.
Helander, E., 1980. Towards a multi-purpose rehabilitation therapist.
    Rehabilitation Great Britain, 1: 26-29.
Kushlick, A., 1976. Evidence to the committee of inquiry into mental
    handicap nursing and care from the Health Care Evaluation
    Research Team, Winchester. Unpublished research report. Health

Care Research Team, Winchester.

Leach, J., 1979. Providing for the destitute. In: wing, J.K. and Olsen, R. (Eds.), "Community Care for the Mentally Disabled". Oxford University Press, Oxford.

Leff, J., Kuipers, L. and Berkowitz, R., 1982. A controlled trial of social intervention in the families of schizophrenic patients. Brit. J. Psychiat., 141: 121-134.

Moores, B. and Grant, G.W.B., 1977. Feelings of alienation among nursing staff in hospitals for the mentally handicapped. Int. J. Nursing Studies, 14: 5-12.

Moos, R.H., 1973. Conceptualisation of human environments. Amer Psychol., 28: No.8. 652-665.

Polsky, R.H. and Chance, M.R.A., 1980. Social interaction and the use of space on a ward of long-term psychiatric patients. J. Nervous and Mental Disease, 168: 550-555.

Porterfield, J. and Blunden, R., 1978. Establishing an activity period and individual skill training with a day setting for profoundly mentally handicapped adults. Research Report No. 6. Mental Handicap in Wales Applied Research Unit, Cardiff.

Reppucci, A. and Saunders, J.T., 1974. Social psychology of behaviour modification: problems of implementation in natural settings. Amer. psychol., September: 649-660.

Rowbottom, R. and Hey, A., 1978. Organisation of services for the mentally ill: working paper. Brunel Institute of Organisational and Social Studies, Uxbridge.

Schein, E.H., 1971. Occupational socialisation in the professions: the case of role innovation. J. Psychiat. Res., 8: 521-530.

Shepherd, G., 1980. The treatment of social difficulties in special environments. In: Feldman, P. and Orford, J. (Eds.), "Psychological Problems: the Social Context". Wiley, Chichester.

Slater, R. and Gill, A., 1981. Environmental personalisation in institutional settings. Paper presented at 12th International Congress of Gerontology, Hamburg.

Smith, A., 1977. The unfaced facts. New Universities Quarterly: Health Care and the Community, 31: 133-145.

Towell, D., 1978. Large institutions - problems and solutions. Health and Soc. Services Review, October: 359-367.

Towell, D., 1981. Challenges in the management of long-term and community care. (Series of 4 articles). Health and Social Services Journal. July 31: 921-922. August 7: 964-965. August 14: 1000-1001. August 21: 1026-1027.

Wing, J.K. and Brown, G.W., 1970. "Institutionalism and Schizophrenia". Cambridge University Press, Cambridge.

Wood, P.H.N., 1980. Appreciating the consequences of disease: the international classification of impairments, disabilities and handicaps. WHO Chronicle, 34: 376-380.

FROM TOKEN ECONOMY TO SOCIAL INFORMATION SYSTEM: THE EMERGENCE OF

CRITICAL VARIABLES

Douglas Fraser

Senior Clinical Psychologist
Tayside Area Clinical Psychology Department
Royal Dundee Liff Hospital
Dundee DD2 5NF

"That a high-level technology calls for a high level of humanism must not deter us from the task of developing both capabilities". Thomas S. Ball (1968, p. 232).

The long-term wards of psychiatric hospitals are characterised by an extremely low level of social stimulation. In addition, a widespread mood of apathy may all too often be apparent both in the behaviour of the patients and in the behaviour of those who are responsible for their rehabilitation. This apathy on the part of the patients is seen to result from the debilitating effects that prevailing institutional practices have upon individuals. Wing and Brown (1970) have argued that a substantial proportion of the morbidity shown by long-term patients is a direct product of their environment. They have shown that an impoverished physical and social environment is very highly correlated with what they term a "clinical poverty syndrome". That is to say, patients under such circumstances tend to exhibit social withdrawal, a lack of or inappropriateness of emotional responsiveness and poverty of speech. Basic self-care skills such as dressing, washing and feeding may be partially lost and there is usually a marked deterioration in former occupational skills. The apathy on the part of the caring staff in such situations may be due to the fact that traditional approaches such as milieu therapy and occupational therapy have made little headway in tackling these problems. It is perhaps surprising then to find that a system which has evolved over the past fourteen years and which has achieved considerable success in this area has been greeted in some quarters with unbridled acclaim and in others with severe scepticism. The system is usually referred to as the token economy and it represents a large scale application of operant

learning principles to the modification of disordered or dysfunctional behaviour.

Bandura (1969) has described the three major characteristics
of token economy programmes:

1. Behaviour necessary for efficient day-to-day functioning (e.g.
   appropriate social responses, attention to personal care,
   performance of simple domestic tasks etc.) are specified as
   responses to be strengthened.

2. A form of currency (usually plastic or metal tokens) is
   established. Presentation of these tokens to the patient is
   made contingent upon the performance of adaptive behaviours.

3. An exchange system is instituted in which a specified number
   of tokens is required for the purchase of various desired
   objects (e.g. sweets and cigarettes) activities (e.g. watching
   television) and privileges (e.g. access to privacy).

This process of linking behaviour which occurs with a low
frequency (social interaction, personal care etc.) to behaviour
which occurs with a high frequency (e.g. smoking, watching television) is claimed to invest a previously innocuous stimulus, the
token, with powerful reinforcing properties. More specifically,
the token is said to derive such conditioned reinforcing properties
in two ways:

1. Through association with intrinsically reinforcing stimuli and
   activities, token presentation becomes reinforcing in its own
   right. The token thus becomes a conditioned reinforcer.

2. As the presentation of a token signals the availability of a
   high frequency behaviour it becomes a discriminative stimulus
   for reinforcement.

To sum up, the token is seen as a conditioned reinforcer for
the low frequency behaviour which precedes its presentation and as
a discriminative stimulus which occasions a subsequent high frequency
response. In a later section of this paper I intend to question
these assumptions concerning the mechanisms of action of token
presentation and, indeed, to argue that they represent unnecessary
theoretical elaborations but, for the moment, let us concentrate
on oft voiced objections to the use of token economy techniques.

Token economy procedures have proven uniquely effective in
overcoming self-care deficits and a wide range of other behavioural
problems which characterise long-term psychiatric patients and
other populations (Ayllon and Azrin, 1968; Kazdin, 1977).
Nevertheless they have been subjected to intense scrutiny and have

probably received more criticism than any other psychotherapeutic procedure currently in use. It has been suggested that this situation has arisen because the therapeutic goals in a token economy are clearly and explicitly formulated, because the results are objectively measureable and because behaviour is much more often effectively modified than in traditional forms of therapy. However, an examination of the main criticisms of token economy systems reveals that the arguments centre not around techniques, procedures and results but rather around ethical issues. In this context two major objections are commonly voiced.

The first is that token economy systems are dehumanising. This line of argument is essentially directed at the model of man which operant theory would appear to suggest i.e. that of an individual whose behaviour is strictly controlled and determined by extraneous events. This view of man and the implication that we can radically change behaviour merely by programming certain consequences may appear to undermine the concepts of free will and responsibility which are so highly valued in our society.

In defence of token economy systems it might plausibly be argued that procedures which characteristically make consequences quite explicit and consistent, actually facilitate responsible decision making and choice. However, the question of coercion may justifiably be raised at this point. It appears that, more often than not, the only choice which the patient can realistically make is to conform to a basically inhumane system, for to do otherwise would result in a loss of his rightful pleasures and privileges. This leads us on to the second major objection to token programmes.

This is that token economy procedures are inhumane. The criticism that token economy procedures are inhumane clearly has both moral and legal implications. It is usually founded on the basis that, in order to ensure that the objects and activities for which patients may exchange tokens remain strongly reinforcing, patients may be deliberately deprived of these in the absence of a sufficient number of tokens with which to effect a purchase. In his review of the legal implications of token economies Wexler (1974) points out that many programmes establish a deprivation situation by placing patients initially in closed wards of low status, equipped with sub-standard furnishings in which they must earn sufficient tokens to pay for their meals, their beds, their toilet articles and their clothing. He goes on to discuss the dilemma of those responsible for the administration of token economy programmes following recent legal action in the United States: "...the behaviour modifier suggests that chronic psychotics respond initially only to the most primitive reinforcers and, therefore, only their contingent availability can motivate the development of socially adaptive behaviour. It follows, the behaviourists claim, that if the basics are made freely available as rights rather than reinforcers, chronic psychotics may be destined to spend their lives functioning poorly in an institution-alised setting, whereas if these basic rights are converted into contingent reinforcers, there may be a real prospect of clinical improvement and discharge." (p. 292). Thus the conflict centres round the issue that in order to effect changes in the patient's condition we may have to deprive him of some of his rights.

However, recent evaluative studies of the token economy would seem to suggest that we require a radical revision of our ideas concerning the processes occurring in token economies when changes in behaviour take place. This evidence would seem to call for the redesigning of programmes of rehabilitation, largely divorced from the token economy model. Let us now examine the evidence.

The partialling out of the effective ingredients of a token economy is an issue of high priority if one is to attempt to establish the necessary and sufficient conditions for behavioural change. In this context one would wish to examine not only the independent variables which are normally viewed as constituting the basis of a token economy, but also the uncontrolled variables which, as Suchotliff, Greaves, Stecker and Berke (1970) point out, are introduced concomitantly with the reinforcement procedure and which could also account for the results achieved.

One study which attempts some control over the variables which had remained uncontrolled in studies of the token economy is that of Heap, Bobbitt, Moore and Hord (1970). Self care skills and grooming behaviour were the dependent variables in this study.

Four sequential conditions, each of 14 days duration were applied: (1) A baseline period of observation only, (2) checking of behaviours informally and without comment, (3) checking but with verbal reinforcement contingent upon successful completion of target behaviours, and (4) checking plus verbal reinforcement plus token delivery upon successful completion of target behaviours. The percentage of patients showing appropriate self care behaviours was approximately 2% during baseline. There were no significant changes during the second condition but there was approximately a 20% increase during the third condition and approximately a 50% increase during the fourth condition. Similar improvements were noted in grooming behaviour under the same four conditions. The results of this study appear strikingly in favour of the token/verbal rein-forcement combination over verbal reinforcement alone. However, the cumulative effects of the treatment programme are not controlled for in this sequential design, that is, one does not know whether continuing verbal reinforcement alone for a sufficiently long period would have resulted in an equally large increase as was evidenced with the token/verbal reinforcement combination.

Baker, Hall and Hutchinson (1974), began their pilot study of the token economy with some appreciation of possible uncontrolled variables: "The particular ward may receive more attention from professional staff, with the consequent improvements in staff morale and attitudes towards the patients. The nurses increase their efforts and provide a better standard of care for patients. They may now expect positive results. New activities and ward routines may be set up. In amongst all this, the hitherto neglected patient receives far more stimulation and attention than usual." (p. 368). Baker et al. (1974), selected seven patients, on the basis of several criteria, for removal from their original long-stay wards to a specialised token economy unit. They were observed in this setting for a period of six weeks. Following this, an activity programme was introduced in which patients were exposed to far more stimulation than usual: an Occupational Therapy Programme was begun; trips to the cinema and to town were organised; social evenings were arranged. After three weeks, tokens were introduced non-contingently for a seven week period. Contingent tokens were then introduced, being earned for the satisfactory performance of various ward tasks which gradually increased in number and variety. Contingent tokens were in effect for fourteen weeks following which baseline conditions were reintroduced.

From their results Baker et al. (1974) concluded that there was little evidence that a specific token contingency was the main factor in changing the patients' target behaviours. The greatest change for most patients occurred during the early stages of the experiment.

Although Baker et al. (1974) conclude that token reinforcement did not emerge as the critical therapeutic agent they were unable to isolate the factors that were of greatest importance. Nevertheless, two possible critical variables which emerge from an examination of their programmes are: (1) an increase in the frequency of instructions given by nurses and (2) a corresponding increase in the availability of social reinforcement. Either variable or a combination of the two could be crucial in explaining the results of this study.

Fernandez (1971), using an A-B-A design in the first two studies conducted by him in a free operant environment, noted that there were no reversals to base-rates when base-line conditions were reinstated after a period of contingent token reinforcement. Following from the above results, Fernandez (1972) argues that the introduction of "contingent token reinforcement" in his studies in all probability involved the introduction of no less than five intended variables, which in turn served to trigger off the action of other unintended (though not unexpected) variables which could have acted either independently or synergistically over time, and brought about the marked behavioural improvement, ordinarily attributed to contingent token reinforcement. The following are some of the variables (both intended and unintended) which Fernandez (1972; 1974a) lists: (1) Instructions given to subjects at the start of the contingent reinforcement phase, (2) contingent token reinforcement for performing desirable behaviours, (3) concomitant "attention" from the staff during contingent token reinforcement, (4) the contingent withdrawal of tokens as response costs, (5) concomitant "attention" from staff during the implementation of response cost procedures, (6) unintended verbal reinforcement from the staff during implementation of all token contingencies, (7) the reinforcing effect of other unintended non-verbal cues emanating from the staff in response to the behaviour of the patients, (8) the effect of observational learning facilitated by incentive variables, (9) contingent verbal/social reinforcement delivered by the relatives of the patients who visited the Unit and reviewed the "progress" of the patients, (10) peer dispensed verbal/social reinforcement, (11) the presumed "intrinsic reinforcement" obtained through the performance of certain behaviours, which were initially instated or strengthened through contingent token reinforcement, (12) the "self-reinforcement" phenomenon and (13) "experimenter-expectancy effects".

Fernandez (1974b) has since proceeded to extend this list of variables, but in a series of studies conducted since 1968, he has reduced the number of variables to manageable proportions for the purposes of experimental investigation. Recent unpublished studies have made use of a sequential design in which a specified variable was initially introduced and allowed to exert its effect for a specified period of time before yet another variable was introduced and added in. In this way an attempt was made to investigate the independent and synergistic effects of a number of specified variables. One such study (Fernandez, 1974a) investigated the role of the following seven variables: (1) individual and group counselling, (2) the instructional control of behaviour, (3) prompting and verbal reinforcement from the staff, (4) non-contingent token reinforcement and the contingent withdrawal of non-contingent tokens, (5) visual and verbal "performance feedback" provided to patients depending on their performance, (6) modelling effects, and (7) contingent token reinforcement and the contingent withdrawal of contingent tokens.

It is inevitably presumptuous to attempt to summarise the findings from a substantial body of research such as that carried out by Fernandez over a ten year period. Bearing this in mind, the major findings from his studies would appear to suggest that: (a) changes in some target behaviours can be brought about by using instructions alone. (b) the majority of target behaviours show most change when instructions are combined with prompting and verbal reinforcement delivered by nursing staff.

Further studies by the present author and his colleagues
(Fraser et al., 1981; Fraser et al., 1982) have added considerable
support to the findings of Fernandez' series of studies. The first
study (Fraser et al., 1981) involved an examination of the effectiveness of instructional training and response cost procedures in
reducing the frequency of performance of a range of inappropriate
behaviours in a group of nine long-term schizophrenic patients in
three distinct settings. Instructional training was found to be
generally effective in controlling inappropriate behaviour. The
effects of a combined instructional training and response cost
procedure in further reducing the level of performance of inappropriate behaviour were confined to a small sub-group of patients
and were only demonstrated in one specific setting.

The second study (Fraser et al., 1982) isolated instructions
as the most potent variable in teaching self help skills to long-
term schizophrenic patients. Buss and Lang (1965) and Storms and
Broen (1969) have suggested that schizophrenics are likely to
benefit from clear and detailed explanations, from extra information
about the expectations of others and from informative feedback
regarding the appropriateness of their behaviour. It may be argued
that the structured application of such a social information system
provides the necessary and sufficient conditions for behaviour
change in long-term schizophrenic patients. This assertion gains
considerable support from the series of studies by Fernandez and
from the studies conducted by the present author and his colleagues.
The token economy is therefore seen to achieve its effects solely
through the elaborate social information system which is embodied
in its application and the conditioning theory of its mode of
operation must, as a result, surrender to Occam's razor since there
has been no reliable evidence to date that contingent token presentation is a critical therapeutic variable.

Briefly, the therapeutic process may be viewed as follows:
in a social context the patient is systematically provided with
information concerning his actions and their likely outcome for
himself and for others. Behaviour change thus comes about through
an informed appraisal of social consequences rather than via a
hypothetical conditioning process or through an attempt to regain
pleasures and privileges which are the patient's by right. In
structuring a programme of rehabilitation along the lines suggested
by these recent findings one would be inviting the patient to
engage in a situation which involves a fair approximation to normal
social exchange. One would also be providing reinforcers which
are freely available in the outside community: approval, praise
encouragement and support, with no need of recourse to a highly
contrived situation which requires an elaborate transitional period
from tokens to these naturally occurring reinforcers if effective

rehabilitation is ever to be achieved. It might still be contested
that the token economy system as it has been implemented in psychiatric hospitals has justified techniques of deprivation and a
situation of marked power imbalance by virtue of the results which
have been achieved. However, I would wish to argue that we cannot
continue to defend coercive systems by reference to their results
since we have clearly demonstrated that programmes which involve no
deprivation of basic rights and privileges achieve comparable results
to those achieved in token economies. In treatment of any kind the
procedures that cause least distress to the patient should always
take priority.

REFERENCES

Ayllon, T. and Azrin, N.H., 1968. "The Token Economy: A
    Motivational System for Therapy and Rehabilitation".
    Appleton-Century-Crofts, New York.
Baker, R., Hall, J.N. and Hutchinson, K., 1974. A token economy
    project with chronic schizophrenic patients. Brit. J. Psychiat,
    124: 367-384.
Ball, T.S., 1968. Issues and implications of operant conditioning:
    the re-establishment of social behaviour. Hosp. Community
    Psychiat, 19: 230-232.
Bandura, A., 1969. "Principles of Behaviour Modification". Holt-
    Rinehart-Winston, New York.
Buss, A.H. and Lang, P.J., 1965. Psychological deficit in
    schizophrenia: 1. Affect, reinforcement and concept attain-
    ment. J. Abnorm. Psychol, 70: 2-24.
Fernandez, J., 1971. The token economy: a learning environment.
    Paper presented at the Third International Symposium on Social
    Psychiatry, Slantchev Bryag, Bulgaria.
Fernandez, J., 1972. Token economies: prosthetic or therapeutic
    environments? Paper presented at the Fourth Annual Southern
    California Conference on Behaviour Modification, Los Angeles.
Fernandez, J., 1974a. Variables which contribute towards the
    behavioural improvement shown by subjects in token programmes.
    Paper presented at the Fourth Annual Conference of the
    European Association for Behaviour Therapy, London.
Fernandez, J., 1974b. Token economies: is contingent token
    reinforcement really necessary? Paper presented at the Eighth
    Annual Conference of the Association for Advancement of
    Behaviour Therapy, Chicago.
Fraser, D., Black, D. and Cockram, L., 1981. An examination of
    the effectiveness of instructional training and response cost
    procedures in controlling the inappropriate behaviour of male
    schizophrenic patients. Behavioural Psychotherapy, 9:
    256-267.

Fraser, D., Black, D., Cockram, L. and Grimes, J., 1982. The
    comparative effectiveness of instructions, verbal reinforcement
    and tokens in teaching self-help skills to long-term schizo-
    phrenic patients. In: Main, C.J. (Ed.), "Clinical Psychology
    and Medicine: A Behavioural Perspective". Plenum, New York.
Heap, R.J., Bobbitt, W.E., Moore, C.H. and Hord, J.E., 1970.
    Behaviour milieu therapy with chronic neuropsychiatric patients,
    J. Abnorm. Psychol., 76: 349-354.
Kazdin, A.E., 1977. "The Token Economy: A Review and Evaluation".
    Plenum, New York.
Storms, L.H. and Broen, W.E., 1969. A theory of schizophrenic
    behavioural disorganisation, Arch. Gen. Psychiat., 20:
    129-143.
Suchotliff, L., Greaves, S., Stecker, H. and Berke, R., 1970.
    Critical variables in a token economy. Proceedings of the
    78th Annual Convention of the American Psychological
    Association, 5: 517-518.
Wexler, D.B., 1978. Token and taboo: behaviour modification, token
    economies and the law. In: Franks, C.M. and Wilson, G.T.
    (Eds.), "Annual Review of Behaviour Therapy, Theory and
    Practice". Brunner Mazel, New York.
Wing, J.K. and Brown, G.W., 1970. "Institutionalism and Schizo-
    phrenia". Cambridge University Press.

WHY DON'T CLINICAL PSYCHOLOGISTS WORKING WITH THE MENTALLY

HANDICAPPED DO PSYCHOLOGY?

C. Cullen   P.A. Woods

Hester Adrian Research   Bryn-y-Neuadd Hospital
Centre   N. Wales
University of Manchester

L. Tennant

Chelmsley Hospital
Birmingham

As clinical psychologists working with mentally handicapped (and other 'chronic' populations) we appear to have found it difficult to identify a definite role for ourselves within the existing pattern of services. At one time we were the profession most expert in assessment of various kinds, and that was itself a clearly identifiable role. For many reasons we became dissatisfied and made moves to become involved in 'treatment', so much so that assessment became a relatively small part of our work. The mode of treatment was almost invariably some form of behavioural intervention, and during the late sixties and early seventies many significant advances were reported. However, it has become apparent that the behavioural treatments familiar to most clinical psychologists, while proving useful, did not often lead to <u>permanent and generalised</u> benefits for mentally handicapped people.

Since clinical psychology is one of the few Health Service professions accustomed to critical self-evaluation, the apparent failure to "solve" serious social problems spurred on the acquisition of a new professional repertoire. It would, of course, have been an eminently sensible move to ask whether we had really exhausted the philosophy behind the behavioural approach. Did most clinical psychologists understand much of it, and were they sure that it could not be useful in understanding complex social systems? The answer is probably "no". However, rather than try to acquire a more comprehensive understanding (which would be quite difficult)

we started to cast around for other easily grasped roles within
which to operate.

That most people want to operate according to canons which take
little effort to understand is important. For as long as clinical
psychologists thought that the behavioural approach involved little
more than "finding things that people like" and then arranging for
these to follow appropriate behaviour, most were "behaviourists".
It should have been apparent from the outset that it was not that
simple - after all there is an increasingly large literature on
behaviourism as a philosophy - but now the naive behavioural approach
has failed to come up with the goods.

The new role into which increasing numbers of clinical psychologists are trying to move is that of adviser/consultant/service
planner. Many see themselves as able to give advice on the way
that services for the mentally handicapped should function. Whilst
this may be a justifiable manoeuvre there do seem to be some problems
to negotiate. We offer the following observations as being worthy
of some consideration:

1.   In general, the advice is often for others to follow rather
     than ourselves. This has important implications for the cred-
     ibility of the advice. For example, if clinical psychologists
     are urging others to foster or adopt mentally handicapped
     children, it would behove them to ask why few of their number
     would follow such advice. The point is not trivial and concerns
     personal credibility. For many years the status of clinical
     psychologists on hospital wards has varied according to the
     feasibility and reality of their advice to direct-care staff.

2.   The advice given is often as general principles which are diff-
     icult to interpret in terms of performers, performances and
     conditions. Kushlick (1975) suggested that this lack of speci-
     ficity was a contributory factor in the failure to implement
     the advice given in the 1971 White Paper "Better Services for
     the Mentally Handicapped". An example drawn from the King's
     Fund Project Paper titled 'An Ordinary Life' will serve to
     further illustrate this point. The authors assert that resid-
     ential services for mentally handicapped people should be based
     on three key principles. Principle Two is that "mentally hand-
     capped people have a right and a need to live like others in
     the community". Much is made of the idea of 'living like others',
     but later in the section explaining principle two is the state-
     ment that "mentally handicapped people also need special help,
     support, guidance and sometimes protection to enable them to
     enjoy the benefits of community life to the full".

We certainly agree that this is so, but it would hardly be
described as 'living like others'. Michael (1980) has suggested

that this kind of imprecision and vagueness has been partly responsible for the difficulties encountered by behaviour modifiers. They
became content to use terms like 'social reinforcement' - which
actually meant only "being nice" to someone on certain occasions.
Such terms are not helpful and are no better than terms such as
'play therapy', 'as much as possible', 'least restrictive' and so
on.

If the King's Fund paper stated only general principles it
would not have gained the credence it has. It does go on to say
how the principles might be translated into practice, and this leads
us on to our third point.

3. Much of the advice given does not have a sound empirical base.
    Indeed, principle two outlined above is said to be "not a matter
    about which empirical judgements can be made". A lot is made
    of the apparent distinction between 'values' and 'empiricism',
    and it is often asserted that it is important to keep value
    statements and empirical judgements separate.

Our view is that logic ties the two together in a very important
way. The importance in making value statements is that they are
supposed to lead to action (by service planners and providers) which
should have certain effects perhaps for mentally handicapped people
(cf. Waller, 1982). It is an empirical matter whether or not the
effects are achieved. If we were unable to say whether or not the
effects were achieved there would be little point in making the
value statements.

To summarise, psychologists should be prepared to follow their
own advice, should aim for specificity in their recommendations,
and, bearing in mind the current state of ignorance concerning
human behaviour, should attempt a scientific understanding of the
functioning of services within which they work.

Let us pause to consider the following service issue. Current
policy in relation to residential facilities for handicapped people
stresses the development of small locally based facilities and in
general psychologists have been vociferous in their support of this
policy. However, a brief survey of recent research illustrates the
way in which clinical psychologists could justifiably be accused
of abdicating their responsibilities. The evidence is confusing
and yet it is our contention that psychologists in general are not
reflecting this fact in their contact with policy making groups.

In a widely cited paper published in 1976, Balla reviewed the
literature relating institution size to quality of care. The
characteristics of care considered included:

a)   Resident care practices
b)   The behavioural functioning of the residents
c)   Discharge rates
d)   The extent of parental and community involvement.

Whilst there was wide variation in the nature of the studies reviewed,
Balla drew some general conclusions. Care practices (measured in
various ways) were said to be "better" in smaller units and there
was more involvement of community based facilities in these units.
However, two other factors emerged. Predictably, there was considerable variation in the quality of care provided even by small units.
Also, there was little evidence that the residents of the units
reviewed (whatever the size of the unit) functioned differently in
any significant way.

In a study of a different nature, Hemming, Lavender and Pill
(1980) reported on the effects of the transfer of adults from a
large hospital to smaller units and concluded that there were significant improvements in management practices, staff/resident interactions, and adaptive behaviour. In contrast, Landesman-Dwyer,
Sackett and Kleinman (1980) investigating the effects of size on
staff and resident behaviour in twenty small group homes observed
that neither staff behaviour nor staff/resident interaction varied
in relation to size, that resident behaviour did vary, and that
residents showed more adaptive social behaviour in the larger units.

Finally, in a paper entitled "On Size and Quality of Residential
Care: A second look", Baroff (1980) re-examined the issues raised
four years earlier by Balla particularly in relation to the
"normalisation" movement. He cites various studies supporting the
view that small units provide better opportunities for the development of appropriate behaviour. Note that this is in contrast with
the findings published by Landesman-Dwyer et al. (1980) but supported
by Hemming, et al. (1980), Balla (1976) having noted no significant
differences.

We do not propose to offer here yet another detailed review
and re-interpretation of the literature but rather to note some
curious and perhaps alarming trends in the available psychological
research. For example, from two of the papers, each of which were
published in 1980, one might conclude that small units are better
(Baroff, 1980) or worse (Landesman-Dwyer, et al., 1980) than larger
units.

"The research literature clearly indicates that
institutions do vary in the quality of life that
they provide and that it is in the smaller setting
that one finds the more resident oriented individ-
ualised experience".

(Baroff, 1980. Emphasis added)

Alternatively,

> "The strongest effects were observed in the
> area of social behaviour. Generally residents
> in the larger group homes engaged in more
> social behaviour than did those in smaller
> group homes. Further, more residents in large
> group homes interacted more with peers; were
> more likely to have a best friend and spent
> more time with their best friends than did
> residents in smaller group homes".

> (Landesman-Dwyer et al., 1980)

Each of these authors cite the earlier report of Balla (1976), in
supporting their own (opposing) views:

> "Care is more adequate in smaller community
> based institutions especially those under
> 100 population".

> (Balla, 1976 as reported in Baroff, 1980)

> "There is little evidence to suggest that
> the behavioural functioning of residents is
> different in institutions of different size".

> (Balla, 1976, as reported in Landesman-
> Dwyer et al., 1980)

How do these differing views arise? Clearly the dependent variables
specified and observed are not always the same. Particularly popular
are (i) measures of care practices (often based on questionnaires),
(ii) of staff/resident interaction, and (iii) of the behaviour of
residents. In this respect if there is any common feature emerging
from the four studies summarised above it is that there is no
necessary link between those factors despite the fact that it sometimes is convenient to assume that links exist.

   Further complexities emerge when differing independent variables
are evaluated. Hemming et al. (1981) evaluated the effect of the
transfer of a group of residents from larger to smaller units
whereas the other studies compared different groups of residents
living in a range of units. These authors noted improvements which
run counter to the observations of both Balla (1976) and Landesman-
Dwyer et al. (1980).

If one is committed to the view that small units are 'better' than larger units regardless of any evidence, and if, for the sake of argument, it could be shown that for some people larger units might sometimes be preferable, then two avenues of escape may be taken. One is to argue that the smaller units are not really the kind you had in mind. They are quite inadequate and you knew that all along. Your small units are actually quite different, and would be much better. The second avenue is to appeal to complexity and to argue that it is not possible to look at one part of a complex service in isolation. Systems are not amenable to a simple causal analysis. We contend that of course they are not amenable to a simple causal analysis, but the possibility of a scientific understanding remains.

We ought to make it clear that we are not advocating that the status quo is maintained until we have strong empirical support to justify any move. That cannot be so given the appalling conditions under which many of our mentally handicapped citizens live. But we are mindful of our failure so far, as clinical psychologists, to support or contribute to much sustained social change. It could just be that one of the reasons is that we know so little of what currently causes and maintains complex human behaviour. Stolz (1981) makes just this point when she writes:

"Bevan (1976) summed up the situation:

'When the Pentagon develops a new weapons system, the research and development process involves an elaborate sequence of testing and comparing alternative technologies, retaining finally only the one that comes off best in comparative testing. In contrast, when our government confronts a major social problem in the civilian sector, its solution is usually intuitive and immediate and, often to our ultimate sorrow, implemented on a full scale.'

"Exemplifying just that strategy (if leaping to an unevaluated solution can be called a strategy), the report of the Joint Commission on Mental Illness and Health ... on the conditions in state mental hospitals led to the first of a series of laws establishing what has become an extraordinarily expensive system of community mental health care ... What had been proved scientifically about the efficacy of community-based versus institutional treatment in 1961, when the report was pub- lished, or in 1963, when the first law was

passed? Very little. However, the pressure
of demands for care outside state institutions
led policymakers to set up the community mental
health system, even in the absence of any
relevant data.

"In 1977, the National Institute of Mental
Health began a pilot test of a new type of
contract given directly to states to assist
them in developing community networks to care
for the chronically mentally ill ... The
intent was to collect data from a few states,
evaluate the mechanism and the procedures
developed, and then, if the initial projects
were shown to be successful, expand the
program by awarding contracts to additional
states. However, in 1978, before any meaningful data could be collected from the pilot
evaluation, New York State funded a $15.1
million program implementing the untested
experimental model in 46 of the 62 counties
in the state."

(Stolz, 1981, p. 494)

Clinical psychologists should have a particular kind of
expertise which is otherwise lacking in mental handicap services.
That expertise in our view revolves around scientific understanding
of the behaviour of people providing and people receiving the
service. It should be possible for clinical psychologists to
identify procedures and conditions which lead to increases in desirable behaviour for mentally handicapped people, and to investigate
ways of sustaining these. That kind of analysis can be carried out
in whatever setting the psychologist works, but at the moment it
seems to us to be premature to assert that we know which is the
most suitable form of service provision.

Psychologists are becoming increasingly reluctant to work in
institutions. If we accept that clinical psychologists ought to be
trying to understand the reasons why things are as they are then
this reluctance is an error. It is a mistake because it ignores an
opportunity to understand how remarkably stable patterns of behaviour
come about. Institutions are very good at establishing and maintaining inappropriate resident behaviour such as pacing or sitting
aimlessly; having no regard for privacy; engaging in antisocial or
disruptive activities; depending on others for the completion of
basic hygiene routines, and so on. For staff, the institution also
maintains strong behaviours such as acting as waiters and waitresses;
tidying linen rooms and store cupboards; treating adults as if they

were children; reacting promptly to disruptive behaviour but ignoring
adaptive behaviour, and so on. To restate, institutions are very
good at these things. If we begin to understand this then this
might give us some guidance on establishing and sustaining appropriat
repertoires.

What, then, does the clinical psychologist qua clinical psychologist have to offer mental handicap services? From the brief
survey of the literature on size we have reviewed, it seems that
there is still a pressing need for information on which environmental
changes and conditions are 'best' for mentally handicapped people.
We may know what we don't want (large, dehumanising institutions)
but it is not at all clear exactly what we do want.

Apparently the evidence available to service planners and others
is at best confusing and often contradictory. Obviously, planning
decisions must be taken based upon the best available information
and psychologists very properly contribute to these decisions.
However, we share with Balla (1976) the conviction that "careful
empirical studies will ultimately provide the best avenue for the
construction of a social policy that will improve the quality of
life for retarded individuals in whatever type of facility they are
found". Psychologists will hold their own views but must provide
the means of evaluating new service proposals and attempt to understand the features of existing services. It may be that a concern
with the functions of service provisions rather than their structures
will be helpful. Institutional practices have been documented and
demonstrated in large units. Equally, small units have been shown
to be capable of supporting the worst in institutional practices.
There appears to be some doubt as to whether permanent gains in
resident behaviour occur and some confusion concerning the determinants of staff behaviour.

There are obviously many areas in which psychologists might
profitably work investigating relationships between behaviour and
determining environments. Landesman-Dwyer, Sackett and Kleinman
(1980) concluded:

> " ... the behaviour of staff members was not
> closely associated with group-home size or with
> any other variables measured in this study. In
> fact, the picture of staff members' behaviour
> across the 20 group homes was remarkably constant,
> unlike that for residents. This relative independ-
> ence of the behaviour of staff members from that
> of residents warrants more careful evaluation".

(p. 15)

We present here three accounts of work which has been aimed at such an evaluation. It is not presented as complete or definitive, but as the kind of work clinical psychologists working within institutional settings might do. Needless to say, similar investigations could be carried out in many service settings.

Woods and Cullen (in press) have presented data from different clinical settings in which staff behaviour and resident behaviour seem to be unrelated. They report two studies during which appropriate toileting was measured for two profoundly handicapped females. In one, the study lasted for over 80 weeks, and the amount of appropriate urination increased from around 25% to 80%. Whilst this is a clinically significant increase, given the long time scale, day-by-day progress was difficult to detect. In fact there were 'relapses' occasionally, so the nurses carrying out the programme effectively saw no progress. However, they digilently carried on with the procedure, even in the absence of noticeable positive behaviour change.

In a similar setting, the appropriate urination of another handicapped woman actually declined over a period of 52 weeks from 72% to around 10%, despite there being an ongoing toileting programme. Direct-care staff in this study had no access to the weekly data, and so never saw the graph showing a gradual skill loss. Nevertheless, as in the previous study, daily changes, and even weekly changes, were variable, sometimes showing a modest improvement, and sometimes a small decline. No overall pattern was evident. Even so, as in the previous example, direct-care staff continued with the programme.

Here, we have two examples where the therapeutic behaviour of direct-care staff was independent of the behaviour of the residents. In the first case, change was too gradual to allow any visible regular improvements, and in the second case the quality of behaviour actually declined. The third example presented by Woods and Cullen (in press) is even more startling. A room management system (cf. Porterfield and Blunden, 1978, for details) was introduced on a ward of thirteen mentally handicapped people. The aim was to increase the amount of adaptive behaviour displayed during an hour-long activity period.

During baseline, before any intervention, there were, on average, only 10% of the residents engaged at any one time. When new toys were made available, with no formal staff intervention, that percentage rose to a maximum of 30%, falling back to 10% in a short time. The room management procedure was introduced, and the proportion of residents adaptively engaged immediately rose to 60%. A brief period of reversal showed the percentage falling to 35%, and the re-introduction of the room management procedure boosted the figure back to 70%.

For about four months the percentage of residents adaptively engaged varied between 50%-70%. This was judged by all the direct-care staff as clinically significant and important, and they all voiced their delight. Moreover, they affirmed their desire to carry on with the room management procedure, even though the period of the formal study was ending, because they could see how much the residents had benefitted.

When the researchers visited the ward fifteen months later, the engagement level was down to 15%. Here is an example where again the behaviour of ward staff appears to be independent of the behaviour of residents. Even with obvious and visible benefits to the residents, direct-care staff did not carry on the therapeutic procedure.

Woods and Cullen were unable to identify the determinants of staff behaviour in these three examples, but it was clear that it was not resident behaviour. They speculated that in the first two cases the presence of a "strong" senior nurse was a major influence, whereas in the final case the "kudos" gained from being a special research project was important.

We have suggested elsewhere that service delivery systems are often pathological rather than constructional in their orientation (Cullen, Hattersley and Tennant, 1981). More specifically in a residential unit the occurrence of certain unwanted but easily defined classes of client behaviour set the occasion for specified parts of staff duties (i.e. when a resident is missing/behaves violently/injures herself or himself ... etc., then certain actions are required of staff). Interestingly, the actions of staff in relation to the main purpose of the establishment (the promotion of adaptive behaviour/opportunities for normal living and so on) are rarely specified and if they are it tends to be in very vague terms (e.g. "facilitates", "encourage", "develop", and so on). In our view a net result here is a service which exists to prevent or, more accurately, cope with difficulties. This in turn generates a stability in patterns of resident behaviour which has a very marked characteristic illustrated in the following accounts of monitored clinical practice.

Examples of unacceptable or problematic behaviour occur with a higher frequency in institutions - to a certain extent institutions are seen to exist to cope with such difficulties. Bendall, Hobbs, Lopez, Moniz and Tennant (1980) described some problems of mainten-ance in a constructionally oriented intervention in a hospital ward. Help had been sought in connection with a middle-aged mentally handicapped woman (A) who had spent much of her life in institutional care. She was recently admitted to the ward and presented manage-ment difficulties for the staff including a persistent tendency to strip off her clothes. Initial observations included sampling her interactions with staff which revealed that during the observation period she was:

- unattended for 63-64% of the period
- engaged with staff in relation to the problem for 33.3% of the period, and
- engaged with staff in relation to adaptive behaviour for 3.3% of the period.

An attempt was made to define a constructional intervention following from an evaluation of the range of A's adaptive behaviour. The resulting strategy included two main facets:

a) An attempt to extend A's concentration through a programme of brief periods of individual training to be carried out and recorded by ward staff.

b) An attempt to manage or reduce the problem behaviour by means of a time out programme.

Figure 1 shows the results of this intervention in relation to (a) and (b) above over a 55-day period. The frequency of the use of time out and of the problem behaviour declined quite markedly reaching a low of less than five incidents within the 5-day period by day 45. The frequency of training sessions increased rapidly initially (obviously since no recorded training was taking place prior to this intervention). However from day 25 through 45 a gradual decline took place. The most interesting feature for the purpose of the present discussion is that the frequency of training sessions appears to follow that of the problem behaviours. As the latter decline or increase so do the former. The authors suggest that pressures on staff contribute to this phenomenon. At the outset this resident was "the most difficult" on that ward. However, as the programme progressed, problem behaviours declined and relative to other residents, A was more manageable. As a consequence another resident became the main focus and the frequency of training for A declined which in turn appeared to produce increases in the problem behaviour. That is, A returned to patterns which were previously successful in gaining staff attention. It seems reasonable to suggest that staff in this kind of situation direct their attention towards those residents whose behaviour would be likely to prompt senior managers to scrutinize staff activities more closely. Crudely, a set of contingencies exist such that certain resident behaviours (those which would injure others or damage property) are the occasion upon which managers look more closely at the activities of their ward staff. Consequently, ward staff, working hard to reduce this possibility, are forced into a pathological orientation which produces cycles of behaviour problems in which a number of residents, in turn, are the most difficult meriting the most staff attention. Typically,

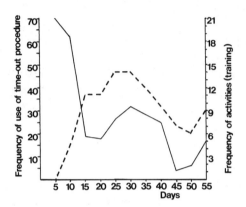

Figure 1:   The relationship between the frequency of use of a time-
out procedure (continuous line) and the frequency of
training activities (broken line) for one mentally
handicapped woman.

some progress is made in reducing the behaviour problem for a
particular individual at which point they merit less attention than
the new "league leader". If this observation has any generality,
one feature of institutional patterns of care is the tendency of
ward staff to be affected to a limited extent by resident developmental gains but more significantly <u>by possible censure from</u>
<u>managers</u>.

A further example carries the implication that this can be a
pervasive feature. An attempt was made by one of the present
authors to evade the problems of the kind of intervention described
above by instituting in conjunction with ward staff a ward-wide
positively oriented programme. The ward in question provided the

living environment for a small number of severely mentally handicapped but physically able women. It was viewed by managers as a difficult ward which typically catered for the most behaviourally disturbed. As a consequence it was relatively well staffed, tended to be protected from the disturbing effects of temporary staff transfers to support other wards ("relieving"), and was maintained with a small number (eight) of residents.

Prior to the instigation of the ward-wide programme there had been a series of problem oriented case conferences producing the kind of circular pattern described above. A decision was made to introduce an "activity training" period to each day, and to avoid instituting new behaviour reduction programmes. The details of the training undertaken are not relevant here. However, as part of the monitoring of progress a retrospective analysis of problem behaviours was made. The basis for these data was the ward incident book which had usefully strict criteria for entries. Figure 2 shows frequencies of incidents (each point representing a total for five days) prior to the beginning of the training periods and at several subsequent points. Although no behaviour reducing interventions had been established there was a marked fall in the overall level of incidents reported. Unfortunately, correlated with this was increasing pressure from managers upon ward staff to accept new (additional) residents coupled with a tendency to view the ward as "easier" and thus more likely to have staff available to be removed for relief duties and so on. The pressure culminated in the admission of two new residents which produced an increase in the number of incidents recorded within the original group of eight (incidents involving new residents being excluded from the data shown).

In this case instigating a ward-wide constructive programme appeared to be effective in reducing the level of problems as well as teaching new skills. Further, to some extent the tendency of staff to work to avoid censure (that is solely on behaviour problems) had been outweighed by providing a positive programme for residents and structure and support for staff. The behaviour of managers more removed from this work was, however, apparently similar to that of ward staff in the earlier example although for them the "league table" comprised wards with associated levels of problem rather than individual residents. In this example the ward was protected (equivalent to the instigation of a programme for an individual) whilst it was "the most difficult". Progress made by staff in managing the ward in some way weakened the concern of managers to continue in this way - presumably other areas in the institution became relatively of more concern. Thus the behaviour of ward staff was punished as a consequence of progress made. Again, it often seems that the actions of staff, in this case more senior staff, are occasioned and proscribed by the occurrence of problem behaviours.

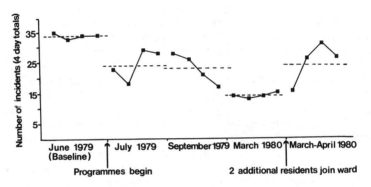

Figure 2:   The number of incidents recorded for the eight residents
of a ward.   The figures for March-April 1980 <u>do not</u> includ
incidents caused by the two additional residents.

Clearly this is an oversimplified view. The behaviours of staff and residents are multiply determined and our conceptualisation of such activity must take account of this fact (some might favour here systems theory and/or ecological accounts (cf. Willems, 1974), alternatively development of the framework presented by Israel Goldiamond (1975) in describing "alternative sets" may prove worthwhile for the radical behaviourist). However, it is evident that many factors in addition to developmental progress made by residents are effective in determining staff behaviour. It is likely that this may be true in residences of varying size and is clearly a worthy area of further investigation for psychologists and others.

Wahler and Fox (1981) have suggested that setting events are important when trying to identify the determinants of behaviour. These are either events or conditions, the presence or absence of which will effect subsequent behaviours. In an institution it is often possible to identify setting events which constrain the acquisition and maintenance of adaptive behaviour by the residents. If these constraints can be removed, then there may be no need to actively arrange contingency management procedures for the behaviours, or, at the very least, removal of the constraints may aid the acquisition and maintenance of adaptive behaviour. This approach goes some way to bridging the gap between the sociology of institutions and the practice of clinical psychology as a 'system-independent' enterprise.

We are aware of few attempts to make a functional analysis of the setting events within institutions. This would involve not only postulating particular conditions as setting events but manipulating those conditions to demonstrate the effect they have on behaviour. Thomas, Burton and Cullen (1982) have presented the preliminary stage of such an analysis, i.e. the identification of certain conditions which might act as setting events for self-care behaviour in an institution. The information was obtained by completing a self-care checklist (Burton, Thomas and Cullen, 1981) for each of the residents of a small institution.

Whenever a person failed to achieve the maximum score on any item, supplementary questions were asked to find out why. Often the answer pointed more to constraints within the institution than to skill deficits on behalf of the residents. For example, for the items aimed at determining whether residents are able to pour hot liquids without spilling, constraints identified might be that it was ward policy not to allow handicapped residents to pour liquids and anyway the hospital did not provide appropriately sized teapots. Here, the residents' behaviour is constrained by two factors: staff behaviour and lack of equipment. (It was instructive that one elderly man who "did not pour hot liquids without spillage" was able to do so perfectly, once he was given a small teapot at mealtimes!)

Data collected in this manner is qualitative, although it is possible to categorise it in several different ways. One way which may have some utility is as follows:

1. Physical environment

:: High cost - here we include aspects of the physical environment which are not easy to change, such as fitting wide doors in a toilet area to allow physically handicapped people in wheelchairs to use the facilities independently.

:: Low cost - some aspects of the environment are relatively easy to change. Providing dispensers which allow measured pieces of toilet paper to be taken at one time obviates the need to keep toilet rolls in the ward office (to prevent the whole roll being put into the toilet).

2. Staff behaviour

:: Rules - some institutions have rules which constrain the acquisition of appropriate behaviour by mentally handicapped people. For example, it is a policy in some hospitals to always have two staff present when a mentally handicapped person is bathing. This constrains acquisition of the repertoire loosely described as "having regard for privacy".

:: Routines - direct-care staff often have habits and routines which have been acquired over many years. Sometimes these may be common throughout an institution, or they may be particular to certain groups of staff only (e.g. certain shifts). An example might be ensuring that shaving of residents is completed before breakfast arrives. In many institutions this means that there is limited time in which to do the task, which in turn means that it is highly un- likely that residents will be given enough time in which to do the shaving themselves.

3. Resident characteristics

:: Physical - some physical characteristics of the residents might prevent them from carrying out some self-care behaviours. It will be difficult (but perhaps possible with the aid of suitable prosthetics) for a person with severe palsy to drink without spillage.

:: Behaviour - problem behaviour may constrain the practice of other behaviours. A person who screams continually is unlikely to be given the opportunity to acquire repertoires necessary for eating in restaurants.

Obviously, some of these 'constraints' will act together and it is often a matter of judgement and empirical evaluation as to what events, repertoires or conditions constitute setting events.

Conclusion

We began by noting the development of the role of the clinical psychologist in the area of service planning. It is our view that psychologists have a particular contribution to make which follows from the possibility of the analysis and evaluation of behaviour in relation to living environments. It is important that we make our views known and vital that these views are based upon an attempt to understand services within which we function. Sometimes we will express or will share values which go beyond our present knowledge and part of our contribution must be to provide some empirical exploration of those views. Our examples have been drawn from services for mentally handicapped people within which the issue of size of residential unit is currently under discussion. We have suggested that the research basis whilst interesting is diverse and that much confusion arises from the inability of psychology to describe accurately the determinants of behaviour (particularly of staff behaviour) in existing settings. We have argued therefore that further study is necessary.

The stage of categorisation described above is, however, only the first stage in a useful analysis. The next step for the clinical psychologist should be to attempt to manipulate these conditions to demonstrate that they achieve measurable effects and are indeed setting events. To do so will require not only a technology of change but a system for measurement (cf. Johnston and Pennypacker, 1981). Both of these will require a systematic application and furtherance of psychology as a discipline.

REFERENCES

Balla, D.A., 1976. Relationship of institution size to quality of care: A review of the literature. Amer. J. Mental Deficiency, 81: 117-124.
Baroff, G.S., 1980. On "size" and the quality of residential care: a second look. Mental Retardation, 18: 113-117.
Bendall, S., Hobbs, S., Lopez, J., Moniz, E. and Tennant, L., 1980. Developing appropriate social behaviour in residential settings. An example of some problems in maintaining treatment gains made by a mentally handicapped adult. Unpublished manuscript.
Burton, M., Thomas, M. and Cullen, C., 1981. "Offerton Self-Care

Checklist". Hester Adrian Research Centre; University of
  Manchester.
Cullen, C., Hattersley, J. and Tennant, L., 1981. Establishing
  behaviour: the constructional approach. In: Davey, G. (Ed.)
  "Application of Conditioning Theory". Methuen, London.
Goldiamond, I., 1975. Alternative sets as a framework for behavioural
  formulations and research. Behaviourism, 3: 49-86.
Hemming, H., Lavender, T. and Pill, R., 1981. Quality of life of
  mentally retarded adults transferred from large institutions
  to new small units. Amer. J. Mental Deficiency, 86: 157-169.
Johnston, J.M. and Pennypacker, H.S., 1981. "Strategies and Tactics
  of Human Behavioural Research". Lawrence Erlbaum Associates,
  Hillsdale, NJ.
Kushlick, A., 1975. Improving services for the mentally handicapped.
  In: Kiernan, C.C. and Woodward, F.P. (Eds.), "Behaviour Mod-
  ification with the Severely Retarded". Associated Scientific
  Publishers, Oxford.
Landesman-Dwyer, S., Sackett, G.P. and Kleinman, J.S., 1980. Rel-
  ationship of size to resident and staff behaviour in small
  community residences. Amer. J. Mental Deficiency, 85: 6-17.
Michael, J.L., 1980. Flight from behaviour analysis. The
  Behaviour Analyst, 3: 1-22.
Porterfield, J. and Blunden, R., 1978. Establishing an activity
  period and individual skill training within a day setting for
  profoundly mentally handicapped adults. J. Practical Approaches
  in Developmental Handicap, 2 (3): 10-15.
Stolz, S.B., 1981. Adoption of innovations from applied behavioural
  research: "Does anybody care?". J. App. Behav. Anal., 14:
  491-505.
Thomas, M., Burton, M. and Cullen, C., 1982. Take a new look at
  your ward: increasing opportunities for learning on wards with
  mentally handicapped residents. Nursing Times, 78: 1068-1070.
Wahler, R.G. and Fox, J.J., 1981. Setting events in applied behaviour analysis: Toward a conceptual and methodological expansion.
  J. App. Behav. Anal., 14: 327-338.
Waller, B., 1982. Skinner's two stage value theory. Behaviourism,
  10: 25-44.
Willems, E.P., 1974. Behavioural technology and behavioural ecology.
  J. App. Behav. Anal., 7: 151-165.
Woods, P.A. and Cullen. C., In press. Determinants of staff
  behaviour in long term care. Behav. Psychother.

VOICES FROM THE INSTITUTION

David Brandon

MIND National Association
for Mental Health

In this paper 1 write about three elements. I write about the
Kings Fund research into patients' views; reveal some results of
some interviews of long stay patients; and draw some general conclusions about the involvement of patients in their own treatment.

Part of a poem by the nineteenth century long stay patient/poet
John Clare, entitled "Written in Northampton County Asylum" is sadly
still relevant:-

> I am! Yet what I am who cares, or knows?
> My friends forsake me like a memory lost.
> I am the self-consumer of my woes:
> They rise and vanish, an oblivious host,
> Shadows of life whose very soul is lost.
> And yet I am - I live though I am toss'd
>
> Into the nothingness of scorn and noise,
> Into the living sea of waking dream
> Where there is neither sense of life, no joys,
> But the huge shipwreck of my own esteem
> And all that's dear. Even those I loved the best
> Are strange - nay, they are stranger than the rest.

Despite Clare's marvellous contribution, the discussion concerning mental illness has been dominated by the babble of
professionals' voices. Voices from within the institution have
hardly been heard.

Perhaps the most comprehensive piece of British research into
all types of patients' views in psychiatric hospitals was completed

by the Kings Fund (1977). It was based on a questionnaire approach used in nine psychiatric hospitals.

The study categorised views into four areas - the ward, care, life in hospitals and treatment. Most patients seemed satisfied with dormitories and day rooms but had many complaints about lack of privacy, poor storage accomodation and, above all, noise. The sanitary provision received far less criticism than in comparable surveys in general hospitals. Most mental hospitals had lovely gardens and grounds and appreciative comments about them were frequently given in response to the question "What do you like best about the hospital?"

Comments about care suggested that patients had a great dependence on their doctors and felt a need to see them at regular intervals. Doctors were greatly appreciated and generally described as 'sympathetic', 'courteous', 'civil', 'pleasant' and 'marvellous'. Patients were also enthusiastic about nurses. Other staff were usually referred to in glowing terms. Very many patients commented that the received insufficient information about their condition from the staff.

Questions about life in hospital indicated that long stay patients tended to be less critical than short stay. Views on meals varied considerably, ranging from stodgy and inedible to excellent. Patients were generally appreciative of the occupation/work element in their lives but over a third of patients complained of a lack of interest, 'nothing to do'; 'it's very boring'. The dullest times were evenings and Sundays.

Fascinatingly, treatment was excluded from the questionnaire but many patients commented on it. Most were appreciative. A minority were critical along the lines of:-

> 'Taking those damn tablets'
> 'Too much of the needle, nasty side effects'
> 'Medication is very strong'
> 'Should move forward from drugs'

A few made specific comments on ECT and group therapy. A minority complained about the lack of treatment for physical illnesses. It is clear from this survey that many patients appreciate the mental hospital as an asylum - 'a place of retreat and security'.

My brief study consisted of ten long interviews with former long stay patients with experiences in hospitals as far apart as West Park, near Epsom; Whittingham, near Preston; and Parkside, Macclesfield.

Eight were males and two female. They were all between fifty-two and sixty-five years old. Between them they had spent more than two centuries in mental hospitals.

It is useful to give an abbreviated version of one interview – Fred Wilkinson[1] who is 60 years old and was formerly a patient in Parkside Hospital, Cheshire.

"My Dad was a gardener and a good natured man. We lived in a small house near Warrington. Mum died when I was ten and Dad when I was just turned seventeen.

"I moved to Crewe to find work. I had a job as a machinist with the loco works. I was there for about ten years living in digs. I hadn't any real friends and got very depressed. The doctors tried to treat me but it was not good, I just seemed to worry over everything, I wasn't the same any more, and so I came into Parkside Mental Hospital in February 1948.

"The first few months I was on the Admissions Ward. They gave me shock treatment to clear up the depression. They put a rubber band around my arm followed by an injection. It was unpleasant. You could watch yourself drifting off. The shock treatment didn't do me any good although I kept on having it.

"Then I moved onto the insulin ward which meant I was improving. They gave me insulin twice weekly – an injection if I remember correctly. It didn't do me any good and on the other hand it didn't make me worse.

"Both there and on the villas, we were either locked in on the wards or surrounded by wire netting. High walls were everywhere. On the wards we mostly sat around which was restful at least. There was nothing much to do. I sat around for years. Up at seven or earlier; breakfast, sit around until dinner, sit around until tea, sit around until lights out. Once a year you were medically examined, between examinations if everything was alright, you were left alone although you were conscious of being watched.

"I used to do odd jobs within the hospital for which we didn't get paid. We worked at an allotment owned by the hospital for about two years. It was just rough gardening and there was no opportunity for advancement. When I realised it was voluntary I stopped working there and just stayed in the ward yard.

"In the mid-nineteen sixties, I started to work outside the hospital. I did gardening jobs for two local ladies which made me

---

[1] All individuals referred to in this paper have been given pseudonyms.

£2.50 a week. That was worth a lot more then and was the first
money I had earned since coming into the hospital.

"Just over ten years ago, I got a job with a firm in Macclesfield. I sprayed the fringes on things like prams. They went
redundant a few years back and I was out of work again. All that
time I had been living within the hospital, returning each evening
from work.

"A few years ago, I got another job working in a local firm.
I fetch and carry and do odd jobs. I like it. At the end of last
year they put me into the self care unit in the hospital and I
started to learn how to cook and take care of myself. Six months
ago, the hospital got a little house near the town centre of
Macclesfield which I share with a younger man, also from the
hospital. We get on fine.

"All those years in Parkside, I didn't make any real friends.
Just a lot of people to say 'hello' to. None of the treatment was
very helpful. The freedom from stress was the most important factor.
I'd got out of my depression and was really ready to leave in the
mid-sixties or even earlier.

"However no-one pushed you. You were left on your own. Once
they had admitted you, they tended to forget.

"I have nothing really to criticise about the hospital. They
tried to be helpful but I was in an apathetic and hopeless situation.
I am happier now, living in the community. I take Largactil three
times a day. I take it as instructed but it's just the same if I
don't. In the community you can do what you like without anyone
watching. Parkside hasn't changed much really. There are less
walls and more lawns and gardens but the routine and the daily
grind is much the same as just after the war."

Now a summary of the others' experiences. Only one had lived
in a side room; the others had ranged from sleeping with three
others to four sleeping in dormitories with more than thirty beds.
In all cases they shared a large day room with usually a quiet room
somewhere nearby. The wards were mainly around twenty-five beds in
size.

From their descriptions, the five patients who had been in
Whittingham Hospital had had the poorest quality environment but
were the least critical. Their remarks varied from 'OK' to
'alright' about the hospital ward.

Two people described the same ward in Springfield Hospital:
"It was the worst ward in the hospital. They got you up at 6.45
a.m. I had to shave in the toilet basin and anyway there was no

mirror in the bathroom. The food was terrible. You had to fight to
get anything at all. It was undercooked and hardly edible." And a
lady patient on the same ward: "It was a very nice ward. I didn't
like the lack of privacy but everywhere was clean. Clothes went
missing - as fast as you bought things they disappeared. The food
was indigestible. I was often sick in the bathroom. There were
only two baths for the whole ward." All five former Whittingham
Hospital patients found the food good to excellent.

When asked what they liked best and least, the responses were
extremely varied. "Social workers - they helped me no end."
"Running the patients' club." "Working in industrial therapy."
"Making jigsaws (in industrial therapy)." "Everything was alright."
"Excursions - going shopping with the OT girls." "Receiving medication in a quiet and orderly queue." "The grounds, walking among
the grass and the trees." "Nothing."

What they liked least was equally varied. "The cafe - it was
a grabhole, pushing and struggling." "The food was indigestible."
"I just didn't like being interned there." "Nothing", said two
patients. "It was faraway from the town, you couldn't go anywhere."
"The noise - you couldn't sleep."

Comments about the staff were mostly favourable. "Good quality
of care. Nursing was excellent and medical attention was first rate.
The medication was heavy and I taught myself to resist it which was
not difficult." "Nursing is now much better than it used to be.
In 1953, it was more like a prison; no sanitation, no hot water for
shaving; bad food." "Nurses were very efficient. I saw the doctors
every six months and they were alright." "The nurses did not bother
us a lot except when ill. If you were not feeling very well, you
stayed in bed. I was medically examined every twelve months.
Social workers were very good." "The nurses were alright. I did
not see much of the doctors. The social workers took us out on
trips to Blackpool." This last patient gave a lurid account of
being kept three months in a padded cell not long after his original
admission. He was attacked by a nurse who began to strangle him
by tightening a towel around his throat.

Doctors were appreciated but seen very infrequently. Medical
visits varied from monthly to annually. Nurses were usually described as kind. Social workers were helpful. Occupational
therapists were appreciated most of all. People's eyes lit up
when they were mentioned.

Only two out of the ten said they had seen a psychologist.
"I saw a psychologist twice. She wanted a diagram for analysis.
She wanted me to put some blocks in a triangle. She asked me how
I see myself on the street. I said as an average person. If you
can do the stated tests in the time limits, she was well pleased

and gave no trouble. She said I was A1."

Routine on the wards was almost monastic. The day began very early - the earliest was 5.30 a.m. and the latest 7.15 a.m. It ended correspondingly early - between 8.45 p.m. and 10.00 p.m. was bedtime. Work in the industrial therapy units was of a routine and monotonous kind and was appreciated much less than the art and discussion groups in OT departments.

Weekends were a problem. There was little to do. "Saturdays and Sundays were very lonely, apart from the cinema on Saturday afternoon. I used to walk round the grounds mostly. They were beautiful."

When asked what kind of treatment they received, the term was understood in the most medical way. "I got Modecate injections and pills and that was all", was the standard reply. Treatment was what the doctor prescribed for you. Only one person mentioned something other than medical under treatment - that was OT.

These ten people lived on the back wards of our mental hospitals. It is difficult to use the term hospital care about what they received. Two of them acted as ancillary staff - helping nurses look after more disabled patients for small amounts of pocket money and extra cigarettes. They received relatively little attention as a group, except within the Occupational Therapy and Industrial Therapy units.

In the main they were comparing present hospitals with those of ten, twenty and thirty years earlier. It had been a grim institution. "Years ago it was horrible. They marched us around the court yards in groups. Every door and gate was locked and the nurses were rough. You don't need a pass to get out now. They're letting people like me out." All these people are glad to be out in the community.

They have learned to keep their heads down. "If you don't draw attention to yourself, they won't do things to you." "If you treat them well they will leave you alone." They have learned a religious acceptance of bad living conditions and difficult ward regimes from which we could all learn.

I interviewed twenty-one patients currently receiving treatment on G3, the psychiatric admission ward of the North Manchester General Hospital. These twenty-one were out of a total of forty-three staying in G3 sometime during the month 15.9.81 to 14.10.81. Twelve interviewees were female and nine male. The average age was 46.8 years - the youngest was 18 and the oldest 82 years. Six of the twenty-one were 65 or over. Of the twenty-two patients not interviewed - seventeen left before I could ask permission and five refused.

Two interviewees had been nurses: one a nursing auxilliary in G3 and another was an RMN. For eleven patients it was their first admission to G3. Four more had had a single previous admission; six had had two or more previous admissions. Eleven had had no other in-patient psychiatric treatment anywhere else. Seven of those were entirely fresh psychiatric admissions. Three of those had been transferred from other wards in the hospital - one after a spinal operation; another after orthopaedic treatment for a broken leg following a suicide attempt; another after medical treatment for blackouts.

Of the nine who had previous in-patient psychiatric treatment elsewhere, five had received it from Springfield Hospital only two hundred yards away, including one patient who had spent sixteen years there. Only four patients had received in-patient psychiatric treatment anywhere else - two from nearby Prestwich Hospital; one in Queens Park Hospital, Blackburn and the other in a Midlands mental hospital.

Length of stay for this current period on G3 depended a great deal on the time of the interview. One person had been in nearly a year and another was admitted at 2 a.m. on the same day as his interview at 8.30 p.m. See Table 1.

On the whole, my interviewees had a longer than average ward stay because I tended to miss all those who came and went fairly quickly. I spent roughly twenty minutes to half an hour with each person, asking about the food, the ward conditions, the staff, what they liked best and least, their treatment and whether they felt they were getting better and why.

FOOD

Two women were on reducing diets. In the main, comments were very favourable. Nine responses were of unstinting praise - "Excellent"; "Very good"; "Great - I never could afford to eat that way at home". Ten others were more qualified in their approval -

Table 1: Duration of Stay on G3 (Before interview)

	No.
Under a week	2
One to two weeks	4
Two weeks to a month	4
One month to six	9
Six to twelve months	2
	21

"Alright"; "Not like home cooking. Quite good for a hospital."
The remaining two were critical:

"Some choice but I don't like the food. Pretty grotty. No taste.
Much better in the staff canteen."

"Rubbish. Breakfast is OK but poor lunch and tea. Poor appearance."

WARD

     Comments about the ward facilities were largely uncritical.
Nine comments were favourable without qualification. They ranged
from "Perfect" to "The facilities are very good" to the milder
"reasonable" and "OK". One lady said: "It is so comfortable I may
have difficulty in leaving."

     One patient said the mixed ward was a good idea and another
criticised mixing the sexes. Other patients complained about the
lack of hot water (four); overcrowding in the TV and dayroom (five);
nowhere to wash clothes on the ward (two) - "The ward washing
machine has been broken for months"; "Too much noise at night";
(two). "Objectionable colours in the rooms" (one); "Dirty toilets"
(two); "Crowded sleeping area" (two); "Inadequate sleeping area
and general arrangements but then psychiatry has always been the
Cinderella of the National Health Service."

NURSES

     Most comments were favourable. They ranged from "perfect" to
"they are all very very good". Nurses were thoroughly appreciated
with particular references to the ward sister. "Sister is best.
She always has time for you." Sixteen comments contain unqualified
praise. The nurses were "unregimented"; "always had time for you";
"have a lot of patience"; "the nursing level is high. Their observation is very good. You are treated as an individual not as a
parcel."

     Four of the remaining comments were really qualified praise.
"Staff are very good. Certain student nurses can't be talked to.
I don't like one particular student nurse who voices dogmatic
opinions not based on experience." "The majority of nurses are
reasonable. The odd one tells bloody lies about you." "Nurses
are in between. Some are OK and some are not. Some are authoritarian and boss you about rather than ask." "Nurses are OK. They
vary a lot." The remaining patient was entirely critical - "They
won't help me. The nurses keep letting me down all the time."

DOCTORS

Most comments were favourable. Eighteen, even more than nurses, were of unqualified praise. "I like the doctors." "The doctors are lovely. You can sit and talk to them and they will listen to you. Sister will tell Dr. what your problems are." "Doctors explain things to you." "Doctors are fabulous." Dr. Tom, the Consultant Psychiatrist, was mentioned by name by most patients. The three remaining comments were "Doctors are good at consultant level. House doctors change too rapidly but they are OK. Levels of treatment for physical illness could be improved. Staffing structure tends to be too hierarchical with the consultant at the top." "Hardly see any doctors." "Only see doctors once a week."

Other staff were very much in the background of these patients' experiences. In the great majority of cases, they were not mentioned unless prompted. Even when reminded, six patients were unable or unwilling to comment on other staff. Other staff are bit players in a G3 drama which is dominated by the heroes and heroines, the doctors and nurses.

Patients were much less enthusiastic about other staff members. Five people commented on OTs - "Nice"; "A bit disorganised although the programmes are quite interesting"; "Not bad"; "Fine"; and "OK". One person was receiving physiotherapy and said that was "OK". Five commented on psychologists. "I don't like them because I don't understand what they are talking about." "OK". "Very good - gave me relaxation tapes." "Good psychologist". "OK - taught me how to relax."

Five people mentioned the domestics. "I like them". "They are nice and helpful". "Very friendly". "Always pleasant". "Always moaning". Five people mentioned social workers. "Helpful". "Excellent". "Not very good - limited psychiatric knowledge. No help with understanding about the Death Grant." "Great social worker". "I saw her about my glasses. She couldn't have cared less. Did nothing."

BEST/LEAST

Each person was asked "What do you like best/least about your stay in hospital?" Most people appreciated the staff and the warm atmosphere. Fourteen people made comments like "talking to the staff"; "relaxing atmosphere" and the "friendliness of both staff and patients".

One person found the company of the other patients" the best experience. Two did not know what to say. Others mentioned "visits from the wife" and "the discos on Mondays and Wednesdays". One patient commented about the Alcoholic Unit - the best thing was a

probation officer "who leads a discussion group and is a really
great guy."

Four people could think of nothing they liked about the
hospital experience. One said "Nothing - you are suffering until
you get home. Hospital is not a holiday". Three people least liked
staff members - "The nurses are no good". "The drama therapist is
awful (on the alcoholics unit)". "I didn't like the attitude of
the Duty Doctor (dragged out of bed at 2 a.m. to admit this patient).
He upset both my wife and myself". Two criticised other patients -
"One patient is catty". "I dislike arguments among the other
patients". Two people felt the worst thing was "not being able to
sleep during the night and not being allowed to get up and make
tea". Two more felt that meal-times were worst - "the worst thing
is carrying the heavy tray all the way back to the trolley". Two
more were critical of the TV room and another said there was noise
at night, some of it coming from the TV which"keeps me awake".
One complained about medication - "Some tablets burn a bit in my
throat". Another was more generally critical about medication -
"I don't like the medicine. All the life seems to go from me."
Two people were even more general - "My own illness" and "Being
here at all".

TREATMENT

I asked "What treatment are you receiving?" mainly to understand what they meant by the term. Eight patients were receiving
treatment concerned with physical conditions - everything from a
broken leg to duodenal ulcers. Only two people were not receiving
some kind of psychotropic medication; two others were receiving
five different varieties. Seven patients had received ECT in G3
during their current stay - varying from four to fifteen sessions.
Two patients mentioned talking to staff within the context of
treatment. Others included "Having a rest"; "Drinking lots of fluid";
"Getting a tonic"; "EEG" and "Having help from nurses in bathing".

Nine patients commented on the nature of their treatment.
Four of these were about ECT. "You go to sleep and don't feel
anything. I feel better after and my relatives say I look younger."
"I have asked for more ECT." "It lifted my depression and helped
disperse some of the blues. The tablets helped as well." "It
didn't bother me. I enjoyed the tea and toast after." Two patients
who were not receiving ECT commented that they had heard bad reports
of it and were determined to resist any suggestion that it be
prescribed for them.

Five patients mentioned drugs. "Valium keeps me going." "I
don't know what the drugs are for. I just take the doctor's advice
and hope for the best." "I get anti-depressant drugs which I do

not need. I am not depressed but heartbroken." (Her husband died
recently.) "If they were killing me I would just take them and not
ask why. They keep changing the tablets because I get dizzy." The
last patient mentioned talking to a "female registrar. We got on
too well so when she left I cut myself. I felt I had no-one to
talk to again."

Only two people were unable to say whether they were feeling
better - one had only been admitted that same day. One said he was
better in some ways, worse in others. Of the others, seven either
felt they were not improving or had reservations about their condition. "I don't feel I'm getting better. ECT is best but I still
feel I want to hurt myself." "They have forgotten me". "I came
in on a compulsory section (25) just because I took an overdose.
I feel its a prison - you feel trapped here. I'm better out."

The remaining eleven felt better. Some attributed that improvement to non-psychiatric causes. "The visitors help a lot."
"Treatment is all equally helpful." "Valium is most helpful."
"ECT is a helpful lifeboat and the drugs stop you sliding back into
the sea again." "Better than any drug is talking to people." "I'm
improving. Regular visits from my lady friend are the main cause
of that." "I'm getting better and I don't know why."

To conclude, there was much appreciation by the patients of the
warmth and safety which G3 provided. It offered a relaxed discipline
with considerable caring which sometimes led to problems. Two
insomniac ladies complained about not being able to make tea during
their sleepless nights. Seven patients complained of boredom. "I
get bored with doing nothing". "Very boring particularly in the
afternoons." "Weekends are boring with nothing to do". Patients
spent most of their time watching TV playing scrabble, drinking
tea and talking. In the main, visits to the day centre were much
appreciated. Three patients complained that they were also bored
there and one commented wryly "There is an enormous difference
between the individual therapy plan and what actually happens."

Many patients saw G3 as a substitute family. Sister Angela
and Dr. Tom were mentioned frequently by name and were certainly
the heads of the household. Their feelings, views and moods had
an enormous effect on the ward atmosphere. In the main, the
'children' were well pleased with their care which was of the very
best traditional psychiatric variety (except for the diagnosed
alcoholic who received a far more psycho-social intervention).
The dangers of this traditional approach are evident from this
study. They lie in reducing other professionals to bit players
with doctors and nurses hogging the stage; in keeping relatives
and families often in the background of 'treatment' so they are
not full partners; in being haphazard about picking up the social
and structural elements of psychiatric patients' problems; in the

Table 2:   Patients' Knowledge of Medication

	No.	
Names of drugs and quantities	7	(includes the two nurses)
Names of drugs but not quantities	6	
Neither drug names nor quantities	6	
Patients not receiving psycho- tropic medication	2	
	21	

infantilisation of some patients indicated by their often hazy
knowledge of their condition and its treatment.

In a recent pamphlet Brandon (1981) I have argued that much of
being mentally ill involves feeling powerless and that in important
ways the existing services confirm that sense of inadequacy. This
is particularly true of long stay patients. They are like off peak
radiator systems in that energy and wisdom only flow one way - from
professionals to the patients and relatives. What patients feel
and think seems not to matter in the health services.

For the last two years, my father in law has been a long stay
patient in a psychiatric hospital. Within the limits of poor
quality surroundings and a shortage of staff, the ward has cared
for him reasonably well. However, there seems no way in which, as
relatives, my wife and I can contribute constructively to improve
the quality of caring. We would like to say that the tannoyed
blaring of Radio One makes it difficult to talk to him; to ask why
we cannot receive a cup of tea when he gets one (to pay for it if
necessary); to worry about the extremely ill fitting nature of some
of the issued clothing. There seems no way in which information
like that can be transmitted except hurtfully.

Levin (1981) makes the strongest case for participation.
'There is more than a little irony in having to present a case for
the people as their own primary source in health. Professionals
in health planning and health services have become accustomed to
thinking about people mostly as sources of pathology, or victims
of pathology and consequently as a 'target' for preventive and
therapeutic services. In effect, we have come to accept a negative
view of trouble, for delaying in seeking care, for 'foolish' beliefs
and practices, and for not 'complying' with medical regimes. This
perspective is part of a professional-industrial construction of
reality that differentiates between providers of health services,
who have the necessary medical knowledge and skills, and consumers
of healh services, who have problems and precious little else.'

REFERENCES

Brandon D., 1981. "Voices from Experience". MIND.
Kings Fund Centre. 1977. "Psychiatric Hospitals Viewed by Their
      Patients".
Levin, L.S., 1981. Self-Care in Health. World Health Forum - an
      International Journal of Health Development. WHO Vol. 2 No.2.

Amphetamine in psychological
    testing, 127, 129, 130
Amylobarbitone in psychological
    testing, 127, 129, 130
Amytal in psychological testing,
    129, 130
Anorexia nervosa
  consumer research, 78-82
  counselling, 81-82, 83-93
    aim, 88-89
    basic issues, not food, 86-87
    control struggle, 84-85
    counter transference, 90
    critical parent, 90-91
    demand for counselling, 85-86
    female predominance, 87-88
    historical factors, 83
    'privileges', 89-90
    resisting help, 85
    self help, 91-92
    therapy, 87-93
    treatment barrier, 83
    understanding, 84
    weight as secondary factor,
      87
  counter-productive measures,
    71-72
  diagnostic criteria, 73-74
  hospital/community management,
    81
  hospital treatment, 77-81
  'illness' or 'abnormal', 68
  introduction to symposium,
    67-72
  long term outcome, 74-78
  menstrual status, 76-77
  mortality rates, 76

Anorexia nervosa (continued)
  non-pathological fasting, 69-70
  pathological fasting, 69, 70
  person oriented/symptom
      oriented approaches, 71
  psychosexual status, 76-77
  self-help (Anorexia Aid),
      91-92, 95-103
    assessment, 100
    behavior modification,
      99-100
    body image, 101-102
    fund raising, 101
    further research, 98-99
    group discussion, 96-97
    group support, 100-101
    'ideal figure', 101
    information sharing, 98
    parents' guilt, 96
    patients' guilt, 96
    recovered anorexics, 97
    social withdrawal, 97
    treatment methods, 99
    tube feeding, 99
  symptomatic treatment dangers,
    70
  weight status, 77-78
  why treat, 68-69
Antidepressant drugs compared
      with cognitive therapy in
      depression, 185-205 (see
      also Depression)
Anti-social behavior and
      low/high class homes,
      62-63 (see also
      Behavior)

Anxiety, self-rated, Beck
        depression scale, 194-196
Aversion therapy in sexual
        deviation, 33, 35-36

Bayesian technique
  defining, 139
  perceptual maze test, 132
  use, 139-141
Beck Depression inventory, 192,
        194
Behavior
  modification, with reference to
        cognitive therapy,
        207-227 (see also
        Cognitive behavior
        modification (therapy):
        Token economy programs)
  pattern in depression, 202, 203
  problems in 'institutions',
        269-270, 272-274
Behaviorism, radical, 210-213
  epiphenomenalist argument,
        211-212
Biofeedback system
  computer controlled, heart
        rate, 147-157 (see also
        Heart rate biofeedback,
        computer-controlled)
  in sexual deviation, 36

Change
  in institutions, 248-249 (see
        also Institutionalism:
        Institutions)
  resistance to, and depression,
        171-177
Chloropromazine in psychological
        testing, 132
Cognitive behavior modification
        (therapy), 207-227
  behaviorism or cognitivism,
        222-223
  experimental evidence, animal
        studies, 209
  and pharmacotherapy compared,
        in depression, 185-205
  aim of study, 187-190

Cognitive behavior modification
        (therapy) (continued)
  and pharmacotherapy compared,
        in depression (continued)
    changes in mood, patterns,
        185-205
    conclusion, 202-204
    correlations of variables,
        190, 191-192
    discussion, 202
    hopelessness, 197-198
    irritability, 196-197
    method, 190
    patients, assessment,
        criteria, 186-187
    patterns of response, 192-202
    results, 190-202
    self-rated anxiety, 194-196
    view of environment, 199-201
    view of self, 198-199
  radical behaviorism, 210
  verbal control, 213-223
    contingency management,
        216-220
    discrimination training,
        220-221
    token economies, 213-216
Computer applications in clinical
        psychology, 107-110
  ability to use, 107-108
  as aid to decision making, 109
  in biofeedback of heart rate,
        109
  controlled biofeedback system,
        heart rate, 147-157 (see
        also Heart rate biofeed-
        back, computer
        controlled)
  and decision making, 135-146
    aim, 144
    Bayesian approaches, 139-141
    design, 144
    diagnostic systems, 138-139
    evaluation, 142-144
    expert systems, 141-142
    modelling, 138
    psychiatric data bases,
        135-136

Computer applications in clinical
        psychology (continued)
    and decision making (continued)
        specific computers, 136–138,
            147
        testing, 136–138
    ethical issues, 109, 117
    microprocessors, 111–119 (see
        also Microprocessors)
    potential, 108–109
    social impact, 107 (see also
        Testing, psychologi-
        cal, automated)
Conditioning and criminality,
        60–63
    genetic factors, 61
    personality factors, 61
Consent, 18–20
    drug abuse, 18–19
    sexual behavior see Sexual
        behavior
Contingency management pro-
        cedures, 216–220
    drinking control, 216
    weight reduction, 217
Court proceedings, psychologist's
        role, 20–21, 43–51 (see
        also Forensic psychology)
Crime
    current theories, 53–63
        conditioning and social
            learning theories, 60–63
        increase in last 10 years,
            53–54
        psychoanalytic hypothesis,
            57–60
        sociological and economic
            theories, 54–57
    definition, 53–54
Criminal behavior, genetic and
        environmental components,
        21
Criminology, role of psycho-
        logists, 17–18
Critical variables, emergence in
        long term care, 253–261
    token economy programs, 253–261
        (see also Token economy
        programs)

Custody of children, psycho-
        logist's role, 43–44

Decision making and computers,
        135–146 (see also Com-
        puters and decision
        making)
Depression
    caused by arrested intellectual
        development, 179–184 (see
        also Intellectual devel-
        opment)
    comparison of cognitive and
        pharmacotherapy, 185–205
    pattern change in mood,
        185–205 (see also
        Cognitive therapy)
    internal events and processes
        introduction, 161–169
        attitude to death, 172
        attitude to future, 173–174
        attitude to others, 172–173
        behavioral aspect, 164
            radical and cognitive
            positions, 164–165,
            185–227
        compared with unhappiness,
            171
        coping, 174–175
        core constructs, 162–163,
            165, 172
        definition, 171
        diagnosis, 161–162
        discussion, 165–168
        forgiveness, 176
        indifference of others,
            176–177
        psychodynamic theory and
            practice, 163–164,
            179–184
        punishment, 173
        resistance to change, 171–177
        self-sacrifice, 175
Desensitization, systematic, in
        sexual deviation, 34–35
Discrimination training, 220–221

Economic theories for
        criminality, 54–57
    personal wealth, 55–56
    and reporting of crime, 56–57

Electroconvulsive therapy,
    290–292
Electrodermal techniques and the
    court, 49–50
Environment
    least restrictive, in residen-
        tial care, 243
    view of, pattern of change in
        depression, 198–199,
        202–203 (*see also*
        Institutions)
Epanutin in psychological test-
    ing, 131, 133
Epiphenomenalist view of
    behaviorism, 211–212
Exposure in sexual deviation, 34

Fading, 34
Forensic psychology, 17–22
    and the clinician, 41–51
        clinical problems, 43–44
        electrodermal techniques,
            49–50
        legal problems, 44–49
        psychometric evidence, 50
        roles, 42
        terminology, 48
Forensic psychology
    court procedures, 20
    rape, 19
    sexual behavior, 18–20
    statements, 20
Future, view, in depression,
    201–202, 203

Genetic factors and criminality,
    61, 62
Grendon Model Prison, 57–58

Haloperidol in psychological
    testing, 131, 132
Hamilton rating scale for
    depression, 192, 193
Hearsay evidence, 48–49
Heart rate biofeedback, computer
    controlled
    data acquisition, 147–150
    equipment, 147–150
    programed data manipulation,
        148–149

Heart rate biofeedback, computer
    controlled (continued)
    programs, 147–150
    specific study, 150–156
        confusing findings, 155–156
        individual differences, 156
        inversion, 151, 155, 156
        off-line data editing,
            151–152
        procedure, 150–151
        results, 152–156
        subjects' feedback display,
            149–150
Heterosexual arousal, techniques,
    33–36
Homosexuality, therapy,
    techniques, 33–36
Hopelessness, pattern, in
    depression, 196–197, 202
Hospital Plan (MOH), 233–236
    consequences of failure,
        235–236
    failure to implement, 234–235
    future plans, 236

Institutionalism, 232
    neurosis syndromes, 244
    possibility of discharge,
        236–237
    psychological methods, 237–238
    reduction, 237 (*see also*
        Hospital Plan: Long term
        care, residential)
Institutions, voices from,
    281–293
    doctors, 289
    ECT, 290–292
    food, 285, 287–288
    general views, 282
    how to improve care, 292
    least/best, 289–290
    nurses, 288
    one patient's story, 283–284
    psychiatric admission ward, 286
    routine, 286
    staff, 285–286, 288–289
    treatment, 286, 290–292
        patients' knowledge of,
            290–292
    wards, 284–285, 288
    work, 284

Intellectual development,
        arrested, causing
        depression, 179–184
    attempted suicide, 179, 180,
        182–183, 184
    frequency, 180–181
    IQ, high, 181
    maternal factors, 183–184
    overcoming, 184
    strangulation of intelligence,
        181–182
    underestimating the patient,
        179–180
Internal events and processes,
        particularly depression,
        introduction, 161–169
        (see also Depression)
Irritability, pattern, in
        depression, 196–197

Jay report, 246–247
Juvenile delinquency,
        psychologist's role, 43

Least restrictive environment in
        residential care, 243
Legal problems, psychologist's
        role, 17–22, 44–49
    adversary bias, 45
    hearsay evidence, 48–49
    legislative differences, 45
    terminology, 48
    weight of evidence, 46–48
Leva Dopa, testing effect, 122
Long term care, 231–239
    clinical features, 232
    'Hospital Plan' (MOH), 233–236
        failure to implement and
            consequences, 234–236
    institutionalism, 232–233, 237,
        281–293
    psychological methods, 237–238
    public policy since 1962,
        233–236
    research evidence, 236–238
    residential, 241–252
        behavioral rather than
            diagnostic formulations,
            242
        caring environment,
            examination, 245–246

Long term care (continued)
        caring personnel,
            examination, 246–247
        clear overall objectives,
            243–244
        constraints upon process of
            change, 248–249
        definition of type of
            intercention, 247–248
        handicapped, specific needs,
            identification, 242–243
        initiatives possible, 249–251
        least restrictive
            environment, 243
        monitoring progress, 244–245
        neurosis syndromes, causes,
            244
        prevention, cure and
            alleviation, 242 (see
            also Institutions)
    size of problem, 231–233

Menstrual status in anorexia
        nervosa, 76–77
Mental capacity, offender,
        psychologist's role, 44
Mentally handicapped, clinical
        psychologist's role,
        263–280
    as adviser/consultant/service
        planners, 264–265
    evaluation of new planning,
        270, 271
    in local small care practices,
        265–267
    problem behaviors, 272–274
    specific studies, 271–272
    support for social change in
        institution, 268–269
    training procedures, 274–279
        summary of outcome, 278–279
    transfer of patients from large
        to small units, 267
    understanding behavior, 269–270
    in relation to environment,
        270–271
Microprocessors in clinical
        psychology, 111–119
    cost, 111, 113–114
    ethical issues, 109, 117

Microprocessors in clinical
    psychology (continued)
  expert systems, 117–119
  political issues, 117
  printers, 115
  sharing multiuser system,
    116–117
  storage, 114–115
  teletext and viewdata, 116
  terminology, 112–113
  TV display, 115
  word length and machine size,
    113–114
M'Naghten's Rules, 47, 48
Modelling, computer, 138
Mortality rates in anorexia
    nervosa, 76

"Nodder" report, 245, 246

Orgasmic reconditioning, 34

Perceptual maze test, 124
  Bayesian technique, 132
  computerizing, 125–127
  single person trials, 127–130
  statistical problems, 130–133
Personality factors and
    criminality, 61
Pharmacotherapy and cognitive
    therapy compared, in
    depression, 185–205
  pattern of change in mood,
    185–205 (see also
    Cognitive therapy)
Pornography effects, 30–31
Post-qualification training, 3–13
    (see also Training
    further)
Practitioner Training
    Sub-Committee, 9
Primary care, clinical psychology
    in, 3
Prison, and psychoanalytic
    treatment of offenders,
    57
Pro-social behavior and low/high
    class homes, 62–63

Psychoanalytic hypothesis, and
    criminal and antisocial
    behavior, 57–60
  recidivism, 57–58
    side effects, 59–60
    treatment effects, results of
      study, 59–60
Psychological testing see
    Testing, psychological
Psychometric evidence in court,
    50
Psychosexual states in anorexia
    nervosa, 76–77

Rape, psychological effects, 19
  physical injury, 25
'Reasonable doubt', 46–47
Recidivism, 57–58
  treatment effect, results of
    study, 59–60

Satiation in sexual deviation, 36
Scientific evidence, 47–48
Self, view of, pattern of change
    in depression, 198–199
Sex education versus sex therapy,
    31
Sexual
  behavior, consent, 23
    children, 18–19
    ethical problems, 19–20
    and inducements or threats,
      18
  crime, 23–29
    against boys, 24–25
    age ranges,
    consenting behavior, 23–24,
      25–27
    court sentences, 24
    deviant behavior, 25, 26–27
    homosexual behavior,
      consenting, 23, 24
    invoking the law, 25–26
    treatment approaches, 27–28
    unlawful intercourse, 24
    age ranges, 24
  deviations, therapy,
    techniques, 33–36
    elimination of deviant
      arousal, 35–36

Sexual (continued)
    deviations, therapy,
            techniques (continued)
        increase of heterosexual
                arousal, 33–35
    dysfunction, therapy, 32
    problems, assessment, 32
Sexually explicit materials, 20
    therapeutic use, 29–39
        in deviations, therapy, 33–36
        implications for use, 36–37
        positive contribution, 30–31
        in sexual dysfunction,
                therapy, 32
        in sexual problems, 32
Shaping, 33
Social learning theories and
        criminality, 60–63
Sociological theories for
        criminality, 54–57

Terminology, legal, 48
Test material, misuse in court,
        50
Testing, psychological, 121–134
    automated, 122–124
        cognitive style, 124–125
        criterion referenced tests,
                123, 127
        design, 125–127
        facilities, 123
        perceptual maze test, 124,
                125–127
            single person trials,
                    127–130
        statistical problems, 130–133
        tests so far programed,
                123–124
    uses, 121–122
Token economy programs, 213–216,
        253–261
    criticisms, 255
    dehumanization, 255
    as inhumane procedures, 255–256
    major characteristics, 254
    reinforcement, 254
    variables, controlled and
            uncontrolled, 256–257
        studies, 256–260

Training, further, for clinical
        psychologists, 3–13
    different types of courses,
            9–11
    financing, 10–11
    future developments, 9–11
    major courses, 8
    needs, 4–5
    post-qualification course, 4
        content, 5–7
        refresher courses, 5, 7
        for senior posts, 5, 6–7
        specialized skill and
                knowledge, 6, 7
    present opportunities, 7–9
Trethowan Report, 3

Unhappiness and depression
        compared, 171

Weight status in anorexia
        nervosa, 77–78
Writing speed, pattern, in
        depression, 202